3D Mesh Processing and Character Animation

Ramakrishnan Mukundan

3D Mesh Processing and Character Animation

With Examples Using OpenGL, OpenMesh and Assimp

 Springer

Ramakrishnan Mukundan (iD)
Department of Computer Science
and Software Engineering
University of Canterbury
Christchurch, New Zealand

ISBN 978-3-030-81356-7   ISBN 978-3-030-81354-3   (eBook)
https://doi.org/10.1007/978-3-030-81354-3

This Springer imprint is published by the registered company Springer Nature Switzerland AG
The registered company address is: Gewerbestrasse 11, 6330 Cham, Switzerland

To my wife
Rema.

Preface

This book expands upon my previous book titled *Advanced Methods in Computer Graphics*, which was published by Springer in 2012. The topics of mesh processing and character animation have attracted a lot of attention in the recent past following the availability of very versatile, powerful, and easy-to-use software libraries, and many online sources of three-dimensional mesh models and rigged character models. Even though these topics were discussed in the previously published work by the author, it was later found necessary to collate more information pertaining to the implementations of important methods based on current technology trends and available software libraries in the field. This need was the primary motivation behind writing this book. The book demonstrates the working and practical applications of core methods in the areas of mesh processing and character animation and aims to provide a good foundation on both theoretical and implementation oriented aspects of the discussed algorithms.

The evolution of programmable GPU architectures has led to a huge uptake in the development of real-time computer graphics applications that leverage the power and flexibility of the GPUs. Developers of OpenGL-based applications use the OpenGL-4 Shading Language to write code for the programmable stages of the graphics pipeline. The capability to execute code directly on a massively parallel architecture of the GPU allows programmers to develop highly efficient and fast implementations of compute intensive tasks. In this context, the tessellation and the geometry shader stages of the OpenGL-4 pipeline have been found to be particularly useful for tasks requiring dynamically varying tessellations of mesh surfaces, geometry amplification, and culling. Several mesh rendering algorithms such as terrain rendering and Bezier surface rendering methods require tessellations of surfaces and associated geometry operations. This book aims to fill a growing need for texts detailing shader-based implementations of methods that use tessellation and geometry stages for surface modelling.

I have been teaching advanced courses in computer graphics for the past 20 years. Most of the material in the book including illustrations and code are drawn from my lecture notes, lab work, and exercises handed out to students. The book includes many explanatory illustrations and graphical outputs of programs to help better understand the concepts and processes discussed in each chapter. The content of the course *Advanced Computer Graphics* (COSC422), which I teach at the University of Canterbury in New Zealand, is regularly updated taking into account recent developments in the field. Until a few years ago, topics on mesh processing and character animation were taught using software libraries developed in-house. With the adoption of popular open-source software library packages for both teaching and implementation of graphics algorithms, the study materials used in the course underwent a complete overhaul. The new enhancements made to the course materials along with a large collection of programs developed for demonstrating the working of various algorithms formed the foundation for this book project. It is hoped that this book will serve as a textbook for similar courses on computer graphics that deal with the topics of mesh processing and character animation.

I am very grateful to the graduate students of my course and the staff in the Department of Computer Science and Software Engineering, University of Canterbury, for their encouragement and support. Student feedbacks obtained through classroom interactions and course evaluations were extremely useful for understanding students' learning style preferences, and the ranking of topics based on what students generally perceived as important, interesting, and useful. This feedback was valuable for selecting and organizing topics and material for the chapters of this book.

I would like to thank the editorial team members at Springer-Verlag London Ltd., for their help throughout this book project. My special thanks go to Helen Desmond, Editor—Computer Science, for encouraging me to write this book, and for providing invaluable support throughout the publication process. I would also like to thank the reviewers of the book proposal for their very constructive feedback and valuable suggestions.

I had to set aside a lot of time every day to prepare the manuscript, and often reprioritize other tasks and activities. I am very grateful to my family for their endless support, and greatly appreciate their patience and understanding.

Christchurch, New Zealand   Ramakrishnan Mukundan
November 2021

Contents

Chapter 1
Introduction

Algorithms for three-dimensional character animation and mesh processing are generally covered in an advanced course on computer graphics designed for senior undergraduate or postgraduate students. These algorithms find many applications in real-time animations and geometric modelling. Character animation is one of the topics which students of computer graphics courses often find both fascinating and challenging. Similarly, the field of mesh processing contains methods that produce interesting variations in the structure of three-dimensional mesh objects that are useful for various modelling applications. The availability of versatile and easy-to-use open-source software libraries has made the implementation and exploration of these methods easier and less time consuming. This book aims to provide a solid foundation of both theoretical and implementation aspects of core methods in the above areas.

1.1 Contents Overview

The topics covered in this book can be broadly grouped into three main categories: (i) mesh processing algorithms, (ii) methods for mesh rendering in OpenGL, and (iii) skeletal and character animation. The chapters that belong to each category and the libraries/APIs used for implementing methods discussed in those chapters are shown in Fig. 1.1.

Chapters 2 and 3 deal with data structures and algorithms used for three-dimensional mesh processing. The topics covered in these chapters include the half-edge data structure, adjacency query processing, mesh simplification and subdivision algorithms, and methods used for mesh parameterization and morphing. Chapters 4 and 5 deal with mesh rendering algorithms that use the shader stages of the OpenGL pipeline. The class of rendering algorithms discussed in these chapters includes billboard rendering, tree rendering, terrain rendering, and Bezier surface rendering. Algorithms covered in Chaps. 6–8 are related to the topic of skeletal and character

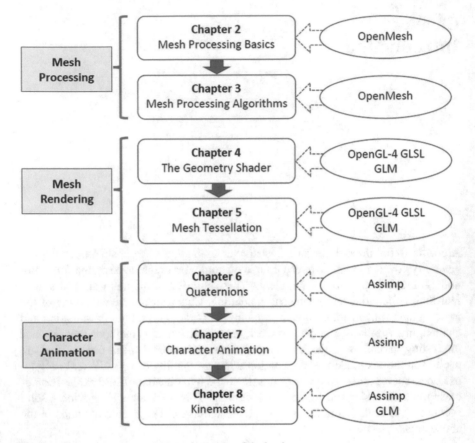

Fig. 1.1 Structure and organisation of contents of the book

animation. Chapter 6 is dedicated to the discussion of the theory and applications of quaternions in animation. Chapter 7 presents methods for animating skeletal structures using motion capture data, and the data structures and algorithms used for animating rigged character models. Chapter 8 outlines an iterative inverse kinematics algorithm for generating goal directed motion of character models.

A large number of illustrations and outputs of programs are included in each chapter to help the reader gain a better understanding of the concepts and processes. Numerous code examples are also included in the text to show the implementations of algorithms.

1.2 Prerequisite Knowledge

The subject matter of this book is drawn from topics in advanced computer graphics, and therefore, familiarity with concepts in introductory computer graphics is desirable. Specifically, the book assumes that the reader is familiar with the following:

- Topics in introductory computer graphics such as transformations, lighting calculations, object modelling, and texture mapping.
- Mathematical concepts that are widely used in computer graphics such as vectors, matrices, barycentric coordinates, and linear interpolation.
- Programming in C/C++ language using OpenGL.
- Shader stages of the OpenGL-4 programmable pipeline, and the computations that are generally performed in each of those stages.
- Implementation of shaders using the OpenGL Shading Language (GLSL) [1] .

1.3 Software Libraries

As shown in Fig. 1.1, the book uses a few open-source software libraries to discuss the implementations of algorithms. The OpenMesh [2] library is used to demonstrate the implementations of mesh processing algorithms presented in Chaps. 2, 3. OpenMesh is a versatile and powerful software library using which mesh queries and operations can be easily performed.

The mesh rendering algorithms covered in Chaps. 4, , 5 use the tessellation and geometry shader stages of the OpenGL-4 pipeline. The OpenGL Mathematics (GLM) [3] library is used in the applications to perform vector operations and to construct transformation matrices. GLM is a very convenient library designed with naming conventions and functionalities similar to that used in OpenGL and the Shading Language (GLSL).

The Open Asset Importer Library (Assimp) [4] is a highly popular software package that supports several well-known 3D model formats and provides data structures and functions useful for developing character animation algorithms. Using Assimp, complex joint hierarchies and materials of rigged character models can be easily loaded into a scene graph-type data structure and animated with an associated set of bone definitions.

The above libraries are all written in C++.

1.4   Supplementary Material

Each chapter is accompanied by a collection of programs and data files that show the implementations of key algorithms presented in that chapter. The files can be downloaded from the following website:

https://www.csse.canterbury.ac.nz/mukundan/Book4/index.html

The "Chapter Resources" section at the end of each chapter gives a brief description of the programs and data files that are available for download. The programs are written entirely by the author, with the primary aim of motivating the reader to explore the implementation of each technique further and to observe and study the outputs and animations generated. The programs could also be used as base code by developers and researchers to build larger frameworks or to try better solutions. A simple programming approach is used so that students with minimal knowledge of C/C++ language and OpenGL would be able to start using the code and work towards more complex and useful applications. None of the software is optimized in terms of algorithm performance or speed.

References and Further Reading

1. J. Kessenich, D. Baldwin, R. Rost, *The OpenGL Shading Language*, Version 4.50, The Khronos Group Inc. 2017. [Online]. Available https://www.khronos.org/registry/OpenGL/specs/gl/GLS LangSpec.4.50.pdf
2. L. Kobbelt, OpenMesh. https://www.graphics.rwth-aachen.de/software/openmesh/. Accessed 1 November 2021
3. OpenGL Mathematics, https://glm.g-truc.net/0.9.9/index.html. Accessed 1 March 2020
4. The Open Asset Importer Library, https://www.assimp.org/. Accessed 15 November 2021

Chapter 2
Mesh Processing Basics

Three-dimensional mesh models are extensively used in computer graphics applications. Various types of modelling, rendering, and animation algorithms use polygonal mesh data. Mesh processing techniques therefore play an important role in the field of graphics algorithms.

This is the first of two chapters on mesh processing methods. This chapter discusses the geometrical and topological aspects related to three-dimensional meshes and their representations. It introduces the OpenMesh [1] library and presents important mesh data structures that are commonly used for operations such as mesh simplification and mesh subdivision. This chapter contains the following sections:

- **Mesh representation**: Gives an overview of data structures used for representing a polygonal mesh.
- **Mesh file formats**: Describes the OBJ, OFF, and PLY formats used for storing mesh data. The OpenMesh library supports these file formats.
- **Polygonal manifolds**: Most mesh models belong to this category. This section deals with the topological characteristics of manifold meshes and some of their important properties.
- **OpenMesh**: Introduces an open-source library for mesh processing. The implementations of mesh processing algorithms are discussed using this library.
- **Mesh data structures**: Provides an outline of important data structures used for processing adjacency queries on mesh objects. The half-edge data structure is most commonly used in applications and also by the OpenMesh library.
- **Mesh traversal**: Describes applications of iterators and circulators in processing adjacency queries.
- **Surface normal computation**: Shows the processes of computing face normal vectors and vertex normal vectors using OpenMesh iterators and circulators.
- **Bounding box computation**: Outlines the method for scale and position normalization of a mesh object, as an example of an application of mesh data structures.

© The Author(s), under exclusive license to Springer Nature Switzerland AG 2022
R. Mukundan, *3D Mesh Processing and Character Animation*,
https://doi.org/10.1007/978-3-030-81354-3_2

- **Triangle adjacency primitive**: This is a special type of adjacency primitive used in shader-based implementations. This section details a method for constructing primitive vertex lists by processing adjacency queries on triangles.

2.1 Mesh Representation

A *polygonal mesh* is a set of vertices and polygonal elements (such as triangles and quads) that collectively define a three-dimensional geometrical shape. The simplest mesh representation thus consists of a vertex list and a polygon list as shown in Fig. 2.1. Polygons are often defined in terms of triangular elements. Since triangles are always both planar and convex, they can be conveniently used in several geometrical computations such as point inclusion tests, area and normal calculations, and interpolation of vertex attributes.

The vertex list contains the three-dimensional coordinates of the mesh vertices defined in a suitable coordinate frame, and the polygon list contains integer values that index into the *vertex list*. An anticlockwise ordering of vertices with respect to the outward face normal direction is commonly used to indicate the front facing side of each polygon. The distinction between the front and the back faces of a polygon becomes important in lighting computations and backface culling operations.

A polygonal mesh comprising entirely of triangles is called a *triangle mesh*. Triangle meshes allow faster hardware accelerated rendering and more efficient mesh processing algorithms. If the polygon list represents a set of connected triangles as in Fig. 2.1, then a compact data structure called a *triangle strip* may be used to represent the model. The first three indices in a triangle strip specify the first triangle. The fourth index along with the previous two indices represents the second triangle. In this fashion, each subsequent index represents a triangle that is defined by that index and the previous two indices.

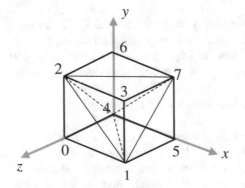

Vertex List			Triangle List		
x	y	z	i	j	k
0.0	0.0	1.0	0	1	2
1.0	0.0	1.0	1	3	2
0.0	1.0	1.0	2	3	7
1.0	1.0	1.0	2	7	6
0.0	0.0	0.0	1	7	3
1.0	0.0	0.0	1	5	7
0.0	1.0	0.0	6	7	4
1.0	1.0	0.0	7	5	4
			0	4	1
			1	4	5
			2	6	4
			0	2	4

Fig. 2.1 A cube and its mesh definition using vertex and polygon lists

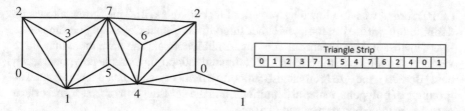

Fig. 2.2 Cut-open view of the cube in Fig. 2.1 showing its representation as a triangle strip

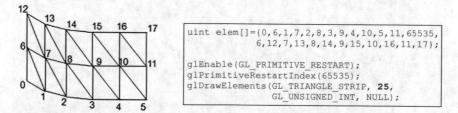

Fig. 2.3 Multiple triangle strips represented by a single element array using a primitive restart index

The representation of a cube as a triangle strip is given in Fig. 2.2. While the triangle list for the cube consists of 36 indices (see in Fig. 2.1), the representation using a triangle strip contains only 14 indices. The triangle strip given in Fig. 2.2 is decoded as the set of 12 triangles {012, 123, 237, 371, 715, 154, 547, 476, 762, 624, 240, 401}. Note that in this representation, the orientation of triangles alternates between clockwise and anticlockwise directions. The change of orientation is usually corrected by reversing the direction of every alternate triangle in the list, starting from the second triangle. Thus, the above list would be correctly interpreted as triangles {012, 213, 237, 731, 715, 514, 547, 746, 762, 264, 240, 041}. If the first triangle is defined in the anticlockwise sense, then all triangles in the corrected list will have the same orientation. When there are multiple triangle strips in a polygonal mesh, it becomes necessary to use either separate arrays of vertex indices, or special indices (usually the maximum integer value) as *primitive restart indices*. OpenGL allows the restart index to be specified using the `glPrimitiveRestartIndex()` function. An example of the use of this function is shown in Fig. 2.3.

2.2 Mesh File Formats

Several file formats are used in graphics applications for storing and sharing mesh data. A number of such file formats represent values in binary and compressed forms for minimizing storage space. In this section, we review some of the popular ASCII file formats that allows easy viewing and editing of mesh data. The *Object*

(.OBJ) format was developed by Wavefront technologies [2]. This format allows the definition of vertices in terms of either three-dimensional Cartesian coordinates or four-dimensional homogeneous coordinates. Polynomials can have more than three vertices. In addition to the basic set of commands supporting simple polygonal mesh data (Box 2.1), the .OBJ format also supports a number of advanced features such as grouping of polygons, material definitions, and the specification of free-form surface geometries including curves and surfaces.

Box 2.1 OBJ File Format

Comments start with the symbol #

    e.g., `# 3D Model definition`

A vertex definition starts with the symbol v and is followed by 3 or 4 floating point values. Each vertex is implicitly assigned an index. The first vertex has an index 1.

e.g.,   `v -1.53 2.06 3.82`

      `v 6.98 -11.3 -0.008 1.0`

Texture coordinates are specified by the symbol `vt` followed by two or three floating point values in the range [0, 1]. Texture coordinates are mapped to vertex coordinates through the face ('f') command. The first set of texture coordinates have an index 1.

e.g.,   `vt 0.25 0.90`

      `vt 0.0 0.5 0.5`

Vertex normal vectors are specified using the `vn` command. The normal components are assigned to a vertex through the face ('f') command. The first set of normal components is assigned an index 1.

e.g.,   `vn -0.256 0.1888 -0.756`

A polygon definition uses a face command that starts with the symbol f and followed by a list of positive integers that are valid vertex indices.

e.g.,   `f 2 3 6`

      `f 15 8 1 22`

The above face command has a more general form `f v/vt/vn v/vt/vn v/vt/vn ...` that can be used to combine texture and normal attributes with vertices. Both `/vt` and `/vn` fields are optional.

e.g.,   `f 2/3/1 3/5/2 6/1/7`

      `f 15/2 8/3 1/5 22/9`

```
f 6//1 7//6 2//12
```

The first example above defines a triangle including references to the texture and normal coordinates at the vertices. The second example attaches only texture coordinate references to each vertex, while the third example uses only the normal vectors.

The *Object File Format* (.OFF) is another convenient ASCII format for storing 3D model definitions. It uses simple vertex-list and face-list structures for specifying a polygonal model. Unlike the .OBJ format, this format does not intersperse commands with values on every line, and therefore can be easily parsed to extract vertex coordinates and face indices. This format also allows users to specify vertices in homogeneous coordinates, faces with more than three vertex indices, and optional colour values for every vertex or face (Box 2.2).

Box 2.2 OFF File Format

The first line should contain the header keyword OFF

This line can be followed by optional comment lines starting with the character #

e.g.,   # Model file for a cube

The first non-comment line should have three integer values n_v, n_f, n_e denoting the total number of vertices, faces and edges. The number of edges (n_e) is always set to 0

e.g.,   8 6 0

The above line is followed by the vertex list. The number of vertices in the list must match the number n_v. The first vertex is assigned the index 0, and the last vertex the index n_v-1.

e.g.,   -1.2 -1.5 -1.3

        1.1 -1.9 -1.7

        . . .

Vertices can also be specified using 4 coordinates in homogeneous form. In this case, the header keyword should be changed to 4OFF.

The vertex list is followed by the face list. Each line contains a set of integers n, i_1, i_2, ..., i_n, where the first integer n gives the number of vertices of that face and the remaining integers give the face indices.

e.g.,   3 2 0 1

        4 1021 558 632 717

Colour values in either RGB or RGBA representation can be optionally added to each face as 3 or 4 integer values in the range [0, 255] or floating point values in the range [0, 1].

e.g.,   `3 1 0 5 255 255 0 0`

`4 15 26 78 9 0.5 0.1 0.25`

The *Polygon File Format* (.PLY) [3] also organizes mesh data as a vertex list and a face list with the addition of several optional elements. The format is also called the Stanford Triangle Format. Elements can be assigned a type (`int, float, double, uint` etc.), and a number of values that are stored against each element. Such information is specified using a list of properties as part of the header (Box 2.3). This file format supports several types of elements and data, and the complete specification is included in the header. Parsing a PLY file is therefore considerably complex than parsing an OBJ or OFF file.

Box 2.3 PLY File Format

The first line in the header should contain the keyword `ply`. The second line specifies the file format using the `format` keyword.

e.g.,   `format ascii 1.0`

Comments begin with the keyword comment

e.g.,   `comment Model definition for a cube`

The total number of vertices, polygons etc. in the model definition is specified using the `element` keyword.

e.g.,   `element vertex 8`

`element face 6`

The type of each element is specified using the `property` keyword. The following commands specify the types of vertex coordinates.

e.g.,   `property float x`

`property float y`

`property float z`

The polygon data is usually defined using a set of vertex indices. The type specification is included in the header as
property int vertex_index

The keyword `end_header` is used to delimit the header information. The vertex and face lists follow this keyword. The first vertex has the index 0.

e.g.,

```
end_header
0.5 0.5 0.5
1.0 0.5 0.5
. .
0 1 2 3
1 0 4 5
. .
```

2.3 Polygonal Manifolds

The model definition files introduced in the previous section contain information about vertices, polygons, colour values, texture coordinates, and possibly many other vertex and face related attributes that collectively specify a mesh geometry. As seen from the examples, list-based mesh definitions often do not store any neighbourhood or connectivity information. The adjacency and incidence relationships between mesh elements define the topology of the mesh and are heavily used by several mesh processing algorithms. This section introduces some of the general and desirable topological characteristics of meshes.

A common assumption in the construction of mesh data structures and related algorithms is that the given mesh is a polygonal manifold. A *polygonal manifold* (specifically, a two-dimensional manifold) is defined as a mesh that satisfies two conditions: (i) no edge is shared by more than two faces, and (ii) the faces sharing a vertex can be ordered in such a way that their vertices excluding the shared vertex form a simple (open or closed) chain. Figure 2.4 shows a few examples of both manifold and non-manifold neighbourhoods on a polygonal mesh surface.

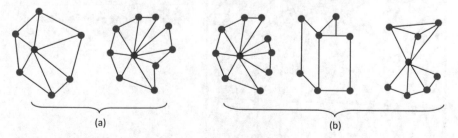

(a)   (b)

Fig. 2.4 Examples of **a** manifold and **b** non-manifold mesh segments

A *non-manifold mesh* may contain edges shared by more than two polygons, or vertices with more than one chain of neighbouring vertices. In a non-manifold mesh, the neighbourhood of a point may not be topologically equivalent (homeomorphic) to a disc, which makes local adjustments surrounding that vertex difficult in many mesh processing algorithms. The methods discussed in this and next chapter assume that the given mesh satisfies the conditions of a polygonal manifold.

The chain of vertices surrounding a vertex in a polygonal manifold is closed if the vertex is an interior vertex, otherwise the vertex is a boundary vertex. In a triangular mesh, the triangles sharing a common vertex form a closed triangle fan for interior vertices, and an open triangle fan for boundary vertices (Fig. 2.4a). An interior vertex is also commonly called a *simple vertex*. An edge that belongs to only one polygon is a *border edge*. Every edge that is not a border edge in a polygonal manifold belongs to exactly two polygons. A closed manifold that does not contain any boundary vertices or border edges is called a *polyhedron*.

Two vertices are adjacent if they are connected by an edge of a polygon. As seen in the previous example, the set of vertices that are adjacent to a vertex in a closed manifold forms a ring. This set is called the *one-ring neighbourhood* of the vertex. The union of one-ring neighbourhoods of every vertex in this set is called its two-ring neighbourhood (Fig. 2.5).

The orientation of the faces of a polygonal manifold is determined by the way in which its vertices are ordered. An anticlockwise ordering of vertices generally corresponds to the front face of a polygon. If two adjacent faces have the same orientation, they are said to be compatible. If every pair of adjacent faces is *compatible*, the mesh is said to be *orientable*.

The number of incident edges of a vertex is called its *degree* or *valence*. Valence is a property commonly associated with only vertices. However, we can also define the valence of a polygonal face as the number of vertices of that face. A mesh in which

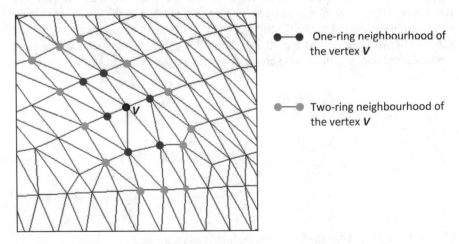

One-ring neighbourhood of the vertex **V**

Two-ring neighbourhood of the vertex **V**

Fig. 2.5 One-ring and two-ring neighbours of a vertex on a manifold mesh

every face has the same number of edges, and every vertex has the same valence is called a *regular* mesh. The number of vertices (V), edges (E), and faces (F) in a closed polygonal mesh are related by the *Euler–Poincaré formula.*

$$V + F - E = 2(1 - g) \tag{2.1}$$

where g, the genus, denotes the number of holes/handles in the mesh. The right-hand side of the above equation is called the *Euler characteristic*. A few mesh objects with varying values of g are shown in Fig. 2.6. It can be easily verified that Eq. (2.1) is satisfied for all three cases. For polyhedral objects without any holes, setting $g = 0$, we get:

$$V + F = E + 2 \tag{2.2}$$

This equation is generally referred to as the *Euler's formula*. The fact that each edge is attached to exactly two vertices is used to prove the *degree-sum formula* (also known as the Euler's handshaking lemma) which states that the sum of the degrees (valences) of all vertices is twice the number of edges.

In a triangular mesh, every face has exactly three edges. If the mesh does not have any border edges, then every edge is counted twice while counting the number of faces. Therefore, the number of faces and edges is connected by the equation $E = 3F/2$. Substituting this in the Euler's formula gives the following properties for a triangle mesh without holes:

$$F = 2V - 4$$
$$E = 3V - 2 \tag{2.3}$$

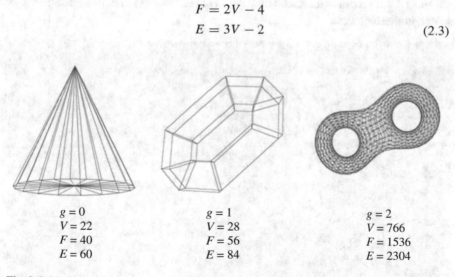

$g = 0$
$V = 22$
$F = 40$
$E = 60$

$g = 1$
$V = 28$
$F = 56$
$E = 84$

$g = 2$
$V = 766$
$F = 1536$
$E = 2304$

Fig. 2.6 Mesh parameters for three models with varying genus values

Thus, for a large triangle mesh, we can easily get an estimate of the number of edges and faces as $F \approx 2\,V$, and $E \approx 3\,V$. The degree-sum formula with these conditions yields the result that the sum of valences in a large triangle mesh is approximately equal to six times the number of vertices. Therefore, the average vertex valence in a large triangle mesh is 6.

2.4   OpenMesh

Mesh operations such as sculpting, repair, simplification, and subdivision are commonly employed in the construction of highly detailed and complex three-dimensional models. These operations require special types of data structures and methods capable of performing local changes in the mesh structure around vertices of a mesh.

OpenMesh is versatile open-source library containing efficient mesh data structures and functions that are useful for mesh processing applications [4, 5]. The next section provides a description of the some of the fundamental data structures that effectively encode local mesh information around vertices, edges, and faces. The data structures and associated methods provide fast neighbourhood access to mesh elements needed for operations such as vertex removal or edge/face subdivision. The OpenMesh initialization step involves the selection of a mesh kernel of either a polygonal type or a triangle mesh type. The kernels define the way mesh entities are internally stored. The examples in Box 2.4 show how OpenMesh kernels are associated with mesh objects, and how data are read in from external mesh files and stored in mesh objects.

Box 2.4 OpenMesh Initialization, Basic Types and Functions

Initialization (general polygonal mesh):

```
#include <OpenMesh/Core/Mesh/PolyMesh_ArrayKernelT.hh>
typedef OpenMesh::PolyMesh_ArrayKernelT<> MyMesh;
MyMesh mesh;
OpenMesh::IO::read_mesh(mesh, "cube.off") //Read mesh data
from file
```

Initialization (triangle polygonal mesh):

```
#include <OpenMesh/Core/Mesh/TriMesh_ArrayKernelT.hh>
typedef OpenMesh::TriMesh_ArrayKernelT<> MyMesh;
MyMesh mesh;
OpenMesh::IO::read_mesh(mesh, "sphere.off") //Read mesh data
from file
```

Basic Types:

```
OpenMesh::Vec3f p = { 1, 2, 3 };    //a point or a vector
OpenMesh::Vec3f n = p.normalize();   //vector normalization
MyMesh::Point  q = { 10, 20, 30 };  //a point
MyMesh::Normal m = { 0.6, 0.8, 0};  //a vector
```

Basic Operations:

```
len = p.length();
glVertex3fv(p.data()); //Using a point in OpenGL
glNormal3fv(n.data()); //Using a vector in OpenGL
d = n1 | n2; //dot product
m = n1 % n2; //cross product
```

Number of vertices: `mesh.n_vertices()`
Number of faces: `mesh.n_faces()`
Number of edges: `mesh.n_edges()`
Attribute query: `mesh.has_face_normals()`
Attribute query: `mesh.has_face_colors()`
Attribute query: `mesh.has_vertex_normals()`

Linear data structures (iterators) and circular data structures (circulators) are the main tools used for mesh traversal and neighbourhood searches. They can be used to process several types of adjacency queries using an efficient mesh data structure known as the half-edge structure. These fundamental techniques are outlined in the following sections.

2.5 Mesh Data Structures

Mesh data structures are designed to perform fast local mesh search in the neighbourhoods of vertices, edges and faces, without having to traverse the whole mesh. They can be used for processing incidence and adjacency queries that are commonly used for gathering information about mesh connectivity and local structure and orientation around vertices. In this section, we consider one face-based and two edge-based data structures.

2.5.1 Face-Based Data Structure

Face-based data structures are primarily used for triangular meshes where both the number of edges and number of vertices per face have a constant value 3. In an ordinary mesh file, each triangle is defined using the indices of its three vertices. A face-based data structure additionally stores references to its three neighbouring triangles (Fig. 2.7). Because of its simple structure, a face data structure can be easily

```
struct Triangle
{
    Vertex *p1, *p2, *p3;
    Triangle *t1, *t2, *t3;
};
```

Fig. 2.7 A face-based data structure for a triangle showing references to its neighbouring faces

constructed from a vertex list and a face list. This data structure does not store any edge-related information, and hence is not particularly suitable for edge operations such as edge collapse, edge flipping, or edge traversal.

Assuming that every polygonal face in a mesh is a triangle, the face-based data structure provides a convenient mechanism to obtain information about all triangles surrounding a vertex. Using this information, we could perform the traversal of the one-ring neighbourhood of a vertex in constant time. The inputs for the algorithm are a vertex v and a triangle containing that vertex. The algorithm iteratively visits the neighbouring triangles, each time checking if the triangle has v as one of its vertices and has not been visited previously. In Fig. 2.8, the triangles indicated by dotted arrows are not visited as they do not contain the vertex v. The vertices of the visited triangles are added to the set of one-ring neighbours of v. A pseudo-code of this method is given in Listing 2.1

Listing 2.1 Pseudo-code for the one-ring neighbourhood traversal algorithm

```
1. Input: v, face   //The triangle has v as a vertex
```

Fig. 2.8 Traversal of the one-ring neighbourhood of a vertex using a face-based data structure

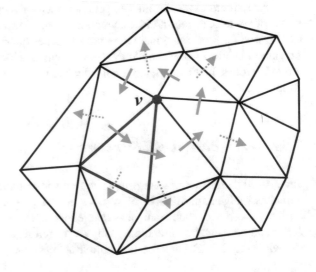

```
2.  S = {}          //Solution set
3.  Add vertices of face other than v to S
4.  t_start = face  //Initial triangle
5.  t_previous = null
6.  t_current = a neighbour of face different from
         t_previous, which has v as a vertex
7.  if (t_current == t_start) STOP
8.  Add vertices of t_current other than v, and not already in v, to S
9.  t_previous = face
10. face = t_current
11. GOTO 6
```

While a face-edge data structure can be easily constructed for triangular meshes, a general polygonal mesh will require more complex structures and methods for processing adjacency queries on its polygonal elements.

2.5.2 Winged-Edge Data Structure

The winged-edge data structure[6] is one of the powerful representations of an orientable mesh that could be used for a variety of edge-based query processing and manipulation of a mesh. In this representation, each face has a clockwise ordering of its vertices and edges. The structure stores several interconnected information pertaining to the neighbourhood of every edge in the form of three substructures: an edge table, a vertex table, and a face table.

An edge PQ and its adjacent faces are shown in Fig. 2.9. The direction of the edge is specified by the start and end vertices, and it enables us to define the left and right sides of the edge. The corresponding references to the polygon L on its left, and R on its right are stored. The edge structure also stores the preceding and

```
struct W_edge
{
    Vertex *start, *end;
    Face   *left,  *right;
    W_edge *left_prev,  *left_next;
    W_edge *right_prev, *right_next;
};
struct Vertex
{
    float x, y, z;
    W_edge *edge;
};
struct Face
{
    W_edge *edge;
};
```

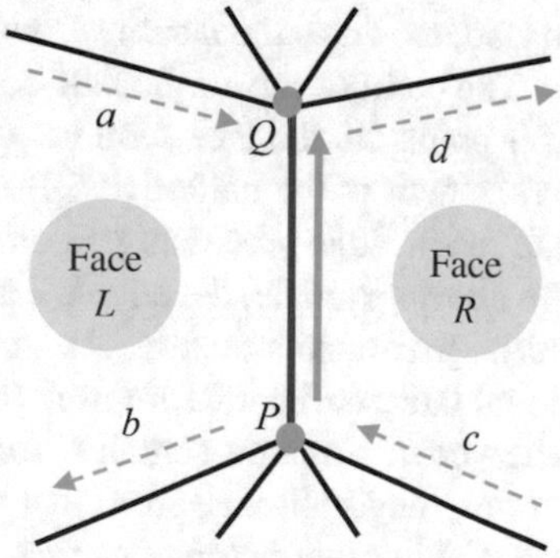

Fig. 2.9 Winged-edge data structure

succeeding edges of PQ with respect to each of these faces. The preceding edge on the left is the edge a, and the succeeding edge on the left is the edge b. Similarly, the preceding edge on the right is c, and the succeeding edge on the right d. Note that on each face, a clockwise ordering of the edges is used. The component values change when the direction of an edge is reversed. The winged-edge structure also requires two additional tables or structures, as shown in Fig. 2.9. The vertex table stores the coordinates of each vertex and one of the edges incident to that vertex. The face table maps each face to one of the edges of that face. These tables provide the entry points to the edge structure via either a vertex or a face. For example, if we are required to find all edges that end at a given vertex v, we first use the vertex table to find one of the edges incident on v, and then use the winged-edge structure to iteratively find the remaining edges. Care must be taken to use the right orientation of an edge; the edge entry for a vertex v in the vertex table may have v as the either the start vertex or the end vertex. Similarly, an edge in the face table may have the face as either its left face or the right face of the edge.

2.5.3 Half-Edge Data Structure

One of the primary limitations of the winged-edge data structure is that the ambiguity regarding the direction of an edge will need to be resolved every time an edge is processed, and this is commonly done using an if-else block to deal with the two possible directions of every edge. The half-edge data structure[7] resolves this ambiguity by splitting every edge and storing it as two half edges, each with a unique direction. A half-edge belongs to only a single face, which is the face on its left side. A half-edge structure stores references to the unique vertex the edge points to, the unique face it belongs to, the successor of the edge belonging to the same face, and the pair of the half-edge having the opposite direction and belonging to the adjacent face (Fig. 2.10). The half-edge structure is essentially a doubly linked list and hence is also known as the Doubly Connected Edge List (DCEL).

The components of the half-edge PQ in Fig. 2.10 are the references to the vertex Q it points to, the face L on its left side, the next edge b on the same face, and the pair which is the half-edge QP in the opposite direction (belonging to the opposite face). Edge processing algorithms often use references to the previous edge (in the above example, the edge a), and this information may also be optionally stored in the half-edge structure. As in the case of the winged-edge structure, two additional tables/structures are used to obtain a half-edge from either a vertex or a face. The vertex structure contains, for each vertex, its coordinates and the reference to an outgoing half-edge from that vertex. The face structure contains, for each face, a half-edge that belongs to that face. From the definition of the half-edge structure, it is clear that for a given half-edge, the start and end points are given by `edge->pair->vert` and `edge->vert` respectively. Similarly, the two faces that border an edge are given by `edge->face` and `edge->pair->face`. As

```
struct H_edge
{
    Vertex *vert;
    Face   *face;
    H_edge *prev, *next;
    H_edge *pair;
};
struct Vertex
{
    float x, y, z;
    H_edge  *edge;
};
struct Face
{
    H_edge *edge;
};
```

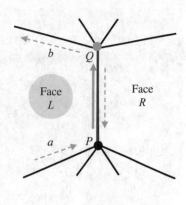

Fig. 2.10 Half-edge data structure

shown in Fig. 2.11, each polygonal face of the mesh contains a set of half-edges oriented in the anti-clockwise sense with respect to the outward normal direction.

OpenMesh stores the vertices, edges, and faces of a mesh and their connectivity information using the half-edge data structure outlined above. References to the half-edge, vertex, and face structures are called *handles*. Handles together with iterators provide the primary mechanism for traversing a mesh. Box 2.5 shows the correspondence between basic operations on the half-edge data structure and OpenMesh functions.

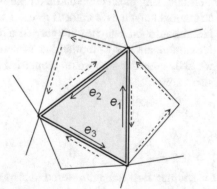

```
e1->next = e2;
e1->prev = e3;
e2->next = e3;
e2->prev = e1;
e3->next = e1;
e3->prev = e2;
```

Fig. 2.11 Half-edges around a polygonal element

Box 2.5 Basic OpenMesh Functions

Type declarations for handles:

```
OpenMesh::VertexHandle verH;
OpenMesh::FaceHandle facH;
OpenMesh::HalfedgeHandle hedH, hedH_n, hedH_p;
OpenMesh::Vec3d point;
```

Half-edge operations:

half-edge → vert: `verH = mesh.to_vertex_handle(hedH);`

half-edge → pair→vert: `verH = mesh.from_vertex_handle(hedH);`

half-edge → next: `hedH_n = mesh.next_halfedge_handle(hedH);`

half-edge→pair: `hedH_p=mesh.opposite_halfedge_handle(hedH);`

half-edge → face: `facH = mesh.face_handle(hedH);`

face → half-edge: `hedH = mesh.halfedge_handle(facH);`

vert → half-edge: `hedH = mesh.halfedge_handle(verH);`

vert coordinates: `point = mesh.point(verH);`

2.6 Mesh Traversal

As seen in the previous section, the half-edge data structure can be used to navigate through a mesh. Three types of mesh elements are used in mesh traversal: (i) a vertex, (ii) a face, and (iii) a directed half-edge. Given a reference to a mesh element, mesh traversal algorithms sequentially visit a neighbouring mesh element using the half-edge data structure. Simple linear data structures known as iterators are used for a sequential traversal of the entire mesh. Neighbourhood searches are carried out by visiting all mesh elements around a particular element using circular data structures known as circulators. In this section, we will consider important properties and applications of both these types of data structures.

2.6.1 Iterators

Iterators provide efficient mechanisms for enumerating elements stored in arrays or lists. OpenMesh supports different types of iterators for vertices, faces, and edges. Dereferencing an iterator gives the corresponding handle. For example, dereferencing a vertex iterator gives a vertex handle using which you may obtain the attribute values of that vertex or access neighbouring elements attached to that vertex. Vertices in a mesh may contain attribute values for normal vectors, colours, and texture coordinates in addition to their 3D position. The code example given in Listing 2.2 prints the coordinates and valences of all vertices in a mesh.

Listing 2.2 Sample application using a vertex iterator

```
typedef OpenMesh::TriMesh_ArrayKernelT<> MyMesh;
MyMesh mesh;
OpenMesh::VertexHandle verH;
MyMesh::VertexIter vit;
OpenMesh::Vec3d p;
int valence;
OpenMesh::IO::read_mesh(mesh, "cube.off")
for (vit = mesh.vertices_begin(); vit != mesh.vertices_end(); vit++)
{
    verH = *vit;
    p = mesh.point(verH);
    valence = mesh.valence(verH);
    cout << p[0] << " " << p[1] << " " << p[2] << " " << valence << endl;
}
```

Face iterators are useful in rendering a mesh, where each face of the mesh is visited and drawn using OpenGL functions. Additional lighting calculations at the vertices of each face may be performed using normal vectors. The code example given in Listing 2.3 prints the number of vertices of each face of a mesh.

Listing 2.3 Sample application using a face iterator

```
typedef OpenMesh::TriMesh_ArrayKernelT<> MyMesh;
MyMesh mesh;
OpenMesh::FaceHandle facH;
MyMesh::FaceIter fit;
int nvert;
OpenMesh::IO::read_mesh(mesh, "cube.off")
for (fit = mesh.faces_begin(); fit != mesh.faces_end(); fit++)
{
    facH = *fit;
    nvert = mesh.valence(facH);
    cout << "Number of vertices = " << nvert << endl;
}
```

OpenMesh provides an edge iterator for accessing all edges of a mesh. Dereferencing the edge iterator gives us an edge handle that could be used to find properties of undirected edge elements of the mesh such as the length, dihedral angle, and the midpoint. Note that the edge handle is not part of the half-edge structure and therefore cannot be used to find the surrounding elements as defined by the half-edge structure. The code example given in Listing 2.4 prints the length and the dihedral angle of all edges of a mesh.

Listing 2.4 Sample application using an edge iterator

```
typedef OpenMesh::TriMesh_ArrayKernelT<> MyMesh;
MyMesh mesh;
OpenMesh::EdgeHandle edgH;
MyMesh::EdgeIter eit;
float len, angle;
OpenMesh::IO::read_mesh(mesh, "cube.off")
for (eit = mesh.edges_begin(); eit != mesh.edges_end(); eit++)
{
    edgH = *eit;
    len = mesh.calc_edge_length(edgH);
    angle = mesh.calc_dihedral_angle(edgH);
    cout << "Edge length = " << len <<
         " Dihedral angle = " << angle << endl;
}
```

2.6.2 Adjacency Queries

The three main components of the half-edge structure (Fig. 2.10), namely half-edges, vertices, and faces, form the primary mesh elements in adjacency queries. Using these mesh elements, we can create nine types of adjacency queries as given in Table 2.1. We use the notation a:- b to mean "find all elements of type b in the neighbourhood of an element of type a". In Table 2.1, the element a is shown in red colour, and the elements b in blue.

Some of the queries may be processed by splitting the query into two simpler queries. For example, the query E:- E may be processed by first processing the query E:- V followed by V:- E. Most of the queries in the above table may be implemented using circulators (discussed in the next section).

2.6.3 Circulators

OpenMesh provides circular data structures known as circulators for performing adjacency queries on vertices and faces. Adjacency queries on edges, on the other hand, can be performed directly using the half-edge structure as shown below. The circulators are used exactly like iterators in a for-loop to enumerate items that are adjacent to the current element. Dereferencing a circulator gives a handle to the enumerated item. The most important circulators and the functions to obtain them from the handle of a given element are listed in Box 2.6. This section describes how the adjacency queries listed in Table 2.1 are implemented using OpenMesh. The pseudo-codes using the pointer notations for the half-edge structure variables are also given for comparison.

Box 2.6 OpenMesh Circulators and Related Functions

Table 2.1 Types of adjacency queries

Query	Description	Example
V:- V	Given a vertex, find all vertices that are adjacent to it. This query finds the one-ring neighbourhood of a vertex	
V: -E	Given a vertex, find all outgoing half-edges from this vertex. This query may be easily modified to find all incident half-edges of the given vertex	
V:- F	Find all faces that share a given vertex	
E:- V	Given a half-edge, find its end vertices	
E:- E	Given a half-edge, find its neighbouring half-edges. The neighbouring edges are either outgoing or incoming half-edges at the vertex pointed to by the given half-edge	
E:- F	Find the faces that share a given edge. For a half-edge, this query generally requires only the face to which the half-edge belongs, but if required, the opposite face may also be obtained easily	
F:- V	Find all vertices of a given face. This information may be directly obtained from a polygon list where each face is specified in terms of indices of its vertices	
F:- E	Given a face, find all half-edges belonging to that face	
F:- F	Given a face, find all neighbouring faces	

Table 2.2 Implementations of adjacency queries using half-edge structure and OpenMesh

Example	Half-edge structure	OpenMesh

V :- V (CW)	```H_edge *e0 = v->edge;```
	```H_edge *edge = e0;```
	```do{```
	``` process(edge->vert);```
	``` edge = edge->pair->next;```
	```} while (edge != e0);```
		```MyMesh::VertexVertexCWIter vvit;```
		```vvit = mesh.vv_cwiter(verH);```
		```for(; vvit.is_valid(); vvit++)```
		```{```
		``` process(*vvit);```
		```}```

V :- V (CCW)	```H_edge *e0 = v->edge;```
	```H_edge *edge = e0;```
	```do{```
	``` process(edge->vert);```
	``` edge = edge->prev->pair;```
	```} while (edge != e0);```
		```MyMesh::VertexVertexCCWIter```
		``` vvit;```
		```vvit = mesh.vv_ccwiter(verH);```
		```for(; vvit.is_valid(); vvit++)```
		```{```
		``` process(*vvit);```
		```}```

V :- E (O)	```H_edge *e0 = v->edge;```
	```H_edge *edge = e0;```
	```do{```
	``` process(edge);```
	``` edge = edge->prev->pair;```
	```} while (edge != e0);```
		```MyMesh::VertexOHalfedgeIter```
		```veit;```
		```veit = mesh.voh_iter(verH);```
		```for(; veit.is_valid(); veit++)```
		```{```
		``` process(*veit);```
		```}```

V :- E (I)	```H_edge *e0= v->edge->prev;```
	```H_edge *edge = e0;```
	```do{```
	``` process(edge);```
	``` edge = edge->pair->prev;```
	```} while (edge != e0);```
		```MyMesh::VertexIHalfedgeIter```
		```veit;```
		```veit = mesh.vih_iter(verH);```
		```for(; veit.is_valid(); veit++)```
		```{```
		``` process(*veit);```
		```}```

V :- F	```H_edge *e0 = v->edge;```
	```H_edge *edge = e0;```
	```do{```
	``` process(edge->face);```
	``` edge = edge->prev->pair;```
	```} while (edge != e0);```
		```MyMesh::VertexFaceIter vfit;```
		```vfit = mesh.vf_iter(verH);```
		```for(; vfit.is_valid(); vfit++)```
		```{```
		``` process(*vfit);```
		```}```

E :- V	```process(e->vert);```
	```process(e->pair->vert);```
		```verH1 =```
		``` mesh.to_vertex_handle(hedH);```
		```verH2 =```
		``` mesh.from_vertex_handle(hedH);```
		```process(*verH1);```
		```process(*verH2);```

E :- E	```H_edge *e0= e->vert->edge;```
	```H_edge *edge = e0;```
	```do{```
	``` process(edge);```
	``` edge = edge->prev->pair;```
	```} while (edge != e0);```
		```verH =```
		``` mesh.to_vertex_handle(hedH);```
		```MyMesh::VertexOHalfedgeIter```
		```veit;```
		```veit = mesh.voh_iter(verH);```
		```for(; veit.is_valid(); veit++)```
		```{```
		``` process(*veit);```
		```}```

E :- F	```process(e->face);```
	```process(e->pair->face);```
		```facH1 = mesh.face_handle(hedH);```
		```e2H =```
		```mesh.opposite_halfedge_handle```
		``` (hedH);```
		```facH2 = mesh.face_handle(e2H);```
		```process(*facH1);```
		```process(*facH2);```

F :- V	```H_edge *e0 =f->edge;```
	```H_edge *edge = e0;```
	```do{```
	``` process(edge->vert);```
	``` edge = edge->next;```
	```} while (edge != e0);```
		```MyMesh::FaceVertexIter fvit;```
		```fvit = mesh.fv_iter(facH);```
		```for(; fvit.is_valid(); fvit++)```
		```{```
		``` process(*fvit);```
		```}```

F :- E	```H_edge *e0 =f->edge;```
	```H_edge *edge = e0;```
	```do{```
	``` process(edge);```
	``` edge = edge->next;```
	```} while (edge != e0);```
		```MyMesh::FaceEdgeIter feit;```
		```feit = mesh.fe_iter(facH);```
		```for(; feit.is_valid(); feit++)```
		```{```
		``` process(*feit);```
		```}```

F :- F	```H_edge *e0 =f->edge;```
	```H_edge *edge = e0;```
	```do{```
	``` process(edge->pair->face);```
	``` edge = edge->next;```
	```} while (edge != e0);```
		```MyMesh::FaceFaceIter ffit;```
		```ffit = mesh.ff_iter(facH);```
		```for(; ffit.is_valid(); ffit++)```
		```{```
		``` process(*ffit);```
		```}```

Circulators:	
Enumeration of vertices connected to a vertex (V :- V):	VertexVertexIter
Clockwise enumeration of vertices connected to a vertex (V :- V):	VertexVertexCWIter
Anti-clockwise enumeration of vertices connected to a vertex (V :- V):	VertexVertexCCWIter
Enumeration of all outgoing half-edges from a vertex (V :- E):	VertexOHalfedgeIter
Enumeration of all incoming half-edges to a vertex (V :- E):	VertexIHalfedgeIter
Enumeration of all faces adjacent to a vertex (V :- F):	VertexFaceIter
Enumeration of all vertices of a face (F :- V):	FaceVertexIter
Enumeration of all half-edges belonging to a face (F :- E):	FaceHalfedgeIter
Enumeration of all faces that are adjacent to a face (F :- F):	FaceFaceIter

Functions for obtaining circulators using handles of mesh elements:		
mesh.vv_iter(verH)	returns a circulator of type	VertexVertexIter
mesh.vv_cwiter(verH)	returns a circulator of type	VertexVertexCWIter
mesh.vv_ccwiter(verH)	returns a circulator of type	VertexVertexCCWIter
mesh.voh_iter(verH)	returns a circulator of type	VertexOHalfedgeIter
mesh.vih_iter(verH)	returns a circulator of type	VertexIHalfedgeIter
mesh.vf_iter(verH)	returns a circulator of type	VertexFaceIter
mesh.fv_iter(facH)	returns a circulator of type	FaceVertexIter
mesh.fh_iter(facH)	returns a circulator of type	FaceHalfedgeIter
mesh.ff_iter(facH)	returns a circulator of type	FaceFaceIter

Examples of the processing of adjacency queries using the half-edge structure in Fig. 2.10 and the corresponding OpenMesh-based implementations are shown in Table 2.1 In the table, the function "doSomething()" represents a generic user defined function that takes an enumerated item as input. Some of the implementations will look very similar to each other, but a careful inspection of the code will reveal subtle differences. For each case, the input mesh element on which the query is performed is indicated in bold font.

2.7 Surface Normal Computation

The orientation of a planar polygonal element in three-dimensional space is given by the direction of its surface normal vector. The normal vector is therefore a very important term used in lighting calculations, collision detection, polygon culling, and non-photorealistic rendering. The normal vector is closely associated with the definition of planar elements. Any plane in thee dimensions is given by a general linear equation of the form:

$$ax + by + cz + d = 0 \tag{2.4}$$

where (a, b, c) represents the direction of the normal vector of the plane. The normalization of this vector gives us the plane's unit normal vector. Since a triangle is always a planar element, the vertices of a triangular region within a polygonal element could be used to find its normal direction as the cross-product of two vectors p and q along the edges of the polygon (Fig. 2.12):

$$\boldsymbol{n}_{\text{face}} = \boldsymbol{p} \times \boldsymbol{q} = \begin{bmatrix} y_1(z_2 - z_3) + y_2(z_3 - z_1) + y_3(z_1 - z_2) \\ z_1(x_2 - x_3) + z_2(x_3 - x_1) + z_3(x_1 - x_2) \\ x_1(y_2 - y_3) + x_2(y_3 - y_1) + x_3(y_1 - y_2) \end{bmatrix} \tag{2.5}$$

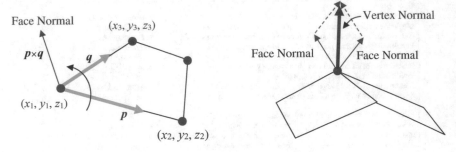

Fig. 2.12 Computation of face normal and vertex normal directions

If the normal vector is assigned to the whole polygonal face including all its vertices, lighting calculations performed on vertices will produce a nearly uniform shade of colour across that polygon. This method of rendering a polygonal mesh using face normal vectors can produce visible discontinuities in shading at polygon boundaries, making the underlying polygonal structure clearly visible.

Vertex normal vectors represent the average normal direction at a vertex and are computed by gathering the face normal vectors of all faces that share that vertex (V:-F):

$$n_{\text{vert}} = \sum_{\text{V: - F}} n_{\text{face}} \tag{2.6}$$

A vertex normal vector may be assigned to each vertex in the definition of an object. Per-vertex normals give a more accurate representation of local orientation of a surface, and thus a smooth shading of the surface. A comparison of the displays of a mesh object produced using face normals and vertex normals is given in Fig. 2.13.

OpenMesh contains functions for computing both face and vertex normal vectors (if not already provided) for an input mesh data. Listing 2.5 gives important parts of the code for rendering a mesh object using face normals. The corresponding code for vertex normals is given in Listing 2.6.

Listing 2.5 OpenMesh code segments of a mesh viewer for rendering mesh data using face normal

```
typedef OpenMesh::TriMesh_ArrayKernelT<> MyMesh;
MyMesh mesh;

void initialize()  //Initialization function
{
   OpenMesh::IO::read_mesh(mesh, "cube.off")
   if (!mesh.has_face_normals())
   {
      mesh.request_face_normals();
      mesh.update_face_normals();
   }
   ... //Other OpenGL initialization
```

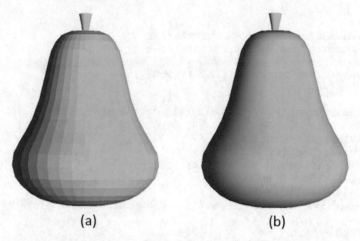

Fig. 2.13 Rendering of a mesh object using **a** face normals and **b** vertex normals

```
}

void drawObject()    //Called in the display function
{
    MyMesh::FaceIter fit;
    MyMesh::FaceHandle facH;
    MyMesh::FaceVertexIter fvit;
    MyMesh::Normal normal;
    MyMesh::Point p;
    for (fit=mesh.faces_begin(); fit!=mesh.faces_end(); fit++)
    {
      facH = *fit;
      normal = mesh.normal(facH); //Get face normal
      glNormal3fv(norm.data());    //Call OpenGL function
      glBegin(GL_TRIANGLES);
      for (fvit = mesh.fv_iter(facH); fvit.is_valid(); fvit++)
      {
         p = mesh.point(*fvit);   //Vertex data
         glVertex3fv(p.data());   //Call OpenGL function
      }
      glEnd();
    }
}
```

Listing 2.6 OpenMesh code segments of a mesh viewer for rendering mesh data using vertex normal

```
typedef OpenMesh::TriMesh_ArrayKernelT<> MyMesh;
MyMesh mesh;

void initialize()  //Initialization function
{
    OpenMesh::IO::read_mesh(mesh, "cube.off")
    if (!mesh.has_vertex_normals())
```

```
    {
       mesh.request_vertex_normals();
       mesh.update_vertex_normals();
    }
    ... //Other OpenGL initialization
}

void drawObject()   //Called in the display function
{
    MyMesh::FaceIter fit;
    MyMesh::FaceHandle facH;
    MyMesh::FaceVertexIter fvit;
    MyMesh::Normal normal;
    MyMesh::Point p;
    for (fit=mesh.faces_begin(); fit!=mesh.faces_end(); fit++)
    {
     facH = *fit;
     glBegin(GL_TRIANGLES);
     for (fvit = mesh.fv_iter(facH); fvit.is_valid(); fvit++)
     {
       normal = mesh.normal(*fvit);  //Get vertex normal
       glNormal3fv(norm.data());    //Call OpenGL function

       p = mesh.point(*fvit);       //Vertex data
       glVertex3fv(p.data());       //Call OpenGL function
     }
     glEnd();
    }
}
```

2.8   Bounding Box Computation

Mesh processing algorithms often require the computation of the bounding box of
a three-dimensional mesh to determine the range of values of vertex coordinates.
The bounding box is also useful for centring and scaling mesh models to fit within
a standard view frustum of the camera. OpenMesh provides two useful functions
minimize(point) and maximize(point) that help in simplifying the code
for computing the bounding box of a mesh model as shown in Listing 2.7.

Listing 2.7 Computation of the bounding box of a given mesh object

```
void getBoundingBox(float& xmin, float& xmax,
                    float& ymin, float& ymax,
                    float& zmin, float& zmax)
{
   MyMesh::VertexIter vit = mesh.vertices_begin();
   MyMesh::Point pmin, pmax;

   pmin = pmax = mesh.point(*vit);

   for (vit = mesh.vertices_begin()+1; vit != mesh.vertices_end(); vit++)
   {
         pmin.minimize(mesh.point(*vit));
         pmax.maximize(mesh.point(*vit));
   }
   xmin = pmin[0];  ymin = pmin[1];  zmin = pmin[2];
   xmax = pmax[0];  ymax = pmax[1];  zmax = pmax[2];
}
```

The parameters of the bounding box could be used to translate the model to the origin and to scale it to fit within a standard view frustum with the view coordinates in the range $[-1, +1]$. The code for translation and scaling of a mesh object is given in Listing 2.8.

Listing 2.8 Scale and position normalization of a given mesh object

```
getBoundingBox(xmin, xmax, ymin, ymax, zmin, zmax);

//Centroid of the box
float xc = (xmin + xmax)*0.5;
float yc = (ymin + ymax)*0.5;
float zc = (zmin + zmax)*0.5;

//Max dimension of the box
OpenMesh::Vec3f box = { xmax - xc, ymax - yc, zmax - zc };
modelScale = 1.0 / box.max();

//Scale the model
glScalef(modelScale, modelScale, modelScale);

//First translate the model to the origin
glTranslatef(-xc, -yc, -zc)

//Draw the model
drawMesh();
```

2.9 Triangle Adjacency Primitive

The triangle adjacency primitive (GL_TRIANGLES_ADJACENCY) [8] is a special type of geometric primitive defined in OpenGL-4. It consists of a triangle and three adjacent triangles and is defined by six vertices $V_0 \dots V_5$, as shown in Fig. 2.14a.

An element (or index) array $\{0, 1, 2, 3, 4, 5\}$ represents a triangle adjacency primitive containing the main triangle $\{0, 2, 4\}$ and its adjacent triangles. The geometry

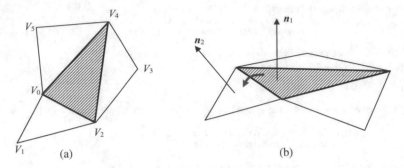

Fig. 2.14 Triangle adjacency primitive and its usefulness in characterizing edge conditions

shader receives all six vertices in a built-in array gl_in[i].gl_Position, $i =$ 0.0.5. If the geometry shader is not present, only the main triangle given by indices {0, 2, 4} is rasterized in the rendering pipeline.

The adjacency information is valuable for deriving several characteristics associated with the edges of the main triangle [9]. It can be used to find the dihedral angle between adjacent faces, identify crease and silhouette edges, and also estimate the direction of local curvature. As an example, if $n_1 \cdot n_2 < 0.5$ in Fig. 2.14b, then the dihedral angle between the corresponding triangles is greater than 60 degrees, and the common edge between the triangles could be classified as a crease edge. Similarly, if a triangle is front-facing (i.e. $n_1 \cdot v > 0$, where v is the view vector) and its adjacent triangle is back-facing ($n_2 \cdot v \leq 0$), then the common edge could be classified as a silhouette edge.

In order to use primitives of the above type, vertices and their attributes will need to be collected in groups of 6. This grouping of vertices can be performed easily with the help of a face-halfedge circulator. As we traverse a mesh using a face iterator (see Listing 2.5), we get the face handles of each triangle by dereferencing the face iterator (facH = *fit). A face-halfedge circulator with this handle as the input would provide the references (handles) to the three half-edges bordering the face. For each half-edge, we can then find the source vertex and the vertex on the opposite face.

If any of the edges of the current triangle is a boundary edge, the corresponding half-edge's opposite half-edge (the dashed edge in Fig. 2.15) will satisfy the condition mesh.is_boundary(). If the condition is satisfied, the vertex on the opposite triangle (vertex V_3 in Fig. 2.15) will not exist. This type of boundary conditions is indicated by repeating the element index in the triangle adjacency primitive. As an example, if the dashed edge in Fig. 2.15 is a boundary edge, the index of V_3 is set as equal to the index of V_2. The code for collecting the vertices of each triangle-adjacency primitive using a face-halfedge circulator is given in Listing 2.9.

Listing 2.9 Construction of vertex data for triangle adjacency primitives

```
indx = 0; //Vertex element index
for (fit = mesh.faces_begin(); fit != mesh.faces_end(); fit++)
{
```

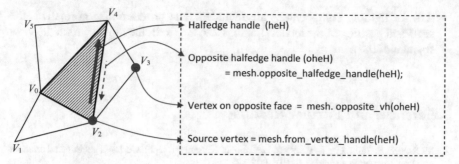

Fig. 2.15 Formation of a triangle-adjacency primitive using a face-halfedge circulator

```
facH = *fit; //Face handle
for (fhit = mesh.fh_iter(facH); fhit.is_valid(); fhit++)
{
heH = *fhit; //Halfedge handle
oheH = mesh.opposite_halfedge_handle(heH);
verH1 = mesh.from_vertex_handle(heh);
elems[indx] = verH1.idx();
if (!mesh.is_boundary(oheH)) //Interior edge
{
verH2 = mesh.opposite_vh(oheH);
elems[indx + 1] = verH2.idx();
}
else //Boundary edge
elems[indx + 1] = elems[indx]; //Repeated vertex
indx += 2;
n}
}
```

The triangle adjacency primitive finds applications in non-photorealistic rendering of a mesh model, where the prominent edges of the model are highlighted and a special type of shading model or texture mapping applied to create an artistic/expressive style in the way the model is displayed. The implementation of a non-photorealistic rendering algorithm using the geometry shader is discussed in detail in Chap. 4.

2.10   Chapter Resources

The folder "Chapter 2" on the companion website contains the following data files and the source code of a program.

- MeshFiles.zip: The zip file contains a few mesh models in OFF and OBJ formats, that were used as examples in this chapter.
- MeshViewer.cpp: This program uses the OpenMesh library for loading a mesh file. OpenMesh iterators and circulators are used for rendering the model. Options for using either face normal vectors (Listing 2.5) or vertex normal vectors (Listing

2.6) for lighting computations are included. The program also normalizes the scale and position of the model (Listings 2.7, 2.8) to fit the model within the view frustum of the camera.

References and Further Reading

1. M. Botsch, S. Steinberg, S. Bischoff, L. Kobbelt, R. Aachen, OpenMesh—a generic and efficient polygon mesh data structure, 02/10/2002
2. P. Bourke, Object Files. http://paulbourke.net/dataformats/obj/. Accessed 10 November 2021
3. J. Burkardt, PLY Files. https://people.sc.fsu.edu/~jburkardt/data/ply/ply.html. Accessed 10 November 2021
4. M. Botsch, L. Kobbelt, M. Pauly, P. Alliez, B. Lévy, *Polygon Mesh Processing*. (AK Peters/CRC Press (in English), 2010), p. 250
5. F. Guggeri, S. Marras, C. Mura, R. Scateni, Topological operations on triangle meshes using the OpenMesh library (2008). https://doi.org/10.2312/LocalChapterEvents/ItalChap/ItalianChapConf2008/073-080
6. B. Neperud, J. Lowther, C.-K. Shene, Visualizing and animating the winged-edge data structure. Comput. Graph. **31**(6), 877–886 (2007). https://doi.org/10.1016/j.cag.2007.08.009
7. M. Botsch, M. Pauly, C. Rossl, S. Bischoff, L. Kobbelt, Geometric modeling based on triangle meshes, in *Presented at the ACM SIGGRAPH 2006 Courses*, Boston, Massachusetts (2006). [Online]. Available https://doi.org/10.1145/1185657.1185839
8. G. Sellers, R.S. Wright, N. Haemel, Primitive processing in OpenGL, in *OpenGL SuperBible: Comprehensive Tutorial and Reference*, 6th ed. (Addison-Wesley Professional, 2013). [Online]. Available https://www.informit.com/articles/article.aspx?p=2120983&seqNum=2
9. P.V. Sander, D. Nehab, E. Chlamtac, H. Hoppe, Efficient traversal of mesh edges using adjacency primitives. ACM Trans. Graph. **27**(5), 144 (2008). https://doi.org/10.1145/1409060.1409097

Chapter 3
Mesh Processing Algorithms

In the previous chapter, we explored ways to traverse a mesh and perform adjacency queries using iterators and circulators of the OpenMesh library. We also discussed the advantages provided by mesh data structures such as the half-edge data structure, and some of their basic applications.

In this chapter, we will consider a few important algorithms in the area of mesh processing, including two main operations performed in several applications: mesh simplification and mesh subdivision. This chapter contains the following sections:

- **Mesh simplification**: Gives an overview of vertex decimation and edge collapse operations used for mesh simplification.
- **Mesh subdivision**: Explains the process of subdivision used for constructing interpolation and approximation surfaces.
- **Mesh parameterization**: Outlines the concepts behind planar and spherical embedding of polygonal meshes.
- **3D morphing**: Presents a few methods for generating a shape morph between two mesh objects.

3.1 Mesh Simplification

Mesh simplification algorithms aim to reduce the geometric complexity of a mesh without altering the essential shape characteristics [1]. These methods are designed to take meshes containing a large number of polygons and convert them into meshes with a relatively smaller number of polygons. Mesh simplification is commonly used in the construction of level-of-detail representations of objects with a high polygon count. Most of the algorithms try to preserve the topology of the mesh by making sure that the resulting mesh has the same Euler characteristic (Eq. (2.1)). In this section, we outline two important methods based on the local simplification strategy that progressively remove vertices or edges until the required level of simplification is achieved [2]. In general, simplification methods use a cost function to select the

© The Author(s), under exclusive license to Springer Nature Switzerland AG 2022
R. Mukundan, *3D Mesh Processing and Character Animation*,
https://doi.org/10.1007/978-3-030-81354-3_3

most appropriate vertex or edge for removal and also impose a set of constraints on vertices or edges for deletion.

3.1.1   Error Metrics

Error metrics in a mesh simplification algorithm are used to specify the cost associated with the removal of a vertex or an edge [3]. The metric associated with a mesh element may also take into account shape and topological features of the mesh that should be preserved during a simplification operation. In general, an error metric provides a coarse measure of the deviation introduced in the geometrical shape of a mesh.

One of the commonly used criteria for vertex decimation is the near-planarity of the neighbourhood of a vertex. A nearly planar region could be represented by a few triangular elements covering the region instead of many smaller triangles. Consider an interior vertex v surrounded by a closed triangle fan as shown in Fig. 3.1. The planarity of the surface region around the vertex can be measured as its distance d from the average plane of its neighbourhood (triangle fan). The average plane is computed as given below, using the local area-weighted average of the surface normal vectors n_i and the centroids p_i of all triangles sharing the vertex v.

If there are k triangles that have a common vertex v $(k \geq 3)$, and if A_i, n_i, p_i denote the area, normal vector and the centroid, respectively, of the ith triangle, then the area-weighted average normal and the area-weighted average point are computed as follows:

$$n_{avg} = \frac{\sum_{i=1}^{k} A_i n_i}{\sum_{i=1}^{k} A_i}$$

$$p_{avg} = \frac{\sum_{i=1}^{k} A_i p_i}{\sum_{i=1}^{k} A_i} \tag{3.1}$$

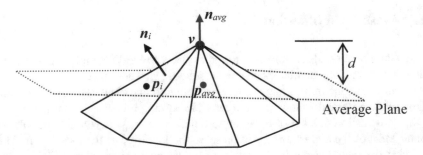

Fig. 3.1 Definition of an average plane and error metric for an interior vertex

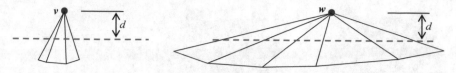

Fig. 3.2 Vertices v and w have the same distance from the average plane but different local curvatures

The equation of the average plane that contains the point p_{avg} and has n_{avg} as the unit normal vector is given by the following dot product between the normal vector and a vector that lies on the plane:

$$n_{avg} \cdot (p - p_{avg}) = 0 \tag{3.2}$$

where $p = (x, y, z)$ is any point that lies on the plane. The cost associated with v is defined as the perpendicular distance (or shortest distance) d of the vertex v from the average plane, given by

$$d = n_{avg} \cdot (v - p_{avg}) \tag{3.3}$$

There are two problems with the above metric. Firstly, the values of d vary with the physical size of the mesh (or scale). Secondly, the definition of d as given above does not accurately represent variations in local curvature around a point. The two examples given in Fig. 3.2 have drastically different curvatures at the vertices, but the same value d computed using Eq. (3.3).

In order to get a better estimate of the local curvature at a vertex v, we normalize the metric d by the length of the largest edge l_e through v:

$$\text{Cost}_1(v) = \frac{d}{l_e} \tag{3.4}$$

The normalization of d makes it a scale invariant and dimension-less quantity, with values between 0 and 1. The pseudo-code for computing the above planarity metric is given in Listing 3.1. This code serves as a good example of the usefulness of mesh iterators and circulators in mesh processing applications.

Listing 3.1 Pseudo-code for computing the planarity metric at vertices of a mesh

```
for each vertex v of the mesh
{
    le = 0
    for each edge e through the vertex v  (V :- E)
    {
        Find the length of the edge
        Update the maximum length le
    }
    for each face f sharing the vertex v  (V :- F)
```

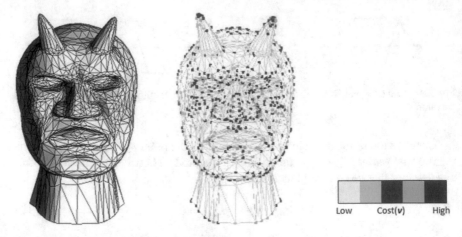

Fig. 3.3 Mesh with the planarity metric at each vertex represented by a colour value

```
{
    Compute the area, normal, centroid of the face
    Update area weighted sum of normals and centroids
}
Compute the distance d of the vertex v from the average plane
Compute  d/(le)
}
```

As an example, the colour encoded values of the planarity metric computed at the vertices of a triangle mesh are shown in Fig. 3.3. The boundary vertices of the mesh are assigned a constant white colour.

If v is a boundary vertex, the error metric for v is defined as the shortest distance d of the vertex from an imaginary line connecting the two opposite neighbours p, q of the vertex along the boundary (Fig. 3.4). These neighbouring vertices are connected to v by edges that have only one bordering face and can be identified using either a winged-edge or half-edge-based ring traversal algorithm.

The shortest distance d of the boundary vertex v from the line PQ can then be obtained as follows:

Fig. 3.4 Definition of an error metric for a boundary vertex

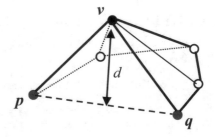

$$\text{Cost}_2(v) = d = \frac{\|(v - p) \times (q - p\|)}{q - p} \tag{3.5}$$

Another cost function that can be associated with vertices and edges is the quadric error metric (QEM). Given a set of k triangles sharing a common vertex v as shown in Fig. 3.1, the cost associated with a vertex p with respect to the triangle fan at v is denoted as QEM(p; v) and is defined as the sum of squares of shortest distances of p from the k triangles. Assume that each triangle containing $v = (x_v, y_v, z_v)$ has a unit surface normal vector $n_i = (a_i, b_i, c_i)$, $i = 1 \ldots k$. The equation of the triangle can be written as

$$a_i x + b_i y + c_i z + d_i = 0, \tag{3.6}$$

where $d_i = -a_i x_v - b_i y_v - c_i z_v$. The shortest distance of the point $p = (x_p, y_p, z_p)$ to this plane is given by

$$d_i(p) = a_i x_p + b_i y_p + c_i z_p + d_i = A_i^T P \tag{3.7}$$

where

$$A_i = \begin{bmatrix} a_i \\ b_i \\ c_i \\ d_i \end{bmatrix}, \quad P = \begin{bmatrix} x_p \\ y_p \\ z_p \\ 1 \end{bmatrix} \tag{3.8}$$

The square of the distance of p to the plane is therefore

$$d_i^2(p) = (A_i^T P)^T (A_i^T P) = P^T (A_i A_i^T) P \tag{3.9}$$

The sum of squares of distances of p to all planes containing v is given by

$$\text{QEM}(p; v) = \sum_{i=1}^{k} d_i^2(p) = P^T \left(\sum_{i=1}^{k} A_i A_i^T \right) P \tag{3.10}$$

The right-hand side of the equation is a quadratic polynomial, hence the name quadric error metric [3, 4]. The summation within the brackets on the right-hand side of Eq. (3.10) can be precomputed and stored for every vertex v.

An approximation of the local curvature around an edge is given by the dihedral angle between the two faces on either side of the edge. If e is an edge containing faces f_1 and f_2, the dihedral angle is given by $\cos^{-1}(n_1 \cdot n_2)$ where, n_1, n_2 are the unit surface normal vectors of faces f_1 and f_2, respectively. Generally, a linear combination of the dihedral angle and the length of the edge $|e|$ is used as the cost associated with the edge e:

$$\text{Cost}_3(e) = k_1\cos^{-1}(\boldsymbol{n}_1 \cdot \boldsymbol{n}_2) + k_2|e| \tag{3.11}$$

where k_1, k_2 are user specified constants. Using OpenMesh, the dihedral angle and the length of an edge with handle 'eh' are calculated as follows:

```
angle = mesh.calc_dihedral_angle(eh);
length = mesh.calc_edge_length(eh);
```

In some implementations, the length $|e|$ is normalized using the maximum value of edge length $|e|_{\text{max}}$ over the entire mesh, to get a scale invariant quantity. The first term is also divided by π to obtain a value in the range $[0, 1]$:

$$\text{Cost}_4(e) = k_1 \frac{\cos^{-1}(\boldsymbol{n}_1 \cdot \boldsymbol{n}_2)}{\pi} + \frac{k_2(|e|)}{|e|_{\text{max}}} \tag{3.12}$$

The computation of inverse cosine function in the above equation can be eliminated by replacing the function with a direct mapping of the value of $\boldsymbol{n}_1 \cdot \boldsymbol{n}_2$ from the range $[-1, +1]$ to $[+1, 0]$:

$$\text{Cost}_5(e) = k_1 \frac{(1 - \boldsymbol{n}_1 \cdot \boldsymbol{n}_2)}{2} + k_2\frac{k_2(|e|)}{|e|_{\text{max}}} \tag{3.13}$$

The mesh in Fig. 3.3 with the edges drawn with colour values representing edge costs as defined above is shown in Fig. 3.5.

Edge collapse operations usually move the end points v, w of an edge towards a common point p somewhere near the middle of the edge to shrink the edge to a point. A cost function for an edge e that is collapsed to a point p can be defined in terms

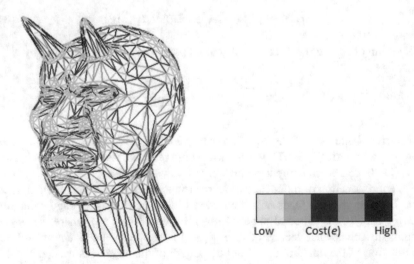

Fig. 3.5 Mesh with the edge cost encoded in colour values

of the QEM metric (see Eq. (3.10)) for p with respect to the end points v and w as follows:

$$\text{Cost}_{\text{QEM}}(e) = \text{QEM}(p; v) + \text{QEM}(p, w) \tag{3.14}$$

3.1.2 Vertex Decimation

The vertex decimation algorithm iteratively removes vertices from a triangular mesh [5] to reduce its polygon count while preserving the topology and shape features of the original mesh. When a vertex is removed, all incident edges of that vertex are also removed leaving a hole in its one-ring neighbourhood. This region will need to be re-triangulated as part of the vertex removal step. The selection of a vertex for removal is generally based on a decimation criterion that ensures that important shape features of the mesh are not affected. The algorithm uses a greedy approach, iteratively selecting the vertex with the current minimum value of an error metric for decimation. An upper threshold for this metric prevents all vertices with values greater than the threshold from being deleted. When a vertex is removed, the error metric values of its adjacent vertices are recomputed based on the re-triangulation of the one-ring neighbourhood.

The one-ring neighbourhood of the deleted vertex will in general form the boundary of a star-shaped polygon (Fig. 3.6). Algorithms for the triangulation of such polygons can be found in [6]. Convex polygons are special types of star-shaped polygons where every internal angle is at most $180°$. Convex polygons can be easily

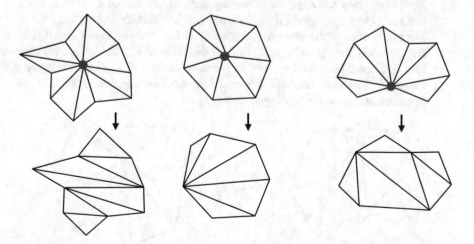

Fig. 3.6 Removal of internal and boundary vertices and the triangulation of the resulting polygons

triangulated from any vertex, but such a triangulation may not always give the optimal value for the minimum angle of the triangles.

In a closed triangle mesh, when a vertex is removed and the resulting polygonal element re-triangulated as shown above, the total number of triangles in the mesh reduces by 2. This can be verified in the first two cases shown in Fig. 3.6. According to Euler's formula (Eq. (2.2)), the removal of a vertex causes the number of edges to reduce by 3.

3.1.3   Edge Collapse Operation

An edge collapse is a relatively simpler operation compared to vertex decimation. Here, a local curvature-based cost function is associated with every edge and used for selecting an edge for removal. An edge and its two incident faces are removed by moving the edge's end points towards each other, till they coincide, collapsing the edge. The result of one edge collapse operation is illustrated in Fig. 3.7, where the edge PQ is collapsed by moving P and Q towards a common point P'. Note that the new vertex P' may in general be somewhere in between the original positions of P and Q.

The main topological restrictions used by the edge collapse algorithm in selecting edges are shown in Fig. 3.8. The bottom row of the figure shows the result of the edge collapse operation in each of the following cases:

(a)   The selected edge belongs to a triangle for which the other two edges are boundary edges. Collapsing this edge results in a topologically inconsistent configuration that contains an isolated vertex.

(b)   Both vertices of the edge are boundary vertices, but the edge itself is not a boundary edge. Collapsing this edge results in a non-manifold vertex.

(c)   The intersection of the one-ring neighbourhoods of vertices P and Q normally contains only the opposite vertices A, B of the edge PQ. In the special case shown in the figure, the intersection contains vertices A, B, C, D. Collapsing the edge PQ removes six faces instead of just two. In general, the edge collapse operation results in the folding of triangles.

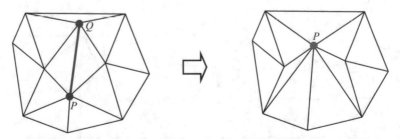

Fig. 3.7   Edge collapse operation performed by moving the vertices P and Q towards P'

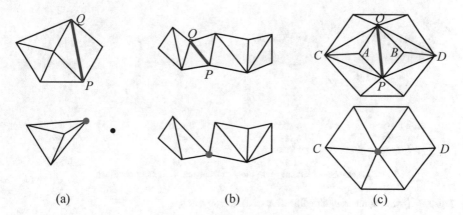

Fig. 3.8 Configurations not suitable for the edge collapse operation

3.1.4 Mesh Simplification Using OpenMesh

OpenMesh uses a cost-driven half-edge selection and collapse operation for simplifying a mesh. The mesh decimation framework includes a set of decimating modules that specify the cost function to be used in the simplification operation. A sample program highlighting the main implementation aspects is given in Listing 3.2.

Listing 3.2 Mesh simplification using OpenMesh

```
#include <OpenMesh/Core/IO/MeshIO.hh>
#include <OpenMesh/Core/Mesh/TriMesh_ArrayKernelT.hh>
#include <OpenMesh/Tools/Decimater/DecimaterT.hh>
#include <OpenMesh/Tools/Decimater/ModQuadricT.hh>

typedef OpenMesh::TriMesh_ArrayKernelT<> MyMesh;
typedef OpenMesh::Decimater::DecimaterT<MyMesh> MyDecimater;
MyMesh mesh;
typedef OpenMesh::Decimater::ModQuadricT<MyMesh>::Handle HMod-
Quadric;
MyDecimater decimater(mesh);
HModQuadric hModQuadric;

int main()
{
OpenMesh::IO::read_mesh(mesh, "Camel.off")
decimater.add(hModQuadric);
decimater.initialize();
decimater.decimate_to(tverts[iter]);
mesh.garbage_collection();

return 0;
}
```

In Fig. 3.9 we can see the decimation framework of OpenMesh in action in progressively simplifying a closed triangle mesh.

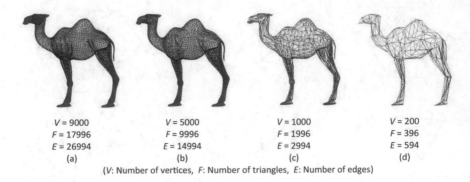

$V = 9000$ $V = 5000$ $V = 1000$ $V = 200$
$F = 17996$ $F = 9996$ $F = 1996$ $F = 396$
$E = 26994$ $E = 14994$ $E = 2994$ $E = 594$
   (a)   (b)   (c)   (d)

(V: Number of vertices, F: Number of triangles, E: Number of edges)

Fig. 3.9 Different levels of simplification of a triangle mesh

3.2 Mesh Subdivision

Mesh subdivision methods increase the polygon density of a mesh by iteratively splitting polygons and applying a set of rules for repositioning polygon vertices in each step [7]. Every subdivision step increases the number of edges, vertices and polygons in a mesh without grossly distorting the overall shape or topological characteristics. Mesh subdivision algorithms are used for geometric modelling of complex surfaces from simple coarse meshes through successive refinement, smoothing and approximation. Subdivision algorithms provide us the capability to alter the level of detail of a polygonal mesh from very coarse to highly tessellated and smooth object models [8]. Such methods are therefore also called scalable geometry techniques.

Before considering subdivision algorithms for polygonal meshes, we review the fundamental aspects of iterative polygonal line subdivision methods used for creating subdivision curves.

3.2.1 Subdivision Curves: Interpolation Versus Approximation

An iterative refinement of a polygonal line can be made to converge to a parametric curve by creating new points in between existing points and suitably transforming the points in each iteration. The initial polygonal line used in this process defines a coarse shape of the desired subdivision curve and is called the base polygonal line or the control polygonal line. Its vertices are often referred to as control points. In this section, we consider two types of subdivision curves:

I.   *Interpolation curves*: In each iteration, the points that are currently on the polygonal line are kept fixed, and only the newly generated points are transformed using a linear combination of existing neighbouring points. In particular, the points on the control polygonal line remain fixed throughout the process, and therefore, the subdivision curve passes through all control points.

II. *Approximation curves*: As in the case of interpolation curves, the newly gener-ated points in each iteration are transformed using a linear combination of neighbouring points. Existing points (points from the previous iteration) are also transformed using a linear combination of their neighbours. This two-step transformation of points may result in an approximating curve that does not pass through any of the control points.

We will now consider the basic principles behind the design of interpolation curves. One of the most commonly used interpolation schemes is a linear interpola-tion between two quantities such as two points or colour values or normal vectors. This single-parameter interpolation gives a convex combination of the interpolated quantities. The interpolated quantities are denoted by P_1, P_2 and the parameter by t in Eq. (3.15). The coefficients of the interpolated quantities are $(1 - t)$ and t.

$$P = (1 - t)P_1 + t P_2, \quad t \in [0, 1] \tag{3.15}$$

In a convex combination of points, each coefficient (weight) is a positive value in the range [0, 1], and the sum of the coefficients is always 1. Even though the above formula could be easily extended to include any number of control points $P_1 \ldots P_n$, such an interpolation mechanism using convex weights is not suitable for generating subdivision curves since the points P resulting from the interpolation always lie within the convex hull of the control points. This problem can be clearly seen in Fig. 3.10, where four points $Q_1 \ldots Q_4$ form the control polygonal line (and also their convex hull because of the polygon's convex shape). In this example, if $P_1 \ldots P_4$ are four consecutive points on the polygonal line in any iteration, a new point P between P_2 and P_3 is generated using the following convex combination of its immediate neighbours:

$$P = \left(\frac{1}{6}\right)P_1 + \left(\frac{2}{6}\right)P_2 + \left(\frac{2}{6}\right)P_3 + \left(\frac{1}{6}\right)P_4 \tag{3.16}$$

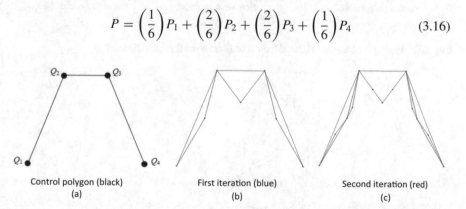

Control polygon (black)   First iteration (blue)   Second iteration (red)
(a)   (b)   (c)

Fig. 3.10 Example of a bad interpolation using a convex combination of neighbouring points

We require the interpolated subdivision curve to have a better, smoother shape defined by the control points, at the same time passing through all control points. As shown above, we will assign a higher weight to the closest neighbours (P_2, P_3), but a negative weight to farther neighbours (P_1, P_4), making sure that the sum of weights is 1 (Eq. (3.17)).

$$P = \left(\frac{-1}{16}\right)P_1 + \left(\frac{9}{16}\right)P_2 + \left(\frac{9}{16}\right)P_3 + \left(\frac{-1}{16}\right)P_4 \qquad (3.17)$$

The above interpolation scheme produces new points that lie outside the convex hull of the control points in such a way that in each iteration the polygonal line is progressively refined to a smoother curve passing through the control points (Fig. 3.11).

Let us now consider the process of generating an approximating curve. For this, we will use a polygon (Fig. 3.12a) as the control polygonal line. Since, in each iteration, every point on the current polygon is transformed, we will use the notation P_i^j to denote the ith point on the polygon in jth iteration. The subscript i varies from 0 to $N_j - 1$, where N_j is the number of points on the curve after jth iteration. Using this notation, we can specify the two-step transformation of points on an approximating subdivision curve as follows:

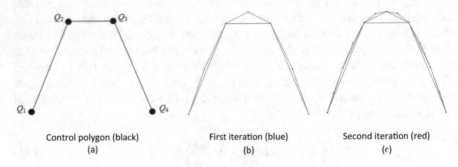

Fig. 3.11 Example of a proper interpolation for generating a subdivision curve

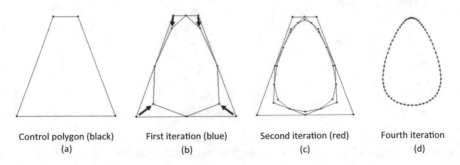

Fig. 3.12 Example of a subdivision curve generated using the approximation method

Transformation of existing points P_i^j in jth iteration:

$$P_{2i}^{j+1} = \left(\frac{1}{8}\right) P_{i-1}^j + \left(\frac{6}{8}\right) P_i^j + \left(\frac{1}{8}\right) P_{i+1}^j \tag{3.18}$$

Insertion of new points in jth iteration:

$$P_{2i-1}^{j+1} = \left(\frac{1}{2}\right) P_{i-1}^j + \left(\frac{1}{2}\right) P_i^j$$

$$P_{2i+1}^{j+1} = \left(\frac{1}{2}\right) P_i^j + \left(\frac{1}{2}\right) P_{i+1}^j \tag{3.19}$$

As seen in the above equations, all points from the current iteration are transformed using Eq. (3.18) in the next iteration, and a new point is added in the middle of every line segment. The equations can be combined into a single matrix equation as follows:

$$\begin{bmatrix} P_{2i-1}^{j+1} \\ P_{2i}^{j+1} \\ P_{2i+1}^{j+1} \end{bmatrix} = \frac{1}{8} \begin{bmatrix} 4 & 4 & 0 \\ 1 & 6 & 1 \\ 0 & 4 & 4 \end{bmatrix} \begin{bmatrix} P_{2i-1}^{j} \\ P_{2i}^{j} \\ P_{2i+1}^{j} \end{bmatrix} \tag{3.20}$$

The first two iterations and the fourth iteration of a simple closed polygonal line are shown in Fig. 3.12. Each iteration doubles the number of points on the curve ($N_0 = 4$, $N_1 = 8$, $N_2 = 16$ etc.). The transformed control polygon converges to a fixed continuous parametric curve known as the limiting curve of the given control polygon.

The transformation in Eq. (3.18) uses a convex combination of 3 points. The transformations for the existing and new points may be generalized to include $2k + 1$ points and corresponding coefficients, where k is a positive number. The coefficients always form a partition of unity. A set of coefficients is called a subdivision mask. A subdivision mask is said to be stationary if its values do not vary with the subdivision level j.

In the following sections, we will extend the above ideas to three-dimensional mesh surfaces and look at subdivision algorithms for mesh interpolation and approximation.

3.2.2 Subdivision of Polygonal Elements

Subdivision algorithms will require the splitting of polygonal elements of a mesh. For simplicity, we will consider only regular subdivisions of triangular and quadrilateral elements of a mesh surface, as shown in Fig. 3.13.

Triangular elements are subdivided using the dyadic split which bisects every edge by inserting a new vertex between every pair of adjacent vertices, increasing

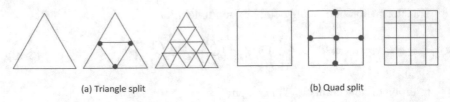

(a) Triangle split   (b) Quad split

Fig. 3.13 Subdivision of polygonal elements of a mesh

the number of triangles by a factor of 4 in each step (Fig. 3.13a). Repeated dyadic splits of a triangle create regular vertices of valence 6. Internal vertices where the valence is not equal to 6 are called extraordinary vertices.

Quadrilateral elements are also subdivided in a similar way, by inserting a new vertex between every pair of adjacent vertices. A new vertex is added for each face also. This process increases the number of quads by a factor of 4 in each step and creates regular vertices of valence 4 (Fig. 3.13b).

A subdivision using a dyadic split may be generalized to a n-adic split where each edge is subdivided into n segments. A 4-adic split creates a subdivision generated in the second iteration of a dyadic split shown above in Fig. 3.13a. If a mesh model consists of k triangles, a n-adic split creates n^2k new triangles in each iteration.

3.2.3   Butterfly Algorithm

The butterfly algorithm [9] extends the 2D interpolation algorithm discussed earlier (see Eq. (3.17)) to a three-dimensional triangular mesh. New points are added by bisecting each edge to obtain a dyadic subdivision of the triangles as shown in Fig. 3.13. The newly added points are further transformed using a weighted combination of neighbouring vertices that exist on the mesh at that iteration. The butterfly algorithm uses an 8-point stencil as shown in Fig. 3.14, to specify the neighbourhood of points used for transforming a new point P on an edge AB.

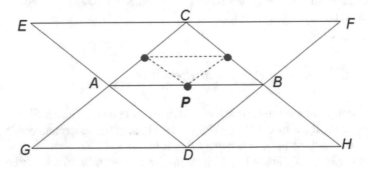

Fig. 3.14 Configuration of 8 neighbouring points used by the butterfly algorithm

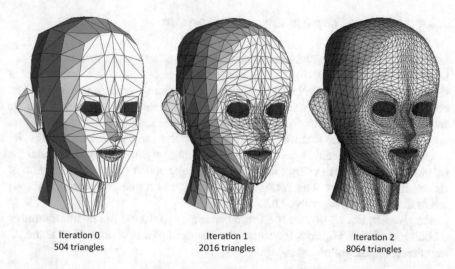

Iteration 0
504 triangles

Iteration 1
2016 triangles

Iteration 2
8064 triangles

Fig. 3.15 Iterative subdivision of a mesh using the butterfly interpolation algorithm

When a new point P is created, its closest vertices A, B are assigned a higher weight compared to the opposite vertices C, D. The corner vertices E, F, G, H are assigned a low negative weight, similar to the 2D example. If we assign a weight 4 for points A, B, a weight 2 for points C, D, and -1 for points $E..G$, the sum of weights equals 8. We normalize the weights by their sum to get the coefficients for the vertices as $\frac{1}{2}, \frac{1}{2}, \frac{1}{4}, \frac{1}{4}, \frac{-1}{8}, \frac{-1}{8}, \frac{-1}{8}, \frac{-1}{8}$. Another set of coefficients commonly used in the butterfly algorithm is $\frac{1}{2}, \frac{1}{2}, \frac{1}{8}, \frac{1}{8}, \frac{-1}{16}, \frac{-1}{16}, \frac{-1}{16}, \frac{-1}{16}$. Note that the sum of coefficients is always 1.

The OpenMesh library includes functions for mesh subdivision using the butterfly algorithm. The main steps in an implementation of the algorithm are given in Listing 3.3. The application of the algorithm on a mesh object is shown in Fig. 3.15.

Listing 3.3 Mesh subdivision based on butterfly algorithm using OpenMesh

```
#include <OpenMesh/Tools/Subdivider/Uniform/ModifiedButterFlyT.hh>
typedef OpenMesh::TriMesh_ArrayKernelT<> MyMesh;
OpenMesh::Subdivider::Uniform::ModifiedButterflyT<MyMesh>
butterfly;
MyMesh mesh;
...
butterfly.attach(mesh);
butterfly(niter); //niter = Number of iterations
butterfly.detach();
mesh.update_normals();
```

3.2.4   Charles-Loop Subdivision Algorithm

In Sect. 3.2.1, we saw a two-dimensional example of an approximation algorithm using Eqs. (3.18) and (3.19). The process comprised of inserting a new vertex at the midpoint of each edge and transforming the existing vertices using a convex combination of their neighbouring points, in each iteration. This method can be adopted for the subdivision of a triangular polygonal manifold, by requiring two subdivision masks: the first mask inserts a new point somewhere near the middle of each edge using a convex combination of existing neighbouring vertices, and the second mask transforms every existing vertex using another convex combination of its one-ring neighbours. This method of subdivision of a triangular mesh is known as the Charles-Loop algorithm [10].

As given in Eq. (3.18), we use the superscript j to denote the iteration number (subdivision level). Figure 3.16a shows the insertion of a new point H after the jth iteration using the following equation:

$$P_H^{j+1} = \left(\frac{1}{8}\right)P_A^j + \left(\frac{3}{8}\right)P_B^j + \left(\frac{3}{8}\right)P_C^j + \left(\frac{1}{8}\right)P_D^j \tag{3.21}$$

Figure 3.16b shows the transformation of an existing vertex G using its one-ring neighbours $G_i, i = 1 \ldots n$:

$$P_G^{j+1} = (1 - n\lambda)P_G^j + \lambda \sum_{i=1}^{n} P_G^j \tag{3.22}$$

The factor λ is chosen such that

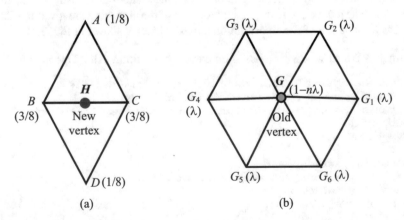

(a)   (b)

Fig. 3.16 Loop subdivision algorithm. The weights assigned to the points are shown in brackets. **a** Insertion of a new point H, **b** transformation of an existing point G

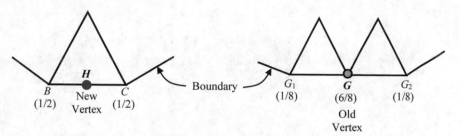

Fig. 3.17 Loop subdivision masks for boundary vertices

$$\lambda < \frac{1}{2n}, \tag{3.23}$$

where n is the valence of G. The above condition ensures that the weight $(1 - n\lambda)$ assigned to the current vertex is greater than the sum of weights $n\lambda$ assigned to its one-ring neighbours. For a regular vertex $(n = 6)$, λ is given a value $1/16$. Equation (3.22) then becomes

$$P_G^{j+1} = \left(\frac{10}{16}\right) P_G^j + \left(\frac{1}{16}\right) \sum_{i=1}^{6} P_G^j \tag{3.24}$$

For boundary vertices, the subdivision masks in Fig. 3.16 are appropriately modified as shown in Fig. 3.17.

The implementation of the Charles-Loop algorithm using OpenMesh is given in Listing 3.4. The similarities between different implementations can be clearly seen by comparing this code with that given in Listing 3.3.

Listing 3.4 Mesh subdivision based on Charles-Loop algorithm using OpenMesh

```
#include <OpenMesh/Tools/Subdivider/Uniform/LoopT.hh>
typedef OpenMesh::TriMesh_ArrayKernelT<> MyMesh;
OpenMesh::Subdivider::Uniform::LoopT<MyMesh> loop;
MyMesh mesh;
...
loop.attach(mesh);
loop(niter); //niter = Number of iterations
loop.detach();
mesh.update_normals();
```

Figure 3.18 illustrates the working of the Charles-Loop algorithm in subdividing a mesh containing 60 triangles.

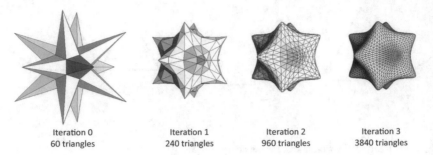

| Iteration 0 | Iteration 1 | Iteration 2 | Iteration 3 |
| 60 triangles | 240 triangles | 960 triangles | 3840 triangles |

Fig. 3.18 Iterative smoothing of a mesh using Charles-Loop subdivision algorithm

3.2.5   Root-3 Subdivision

The $\sqrt{3}$-subdivision scheme [11] combines a triangle split operation and an edge flip operation to generate a smooth surface from a triangular mesh. The iterative algorithm performs the following two steps in every iteration.

- For each triangle, insert a new vertex at its centroid, and split the triangle into three triangles as shown in Fig. 3.19a. This operation performs the subdivision of the mesh, increasing the number of triangles by a factor of three in a single subdivision step. The operation also introduces three new edges, one from each vertex to the centroid, along the direction of a median.
- Flip the old edges as shown in Fig. 3.19b. This operation contributes to the smoothing of the mesh.

We saw earlier in Section 3.2.2 that an n-adic subdivision of a triangle results in n^2 new triangles. Since this algorithm increases the number of triangles by a factor of three in each step, it is referred to as the $\sqrt{3}$-subdivision scheme.

Figure 3.20 shows the outputs of the first three iterations of the $\sqrt{3}$-subdivision scheme for a sample mesh model. Comparison with Fig. 3.18 shows that the Charles-Loop algorithm increases the number of triangles by a factor of 4 in each iteration,

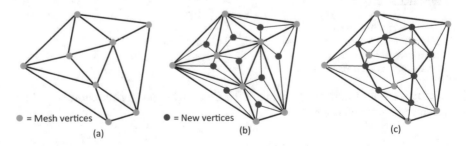

● = Mesh vertices   ● = New vertices

(a)   (b)   (c)

Fig. 3.19 **a** Original mesh, **b** insertion of new vertices and subdivision of triangles, **c** edge flipping operation

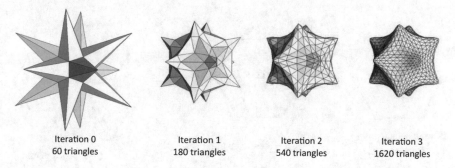

| Iteration 0 | Iteration 1 | Iteration 2 | Iteration 3 |
| 60 triangles | 180 triangles | 540 triangles | 1620 triangles |

Fig. 3.20 First three iterations of the $\sqrt{3}$-subdivision method for a sample mesh model

while the $\sqrt{3}$-subdivision method increases the number of triangles only by a factor of 3 after each iteration.

The implementation of the $\sqrt{3}$-subdivision algorithm using OpenMesh is given in Listing 3.5.

Listing 3.5 Mesh subdivision based on $\sqrt{3}$-subdivision algorithm using OpenMesh

```
#include <OpenMesh/Tools/Subdivider/Uniform/Sqrt3T.hh>
typedef OpenMesh::TriMesh_ArrayKernelT<> MyMesh;
OpenMesh::Subdivider::Uniform::Sqrt3T<MyMesh> root3;
MyMesh mesh;
...
root3.attach(mesh);
root3(niter); //niter = Number of iterations
root3.detach();
root3.update_normals();
```

3.2.6 Catmull–Clark Subdivision

The Catmull–Clark approximation scheme [12] is used to subdivide meshes with arbitrary topology. Unlike the previous method, it produces a mesh that consists primarily of quadrilaterals containing vertices of valence 4. In each subdivision step of the algorithm, the following mesh operations are performed in a sequence:

- A new vertex (face point) is added to each face by computing the average of all vertices of the face (Fig. 3.21a). In the following equation, j denotes the subdivision level, f a face, and n_f the number of vertices of that face, and v_i the vertices of the face. v_f denotes the new face point.

$$v_f^{j+1} = \left(\frac{1}{n_f}\right) \sum_{i=1}^{n_f} v_i^j \tag{3.25}$$

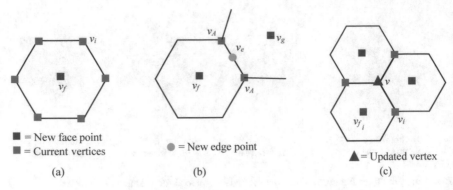

= New face point
= Current vertices   = New edge point

▲= Updated vertex

(a)   (b)   (c)

Fig. 3.21 In each iteration of the Catmull–Clark algorithm, new face and edge points are added and existing vertex positions are updated

- A new edge point is added to each edge by computing the average of the end points of the edge and the new face points of the edge's neighbouring faces (Fig. 3.21b). In the following equation, the new edge point is denoted by v_e. The edge has end points v_A, v_B, and adjacent faces f and g.

$$v_e^{j+1} = \frac{\left(v_f^{j+1} + v_g^{j+1} + v_A^j + v_B^j\right)}{4} \qquad (3.26)$$

- After adding new face and edge points, the position of every old vertex is updated as follows. Let n_v be the number of incident edges of a vertex v, v_i the one-ring neighbours of the vertex v, and v_{f_i} the new face points on the faces surrounding v (Fig. 3.21c). Q_v and R_v denote the average of the new face points and the edge midpoints, respectively. The superscript j denotes the subdivision level.

$$Q_v = \left(\frac{1}{n_v}\right) \sum_{i=1}^{n_v} v_{f_i}^{j+1}$$

$$R_v = \left(\frac{1}{n_v}\right) \sum_{i=1}^{n_v} \frac{\left(v + v_i^j\right)}{2}$$

$$v_{\text{updated}} = \frac{Q_v + 2R_v + (n_v - 3)v}{n_v} \qquad (3.27)$$

The vertex update equation in Eq. (3.27) can be viewed as a convex combination of three points Q, R and v, with weights 0.25, 0.5, 0.25 for a regular vertex. For a vertex of valence 3, the weights are 0.33, 0.67 and 0. On completion of the steps outlined above, the mesh is re-tessellated. New faces and edges are added to the mesh by connecting each new face point to every new edge point located around that face (Fig. 3.22). Insertion of new edge points also splits existing edges. As discussed

Fig. 3.22 Mesh tessellation after one iteration of the Catmull–Clark algorithm

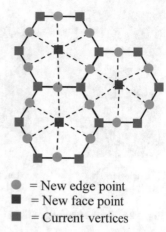

● = New edge point
■ = New face point
■ = Current vertices

earlier, each iteration also updates the coordinates of existing vertices as well as the definitions of incident edges of those vertices. As seen in Fig. 3.22, the newly added faces are all quadrilaterals, and all new edge points have valence 4. Vertices that have a valence other than 4 after the first iteration will continue to have a valence other than 4 in subsequent iterations and will therefore become extraordinary vertices.

The Catmull–Clark subdivision of a cube is shown in Fig. 3.23. The original vertices of the cube always have a valence 3, while all other vertices have a valence 4.

Another example of the Catmull–Clark subdivision process is shown in Fig. 3.24.

The implementation of the Catmull–Clark algorithm using OpenMesh is given in Listing 3.6.

Listing 3.6 Mesh subdivision based on Catmull–Clark algorithm using OpenMesh

```
#include <OpenMesh/Tools/Subdivider/Uniform/CatmullClarkT.hh>
typedef OpenMesh::TriMesh_ArrayKernelT<> MyMesh;
OpenMesh::Subdivider::Uniform::CatmullClarkT<MyMesh> catmull;
```

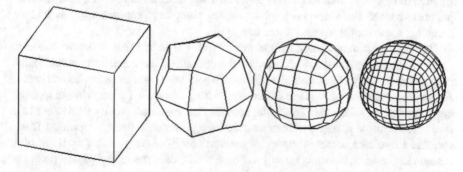

Fig. 3.23 Catmull–Clark subdivision of a cube through three iterations of the algorithm

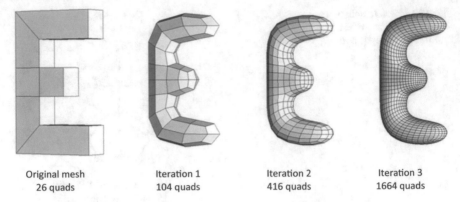

Original mesh	Iteration 1	Iteration 2	Iteration 3
26 quads	104 quads	416 quads	1664 quads

Fig. 3.24   Three iterations of Catmull–Clark subdivision of a mesh model

```
MyMesh mesh;
...
catmull.attach(mesh);
catmull (niter); //niter = Number of iterations
catmull.detach();
catmull.update_normals();
```

3.3   Mesh Parameterization

Mesh parameterization can be broadly defined as the process of generating a mapping of points in a three-dimensional mesh to points belonging to a simpler parametric domain. A parameterization typically associates a unique two-dimensional point to every vertex, thus establishing a mapping from a subset of $\mathfrak{R}^3$ to a subset of $\mathfrak{R}^2$. The two-dimensional domain could simply be a region of a plane, or in a more general case a set of parametric coordinates defined on another surface such as a sphere. The mesh is then said to be parametrically embedded in that domain. Mesh parameterization finds several applications in computer graphics such as texture mapping, mesh morphing and re-meshing [13].

One of the primary goals of parameterization is to achieve a one-to-one and invertible mapping (a bijection) between the domain of the mesh and another parametric domain [14]. Some parameterizations additionally preserve angles and areas. Angle preserving mappings are called conformal, while area preserving mappings are known as authalic [15]. Triangular meshes that are topologically equivalent to a disc have a simple planar parameterization using piecewise linear mappings. If we can find a one–one correspondence of the vertices $P_i = (x_i, y_i, z_i)$, $i = 1...3$, of a triangle to points $S_i = (u_i, v_i)$, $i = 1...3$ on a plane, then the map f of any point (x, y, z) within the triangle is given by the linear function

$$f(x, y, z) = \lambda_1 S_1 + \lambda_2 S_2 + \lambda_3 S_3 \tag{3.28}$$

where $(\lambda_1, \lambda_2, \lambda_3)$ are the barycentric coordinates of the point (x, y, z) with respect to the triangle $P_1 P_2 P_3$. The next section discusses barycentric coordinates in detail.

3.3.1 Barycentric Coordinates

Consider a triangle given by vertices P_1, P_2, P_3. Any point Q inside the triangle can be expressed as a convex combination of its vertices as

$$Q = \lambda_1 P_1 + \lambda_2 P_2 + \lambda_3 P_3, 0 \leq \lambda_1, \lambda_2, \lambda_3 \leq 1, \lambda_1 + \lambda_2 + \lambda_3 = 1, \tag{3.29}$$

The above equation shows that the point Q is uniquely specified by a new set of coordinates $(\lambda_1, \lambda_2, \lambda_3)$ defined by P_1, P_2, and P_3. This local coordinate system is called the barycentric coordinates for the triangle. Barycentric coordinates are also sometimes referred to as trilinear coordinates. From the above equation, it can also be seen that the barycentric coordinates of the vertices of the triangle are given by

$$P_1 = (1, 0, 0)$$
$$P_2 = (0, 1, 0)$$
$$P_3 = (0, 0, 1) \tag{3.30}$$

The centroid C of any triangle has barycentric coordinates $(1/3, 1/3, 1/3)$. The barycentric coordinates of a point Q with respect to P_1, P_2, P_3 have a geometrical interpretation as the ratios of the areas of triangles $QP_2 P_3, QP_3 P_1, QP_1 P_2$ to the area of the whole triangle $P_1 P_2 P_3$. In the following equations, the symbol Δ denotes the signed area of a triangle:

$$\lambda_1 = \frac{\Delta Q P_2 P_3}{\Delta P_1 P_2 P_3}, \quad \lambda_2 = \frac{\Delta Q P_3 P_1}{\Delta P_1 P_2 P_3}, \quad \lambda_3 = \frac{\Delta Q P_1 P_2}{\Delta P_1 P_2 P_3}, \tag{3.31}$$

In a simplified two-dimensional case where $P_1 = (x_1, y_1)$, $P_2 = (x_2, y_2)$, $P_3 = (x_3, y_3)$, $Q = (x_q, y_q)$, the expressions for the barycentric coordinates of Q assume the following form:

$$\lambda_1 = \frac{x_q(y_2 - y_3) + x_2(y_3 - y_q) + x_3(y_q - y_2)}{x_1(y_2 - y_3) + x_2(y_3 - y_1) + x_3(y_1 - y_2)},$$
$$\lambda_2 = \frac{x_q(y_3 - y_1) + x_3(y_1 - y_q) + x_1(y_q - y_3)}{x_1(y_2 - y_3) + x_2(y_3 - y_1) + x_3(y_1 - y_2)},$$
$$\lambda_3 = 1 - \lambda_1 - \lambda_2 \tag{3.32}$$

The above equations for barycentric coordinates of a two-dimensional point Q $= (x_q, y_q)$ can also be interpreted as the solutions of the following linear system obtained directly from Eq. (3.29):

$$\lambda_1 P_1 + \lambda_2 P_2 + (1 - \lambda_1 - \lambda_2) P_3 - Q = 0. \tag{3.33}$$

If any of the above quantities is negative, then the point Q lies outside the triangle $P_1 P_2 P_3$. However, in a general three-dimensional case, the point Q need not lie on the plane of the triangle. Hence, we require the additional condition that the sum of barycentric coordinates equals 1 to ensure that the points are coplanar. Thus, if the conditions $\lambda_1 + \lambda_2 + \lambda_3 = 1$, $0 \le \lambda_1, \lambda_2, \lambda_3 \le 1$ are met, then Q lies on the plane defined by the points P_1, P_2, P_3, and also lies within the triangle $P_1 P_2 P_3$.

The barycentric coordinates of an interior point Q within a triangle can be used to get the interpolated value of any quantity defined at the vertices of the triangle. If f_{P1}, f_{P2}, f_{P3} denote the values of some attribute (such as colour) associated with the vertices, then the interpolated value of the attribute at Q is given by

$$f_Q = \lambda_1 f_{P1} + \lambda_2 f_{P2} + \lambda_3 f_{P3}. \tag{3.34}$$

Using barycentric coordinates we can establish a one-to-one mapping of points from within one triangle to another. For any given interior point Q of the first triangle, we compute the barycentric coordinates. The linear combination of the vertices of the second triangle with the barycentric coordinates of Q gives the coordinates of the corresponding point R inside the second triangle (Fig. 3.25). We can use this mapping to transfer values from the interior of the first triangle to the second. As an immediate application of this transfer method, we can map an image (or texture) from one triangular region to another.

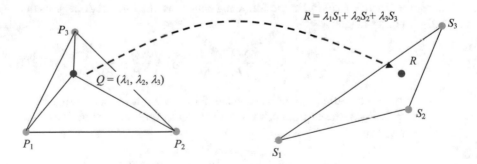

Fig. 3.25 Barycentric mapping of points from one triangle to another

3.3.2 Barycentric Embedding

In the previous sections, we saw that the problem of planar embedding for a triangular mesh reduces to the problem of determining a mapping of the vertices of all triangles to a planar region (Eq. (3.28)). In this section, we consider a physics-based method for obtaining this mapping for an open mesh.

Imagine a three-dimensional triangular mesh fitted with springs along each edge, and rigid links at each vertex where the springs meet. The springs are assumed to have a zero rest length. If we stretch this network of springs and place it on a plane so that the boundary vertices of the mesh are firmly attached to points around a convex polygon, the interior vertices will settle in a minimum energy configuration (Fig. 3.26). We then have a planar embedding of the mesh without any fold-over of triangles.

We denote the map of a vertex V_i (x_i, y_i, z_i) on the mesh by P_i (u_i, v_i), $i = 1 \ldots n$. The potential energy of the spring attached to the edge $P_i P_j$ is proportional to the square of the displacement:

$$E_{ij} = \left(\frac{1}{2}\right) K_{ij} \|P_i - P_j\|^2 \tag{3.35}$$

where K_{ij} is the spring constant. For any point P_i, if N_i denotes the set of indices of its one-ring neighbours, the sum of potential energies of all incident edges of P_i is given by

$$E(P_i) = \left(\frac{1}{2}\right) \sum_{j \in N_i} K_{ij} \|P_i - P_j\|^2, \quad i = 1 \ldots n. \tag{3.36}$$

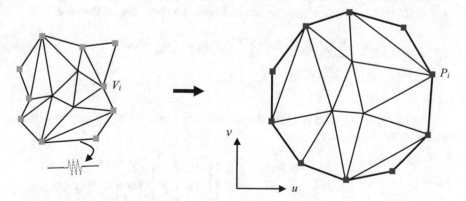

Fig. 3.26 Planar embedding of a mesh

The total potential energy of the system is obtained by adding up the above values for every vertex. We note that every edge is counted twice in the summation and therefore we further multiply the result by half.

$$E = \left(\frac{1}{4}\right) \sum_i \sum_{j \in N_i} K_{ij} \|P_i - P_j\|^2, \quad i = 1 \ldots n. \tag{3.37}$$

For the minimum energy configuration, the partial derivatives of the above expression with respect to the variable P_i must be zero. Hence

$$\sum_{j \in N_i} K_{ij}(P_i - P_j) = 0, \quad i = 1 \ldots n. \tag{3.38}$$

From the above equation, we get

$$P_i = \sum_{j \in N_i} \beta_{ij} P_j, \quad i = 1 \ldots n. \tag{3.39}$$

where

$$\beta_{ij} = \frac{K_{ij}}{\sum_{r \in N_i} K_{ir}}, \quad i = 1 \ldots n. \tag{3.40}$$

Since K_{ij}s are all positive and there are at least two edges incident to a vertex, we have $0 < \beta_{ij} < 1$ for all $j \in N_i$. Thus, Eq. (3.39) expresses P_i as a convex combination of its one-ring neighbours on the planar domain. Let the boundary vertices be given by $P_{m+1}, \ldots, P_n$ for some value of $m < n$. Since these vertices are fixed at known positions around a convex polygon, the only unknowns to be determined are the locations of the interior vertices $P_1 \ldots P_m$. Equation (3.39) can be re-written as follows:

$$P_i - \sum_{\substack{j \in N_i \\ j \leq m}} \beta_{ij} P_j = \sum_{\substack{j \in N_i \\ j > m}} \beta_{ij} P_j = Q_i, \quad i = 1 \ldots m. \tag{3.41}$$

If we set $\beta_{ij} = 0$ for $j \notin N_i$, then the above set of linear equations can be written as a single matrix equation:

$$\begin{bmatrix} 1 & -\beta_{12} & \cdots & -\beta_{1m} \\ -\beta_{21} & 1 & \cdots & -\beta_{2m} \\ \cdots & \cdots & \cdots & \cdots \\ -\beta_{m1} & -\beta_{m2} & \cdots & 1 \end{bmatrix} \begin{bmatrix} P_1 \\ P_2 \\ \cdots \\ P_m \end{bmatrix} = \begin{bmatrix} Q_1 \\ Q_2 \\ \cdots \\ Q_m \end{bmatrix} \tag{3.42}$$

The above equation in fact represents two equations in u and v coordinates of the interior points P_i. Since $0 \le \beta_{ij} < 1$, the $m \times m$ matrix in the above equation is diagonally dominant as well as non-singular. The planar locations of the interior points are therefore given by

$$
\begin{bmatrix} P_1 \\ P_2 \\ \cdots \\ P_m \end{bmatrix} = \begin{bmatrix} 1 & -\beta_{12} & \cdots & -\beta_{1m} \\ -\beta_{21} & 1 & \cdots & -\beta_{2m} \\ \cdots & \cdots & \cdots & \cdots \\ -\beta_{m1} & -\beta_{m2} & \cdots & 1 \end{bmatrix}^{-1} \begin{bmatrix} Q_1 \\ Q_2 \\ \cdots \\ Q_m \end{bmatrix}
\tag{3.43}
$$

The values of $Q_1, \ldots, Q_m$ can be precomputed using Eq. (3.41). A simple choice for β_{ij} is

$$
\beta_{ij} = \begin{cases} 0, \text{ if } j \ne N_i \\ \frac{1}{|N_i|}, \text{ if } j \in N_i \end{cases}.
\tag{3.44}
$$

The above setting is equivalent to assigning a unit value for all spring constants ($K_{ij} = 1$, for $j \in N_i$, for all i). This also implies that for a given i, the value of β_{ij}s are all equal and independent of j. The position of a vertex relative to its neighbours is thus ignored. In fact, Eq. (3.44) places P_i at the barycentric centre of the closed polygon formed by its one-ring neighbours. Also note that the definition of β_{ij} is asymmetric, i.e. $\beta_{ij} \ne \beta_{ji}$. Two examples of barycentric mapping using this method are given in Fig. 3.27. The model of the "house" in Fig. 3.27a has 9 interior vertices and 6 boundary vertices. The model of the "car" in Fig. 3.27c has 12 interior vertices and 20 boundary vertices. The boundary vertices are mapped to equidistant points along the circumference of a circle. The coordinates of the mappings of the internal vertices are computed using Eqs. (3.43) and (3.44).

A few other commonly used metrics for K_{ij} (3.38) are listed in Box 3.1. These metrics capture information about the geometry of the mesh surrounding an edge using distances and angles within the triangles that border the edge. For each metric, the values of K_{ij} are further normalized using Eq. (3.40) to obtain the corresponding values of β_{ij}. The metrics are defined using the angles within the adjacent triangles of the edge $V_i V_j$ of the original mesh.

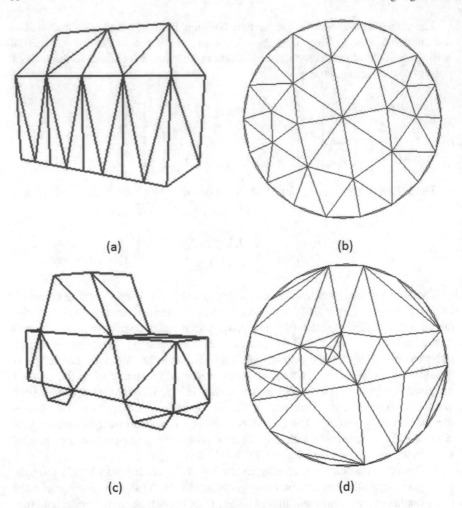

(a)   (b)

(c)   (d)

Fig. 3.27   Barycentric embedding of mesh objects inside a circle

Box 3.1: Commonly used expressions for spring constants (edge weights) K_{ij}

Wachspress Metric [16] :

$$K_{ij} = \frac{\cot \psi_{ji} + \cot \varphi_{ij}}{r_{ij}^2}$$

Discrete Harmonic Metric:

$$K_{ij} = \cot \delta_{ij} + \cot \delta_{ji}$$

Mean Value Metric [16] :

$$K_{ij} = \frac{\tan\left(\frac{\psi_{ij}}{2}\right) + \tan\left(\frac{\varphi_{ji}}{2}\right)}{r_{ij}}$$

The inverse of the matrix in Eq. (3.43) can be computed easily for simple meshes only, when m is small. For large values of m, we can solve the system iteratively by either Jacobi or Gauss–Seidel methods. Rewriting Eq. (3.41) as an update equation for P_i in the $(k + 1)$th iteration in terms of the values of P_j in the previous iteration k, we have the following solution based on the Jacobi method:

$$P_i^{(k+1)} = Q_i + \sum_{\substack{j \in N_i \\ j \leq m}} \beta_{ij} P_j^{(k)}, \quad i = 1 \ldots m, k = 0, 1, \ldots \tag{3.45}$$

The Gauss–Seidel method uses the updated values of $P_1, \ldots, P_{i-1}$ and the previous values $P_{i+1}, \ldots P_m$ to update P_i:

$$P_i^{(k+1)} = Q_i + \sum_{\substack{j \in N_i \\ j < i \leq m}} \beta_{ij} P_j^{(k+1)} + \sum_{\substack{j \in N_i \\ i < j \leq m}} \beta_{ij} P_j^{(k)}$$

$$i = 1 \ldots m, k = 0, 1, \ldots \tag{3.46}$$

The advantage of the Gauss–Seidel method over Jacobi method is that the values of P_i can be sequentially updated in place within the same list without having to maintain two separate lists for the previous and the updated values. In both the above cases, a convergence criterion is used to determine when the iteration must stop:

$$\left| P_i^{(k+1)} - P_i^{(k)} \right| < \varepsilon \quad i = 1 \ldots n, k = 0, 1, \ldots \tag{3.47}$$

where ε is a user specified threshold that is independent of i.

3.3.3 Spherical Embedding

The methods presented in the previous section are suitable for open manifold meshes. A closed manifold mesh, on the other hand, is topologically equivalent to a sphere, and therefore, the natural parameterization domain for such meshes is a sphere. A spherical embedding generates a mapping of vertices of a closed mesh to points on a sphere. As a consequence, triangles of the mesh get mapped to spherical triangles (Fig. 3.28). For a triangular mesh, the mapped set of spherical triangles must form a partition of the sphere. The embedding associates a pair of spherical coordinates (α, δ), $0 \leq \alpha \leq 2\pi, -\pi/2 \leq \delta \leq \pi/2$, with every three-dimensional vertex of the mesh.

$$\alpha_i = \tan^{-1}\left(\frac{u_i}{w_i}\right)$$

$$\delta_i = \tan^{-1}\left(\frac{v_i}{\sqrt{u_i^2 + w_i^2}}\right) \tag{3.48}$$

For simple closed meshes centred at the origin, the vertices can be directly projected to the surface of a unit sphere using coordinate normalization. The spherical coordinates are then extracted from the normalized coordinates (u_i, v_i, w_i) using the following equations.

The above values can be further transformed into the range [0, 1] if they are to be used as texture coordinates. For a general triangular mesh, the iterative solution for the minimum energy equation in Eq. (3.39) can be extended for a mapping onto a

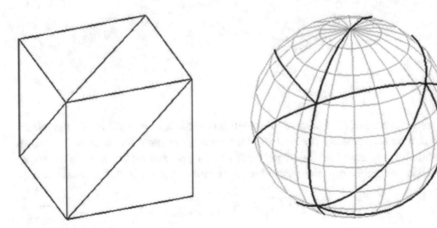

Fig. 3.28 Spherical embedding of a simple mesh

unit sphere as follows:

$$P_i^{(k+1)} = (1 - \lambda)P_i^{(k)} + \lambda \sum_{j \in N_i} \beta_{ij} P_j, \ \|P_i\| = 1, i = 1 \ldots n. \tag{3.49}$$

where $P_i = (u_i, v_i, w_i)$, $i = 1 \ldots n$ are points on the unit sphere, and λ is a damping parameter. The value of λ is usually set to 0.5. The weights β_{ij} are computed using Eq. (3.44). The Gauss–Seidel solver provides the following iterative solution for the above equation:

$$S_i = (1 - \lambda)P_i^{(k)} + \lambda \sum_{\substack{j \in N_i \\ j < i}} \beta_{ij} P_j^{(k+1)} + \lambda \sum_{\substack{j \in N_i \\ j > i}} \beta_{ij} P_j^{(k)}, \quad i = 1 \ldots n.$$

$$P_i^{(k+1)} = \frac{S_i}{|S_i|} \tag{3.50}$$

3.4 3D Morphing

An area of mesh processing where the mesh parameterization and subdivision methods discussed above find applications is 3D morphing. Shape morphing using three-dimensional mesh models produces a transformation from one shape to another as a series of modifications of the mesh structure and transformations of vertices. In this section, we explore a few of the basic algorithms used for 3D morphing.

3.4.1 Shortest Distance and Projection

In 3D morphing, we often encounter the problem of finding the triangle on a mesh surface the lies closest to a given point. As part of the problem's formulation, we get the signed distance of the point from the plane of the triangle, and also the projection of the point on the plane. The triangle is rejected if the projection of the point lies outside the triangle.

Consider a point $P = (x_p, y_p, z_p)$, and a triangle formed using vertices $A = (x_a, y_a, z_a)$, $B = (x_b, y_b, z_b)$, and $C = (x_c, y_c, z_c)$. The surface normal vector $\boldsymbol{n} = (x_n, y_n, z_n)$ of the triangle is given by the vector cross-product $(B - A) \times (C - A)$:

$$x_n = y_a(z_b - z_c) + y_b(z_c - z_a) + y_c(z_a - z_b)$$
$$y_n = z_a(x_b - x_c) + z_b(x_c - x_a) + z_c(x_a - x_b)$$

$$z_n = x_a(y_b - y_c) + x_b(y_c - y_a) + x_c(y_a - y_b) \tag{3.51}$$

The unit surface normal vector $u = (x_u, y_u, z_u)$ is obtained by normalizing n:

$$u = (x_u, y_u, z_u) = \frac{(x_n, y_n, z_n)}{\sqrt{x_n^2 + y_n^2 + z_n^2}} \tag{3.52}$$

The shortest distance D of the point P from the plane of the triangle is given by the equation

$$D = (x_p - x_a)x_u + (y_p - y_a)y_u + (z_p - z_a)z_u \tag{3.53}$$

The above term is also called the signed distance of the point P from the plane, as it assumes a positive value if P is on the same side as n, and a negative value otherwise. In general, if the plane's equation is given in the normal form $ax + by + cz + d = 0$, where $a^2 + b^2 + c^2 = 1$, the signed distance of the point P is given by

$$D = ax_p + by_p + cz_p + d \tag{3.54}$$

The above expression can be thought of as the dot product between the vector (a, b, c, d) and $(x_p, y_p, z_p, 1)$, the latter being the homogeneous representation of P. Note that the unit normal vector to the plane is given by (a, b, c).

The projection Q of the point P on the plane of the triangle (Fig. 3.29a) is straightaway obtained as

$$Q = P - Du \tag{3.55}$$

The projection Q may not always lie within the triangle ABC. A simple point inclusion test is commonly used to determine whether the point Q is an interior point of the triangle. This test involves comparing the signs of the following three quantities (Fig. 3.29b):

$$t_1 = ((B - A) \times (Q - A)) \cdot n$$

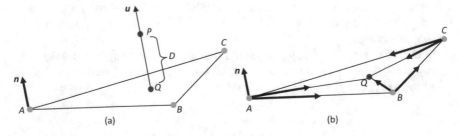

(a)   (b)

Fig. 3.29 Shortest distance and projection of a point with respect to a triangle

$$t_2 = ((C - B) \times (Q - B)) \cdot \mathbf{n}$$
$$t_3 = ((A - C) \times (Q - C)) \cdot \mathbf{n} \qquad (3.56)$$

If the values of the above three quantities have the same sign, then the point Q is inside the triangle. The barycentric coordinates of Q (Eq. (3.31)) could also be used to determine if the point is inside the triangle.

3.4.2 Point Correspondence

3D morphing involves two mesh objects (source and target meshes) of arbitrary size, shape, and topology. A primary goal of most morphing algorithms is to establish a point correspondence between the two meshes. If the meshes have two-dimensional parametric representations, it may be possible to derive a mapping between the parametric domains and find a point on the target mesh corresponding to each vertex of the source mesh (Fig. 3.30). A mapping between two-dimensional parametric domains is easier to achieve compared to three-dimensional mesh spaces.

When a vertex correspondence between the source and the target meshes is established, a correspondence between vertex attributes such as colour and normal vectors is also simultaneously obtained. Shape morphing between the two mesh objects involves an interpolation between corresponding vertex coordinates and their corresponding attributes. Two simple examples of 3D morphing using a mapping of the parametric domains of the source and target meshes are given below.

A cylinder with the base centred at the origin having a radius R and height H has a two-parameter representation (y_s, θ) given by the equations

$$x_s = R \sin \theta, \quad z_s = R \cos \theta$$

$$\theta = \tan^{-1}\left(\frac{x_s}{z_s}\right), \quad 0 \le \theta \le 2\pi, 0 \le y_s \le H. \qquad (3.57)$$

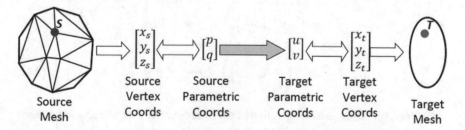

Fig. 3.30 Establishing vertex correspondence through the mapping of parametric domains

Fig. 3.31 Morphing of a cylinder to a sphere

We can use a very similar parametric representation (y_t, ϕ) of a sphere centred at the origin and having a radius R. We consider the sphere as a more general case of a cylinder where the radius of a horizontal slice at height y varies from 0 to R:

$$x_t = r \sin \phi, \quad z_t = r \cos \phi, \quad r = \sqrt{R^2 - y_t^2}$$

$$\phi = \tan^{-1}\left(\frac{x_t}{z_t}\right), \quad 0 \leq \phi \leq 2\pi, -R \leq y_t \leq R. \tag{3.58}$$

The mapping of the two parametric domains required for a 3D morphing of a cylinder to a sphere is given by the equations

$$\phi = \theta, \quad y_t = \left(\frac{2R}{H}\right) y_s - R \tag{3.59}$$

Intermediate outputs of the morphing algorithm incorporating transformations of vertex coordinates, normal vectors, and colour values are shown in Fig. 3.31.

As a second example, consider the morphing of a sphere to a torus. Here, we use a two-dimensional parameterization of a sphere of radius R in terms of spherical coordinates (α, δ):

$$x_s = R \cos \delta \sin \alpha, \quad y_s = R \sin \delta, \quad z_s = R \cos \delta \cos \alpha$$

$$\alpha = \tan^{-1}\left(\frac{x_s}{z_s}\right), \quad 0 \leq \alpha \leq 2\pi.$$

$$\delta = \tan^{-1}\left(\frac{y_s}{\sqrt{x_s^2 + z_s^2}}\right), \quad -\frac{\pi}{2} \leq \delta \leq \frac{\pi}{2}. \tag{3.60}$$

The corresponding parameterization of a torus with outer radius R and inner radius r, is given by the following equations in parameters (ω, φ):

$$x_t = (R + r \cos \varphi) \sin \omega, \quad y_t = r \sin \varphi, \quad z_t = (R + r \cos \varphi) \cos \omega$$

Fig. 3.32 Morphing of a sphere to a torus

$$\omega = \tan^{-1}\left(\frac{x_t}{z_t}\right), \quad 0 \leq \omega \leq 2\pi.$$

$$\varphi = \tan^{-1}\left(\frac{y_t}{\sqrt{x_t^2 + z_t^2} - R}\right), \quad -\pi \leq \varphi \leq \pi. \tag{3.61}$$

The above representations of the shapes allow a straightforward mapping of the parameters:

$$\omega = \alpha, \quad \varphi = 2\delta \tag{3.62}$$

A few stages of the morphing sequence are shown in Fig. 3.32.

3.4.3   Projective Mapping

One way of solving the correspondence problem between two meshes is to project the vertices of one mesh onto the other. This process, known as projective mapping, involves the translation of both meshes to the same location (centre), and the projection of vertices from one mesh to the polygons of the other (see Sect. 3.4.1). When a projection of a vertex is found within a polygon, the polygon is subdivided to form a local mesh structure that contains the projected vertex. The projection of each of the source and target meshes on the other yields two mesh structures with the equal number of vertices, from which the vertex correspondence information needed for morphing could be obtained as detailed below. We illustrate the method of projective mapping using two simple mesh objects, a tetrahedron and a cube (Fig. 3.33a).

Figure 3.33b shows the projection of the vertices of the tetrahedron on the cube. The cube's vertices are projected onto the tetrahedron as shown in Fig. 3.33c. When a projected vertex is inserted inside a triangle, the triangle is split into three smaller triangles. Both the cube and the tetrahedron now have 12 vertices each. Each original vertex on the cube corresponds to its projection on the tetrahedron, and each projection on the cube corresponds to an original vertex on the tetrahedron. The morphing sequence using projective mapping is shown in Fig. 3.34.

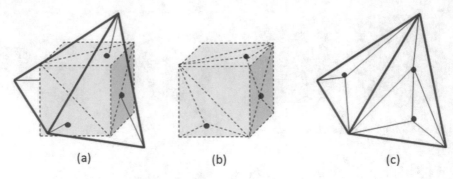

Fig. 3.33 Example of projective mapping

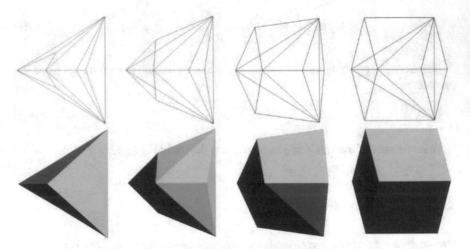

Fig. 3.34 Morphing of a tetrahedron to a cube using projective mapping

3.4.4 Barycentric Mapping

Barycentric mapping could be considered as an extension of projective mapping, where both meshes are mapped to the same parametric space (see Sect. 3.3.1), for obtaining a projection of one mesh on the other. Two open mesh objects are used are used as source and target meshes. Here also, the goal is to obtain an equal number of vertices on both meshes. The boundary vertices of each mesh are mapped to equidistant points along the circumference of a circle as shown in Fig. 3.27. The interior vertices of both meshes are mapped to the interior of the same circle. We thus obtain the barycentric embedding of one mesh overlayed on top of the other. Figure 3.35a shows the overlayed planar embeddings of the mesh objects in Fig. 3.27.

The overlapping two-dimensional mesh structures in the parametric space actually give the projections of vertices of one mesh onto the triangles of the other. In a two-dimensional space, we can easily determine if a point belonging to a mesh is inside

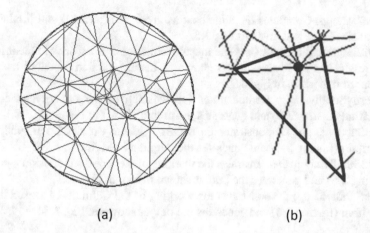

Fig. 3.35 Combined barycentric mappings of two mesh objects

Fig. 3.36 Sample morph sequence generated using barycentric embedding

a triangle belonging to the other mesh (Fig. 3.35b), using barycentric coordinates (Eq. (3.32)). Barycentric coordinates are also used to find the map of a vertex from the two-dimensional domain to the original three-dimensional mesh. If a triangle on a mesh contains a vertex of the other mesh, the triangle is split into three smaller triangles, similar to the projective mapping algorithm (Sect. 3.4.3). When this process of adding vertices and splitting triangles is completed for both mesh objects, we have equal number of vertices on them. Also, each vertex on one mesh corresponds to its map on the other mesh, and thus we also have the point correspondence information required for morphing. A few stages of morph sequence generated using the mesh objects in Fig. 3.27 are given in Fig. 3.36.

3.5 Chapter Resources

The folder "Chapter 3" on the companion website contains the following programs and associated data files. The programs demonstrate the implementation and working of the algorithms presented in this chapter.

- VertexCost.cpp: Computes the planarity metric at each vertex of the input mesh as given in Listing 3.1 and produces an output similar to that given in Fig. 3.3.

- EdgeCost.cpp: Computes the edge cost as given in Eq. (3.12) and produces an output similar to that given in Fig. 3.5.
- MeshSimplification.cpp: Uses the mesh decimation framework of OpenMesh to progressively simplify a mesh as shown in Listing 3.2 and produces an output similar to that given in Fig. 3.9.
- ButterflySubdivn.cpp: Demonstrates the working of the butterfly subdivision algorithm (Listing 3.3) and generates the output shown in Fig. 3.15.
- LoopSubdivn.cpp: Demonstrates the working of the Charles-Loop subdivision algorithm (Listing 3.4) and generates the output shown in Fig. 3.18.
- Root3Subdivn.cpp: Demonstrates the working of the root-3 subdivision algorithm (Listing 3.5) and generates the output shown in Fig. 3.20.
- ClarkSubdivn.cpp: Demonstrates the working of the Catmull–Clark subdivision algorithm (Listing 3.6) and generates the output shown in Fig. 3.24.

References and Further Reading

1. M. Botsch, L. Kobbelt, M. Pauly, P. Alliez, B. Lévy, *Polygon Mesh Processing.* (AK Peters/CRC Press, 2010), p. 250
2. P. Cignoni, C. Montani, R. Scopigno, A comparison of mesh simplification algorithms. Comput. Graph. **22**(1), 37–54 (1998). https://doi.org/10.1016/S0097-8493(97)00082-4
3. M. Garland, P.S. Heckbert, Surface simplification using quadric error metrics, in *Presented at the Proceedings of the 24th Annual Conference on Computer Graphics and Interactive Techniques* (1997). [Online]. Available https://doi.org/10.1145/258734.258849
4. H. Hoppe, New quadric metric for simplifying meshes with appearance attributes, in *Presented at the Proceedings of the Conference on Visualization '99: Celebrating Ten Years*, San Francisco, California, USA (1999)
5. W.J. Schroeder, J.A. Zarge, W.E. Lorensen, Decimation of triangle meshes, in *Presented at the Proceedings of the 19th Annual Conference on Computer Graphics and Interactive Techniques* (1992). [Online]. Available https://doi.org/10.1145/133994.134010
6. J.A. De Loera, F. Santos, *Triangulations—Structures for Algorithms and Applications* (Algorithms and Computation in Mathematics). (Springer, Berlin, Heidelberg, 2010), pp. XIII, 535
7. C.E. Catalano, I. Ivrissimtzis, A. Nasri, Subdivision surfaces and applications, in *Shape Analysis and Structuring*, ed. by L. De Floriani, M. Spagnuolo. (Springer, Berlin Heidelberg, 2008), pp. 115–143
8. M. Sabin, Chapter 12—Subdivision surfaces, in *Handbook of computer aided geometric design.* ed. by G. Farin, J. Hoschek, M.-S. Kim (North-Holland, Amsterdam, 2002), pp. 309–325
9. N. Dyn, D. Levine, J.A. Gregory, A butterfly subdivision scheme for surface interpolation with tension control. ACM Trans. Graph. **9**(2), 160–169 (1990). https://doi.org/10.1145/78956.78958
10. C. Loop, Smooth subdivision surfaces based on triangles, January 1987. [Online]. Available https://www.microsoft.com/en-us/research/publication/smooth-subdivision-surfaces-based-on-triangles/
11. L. Kobbelt, $\sqrt{3}$-subdivision, in *Presented at the Proceedings of the 27th Annual Conference on Computer Graphics and Interactive Techniques* (2000). [Online]. Available https://doi.org/10.1145/344779.344835
12. E. Catmull, J. Clark, Recursively generated B-spline surfaces on arbitrary topological meshes. Computer-Aided Des. **10**(6), 350–355 (1978). https://doi.org/10.1016/0010-4485(78)90110-0

13. M.S. Floater, K. Hormann, Surface parameterization: a tutorial and survey, in *Advances in Multiresolution for Geometric Modelling*, ed. by N.A. Dodgson, M.S. Floater, M.A. Sabin. (Springer, Berlin Heidelberg, 2005), pp. 157–186
14. K. Hormann, M.S. Floater, Mean value coordinates for arbitrary planar polygons. ACM Trans. Graph. **25**(4), 1424–1441 (2006). https://doi.org/10.1145/1183287.1183295
15. G. Peyré, *Numerical mesh processing* (2008). hal-00365931. Available https://hal.archives-ouvertes.fr/hal-00365931/file/Peyre-NumericalMeshProcessing.pdf
16. A. Sheffer, E. Praun, K. Rose, Mesh parameterization methods and their applications. Found. Trends. Comput. Graph. Vis. **2**(2), 105–171 (2006). https://doi.org/10.1561/0600000011

Chapter 4
The Geometry Shader

The geometry shader stage in the OpenGL-4 programmable pipeline [1] is a versatile tool in the processing of three-dimensional mesh surfaces. It allows access to the complete vertex information pertaining to each primitive and provides the functionality to (i) discard primitives as a whole, (ii) modify the shape and structure of a primitive, (iii) generate additional primitives, (iv) process the triangles generated by the primitive generator, and (v) create multiple copies of a mesh object (instancing). Some of the common applications of a geometry shader are geometry culling (e.g. backface culling prior to rasterization), geometry amplification (e.g. generating a surface of revolution using only a base polygonal line as input), creation of texture mapped billboards, and non-photorealistic rendering. This chapter discusses these applications using a geometry shader and contains the following sections:

- **General properties**: Outlines a few important aspects of the geometry shader.
- **Backface culling**: Shows the usefulness of a geometry shader in a mesh rendering application.
- **Surface of revolution**: Demonstrates the usefulness of a geometry shader in generating additional primitives for constructing a surface of revolution from a base polygonal line.
- **Billboards**: Shows an application of a geometry shader for generating view-oriented billboards.
- **Modelling trees**: Presents a fast and simple algorithm for rendering realistic three-dimensional models of trees using the capabilities of a geometry shader.
- **Non-photorealistic rendering**: Discusses methods for highlighting edges of a mesh model using a geometry shader as part of a non-photorealistic rendering algorithm.

© The Author(s), under exclusive license to Springer Nature Switzerland AG 2022
R. Mukundan, *3D Mesh Processing and Character Animation*,
https://doi.org/10.1007/978-3-030-81354-3_4

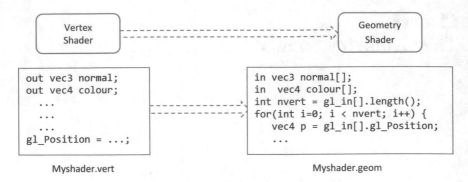

Fig. 4.1 Parameter passing from a vertex shader to a geometric shader

4.1 General Properties

The geometry shader receives inputs from either the tessellation evaluation shader (if the tessellation stage is active) or the vertex shader. The tessellation shader stage is discussed in detail in the next chapter. This chapter discusses applications where the geometry shader receives inputs from the vertex shader (Fig. 4.1).

The geometry shader executes one per input primitive. The most general output of a geometry shader is a triangle strip, of which a triangle and quad are special cases. As shown in Fig. 4.1, the geometry shader receives the vertex positions in the built-in array `gl_in[].gl_Position`. The length of this array (the number of vertices received) is given by `gl_in[].length()`. Each vertex attribute that is output by the vertex shader is gathered in an array having the same variable name in the geometry shader. These arrays are typically processed inside a for-loop as shown in Fig. 4.1. In order to facilitate geometry transformations, lighting calculations, and texture coordinate assignments, the vertex positions and normal vectors are usually sent to the geometry shader in world coordinates (typically using a pass-thru vertex shader), and their conversion to the clip coordinate space is done in the geometry shader. Since the geometry shader is the last shader stage before clipping and rasterization, it is a requirement that each vertex emitted by the shader using the built-in output variable `gl_Position` is in the clip coordinate space.

4.2 Backface Culling

A geometry shader can discard a primitive by simply exiting without emitting any of its vertices. Both view frustum culling and backface culling operations can be performed inside the geometry shader. These operations help reduce the number of primitives processed in the pipeline and provide significant performance gains in real-time applications involving a large number of polygons [2, 3]. Backface culling is normally performed after rasterization by considering the winding order of vertices in screen space. Performing backface culling in the geometry shader further speeds up the process by eliminating the need for rasterizing polygons that are not visible to the viewer.

The sample implementation given in Listing 4.1 converts the vertex coordinates of each triangular primitive to eye coordinate space using the model-view matrix (mvMatrix). If the dot product between the unit normal vector of a triangle and the view vector in the eye-coordinate space is negative, the triangle is treated as a back-facing polygon and not rendered. Note that in eye-coordinate space, the camera is at the origin, and the view vector is given by $-p$, where p is the centroid of the current triangle in eye coordinates.

Listing 4.1 Backface culling using geometry shader

```
void main()
{
  vec4 posn[3], posnAvg;
  vec3 faceNorm, viewVec;
  float ndotV;
  posnAvg = vec4(0,0,0,1);
  for(int i = 0; i < 3; i++)
  {
    posn[i] = mvMatrix * gl_in[i].gl_Position;
    posnAvg = posnAvg + posn[i];
  }
  posnAvg = posnAvg/3.0;  //centroid in eye coords
  viewVec = -normalize(posnAvg.xyz);

  faceNorm = normalize(cross(posn[1].xyz - posn[0].xyz,
                  posn[2].xyz - posn[0].xyz));

  ndotV= dot(faceNorm, viewVec);
  if(ndotV < 0) return;   //Back facing triangle

  for(int i = 0; i < 3; i++)
  {
    gl_Position = projMatrix * posn[i];
    EmitVertex();
  }
  EndPrimitive();
}
```

An output of the above geometry shader-based algorithm for backface culling is shown in Fig. 4.2.

4.3 Surface of Revolution

A surface of revolution is a three-dimensional mesh object obtained by revolving a two-dimensional polygonal line about a fixed axis. As an example, the polygonal

Fig. 4.2 Wireframe model of a mesh object without and with backface culling

line in Fig. 4.3a is rotated about the y-axis at constant angle increments to generate several rotated versions known as slices (Fig. 4.3b). The surface mesh is constructed by connecting pairs of consecutive slices using triangle strips (Fig. 4.3b, c).

We can assume that the polygonal line (or base curve) used in the construction of the surface of revolution is a two-dimensional line strip on the xy-plane. The geometry shader receives segments of this line strip as input, where a line segment is specified by its end points (x_1, y_1) and (x_2, y_2). For each line segment received, the geometry shader constructs and outputs a triangle strip as shown in Fig. 4.4. This is a good example of the use of the geometry shader for geometry amplification.

The shader code given in Listing 4.2 provides a sample implementation of the above process of revolving a line segment about the y-axis to generate and output a triangle strip. An angle increment of $10°$ is used for generating the points on the triangle strip. The variable `mvpMatrix` represents the modelview-projection matrix used for converting the coordinates of vertices from the world space to the clip coordinate space.

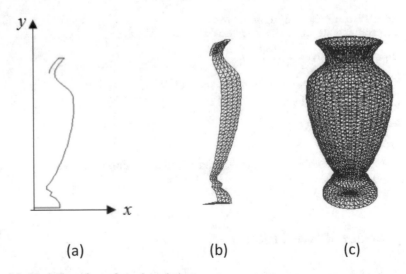

(a)   (b)   (c)

Fig. 4.3 Modelling of a surface of revolution

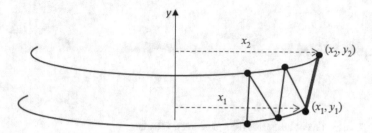

Fig. 4.4 Construction of a triangle strip from an input line segment

Listing 4.2 Surface of revolution using geometry shader

```
layout (lines) in;
layout (triangle_strip, max_vertices = 80) out;
uniform mat4 mvpMatrix;

void main() {
  float x1 = gl_in[0].gl_Position.x;
  float x2 = gl_in[1].gl_Position.x;
  float angle;
  for(int i = 0;  i <= 36; i++)
  {
    angle = radians(i * 10);
      gl_Position  =  mvpMatrix  *  vec4(x1*cos(angle),  y1,  -
x1*sin(angle), 1);
    EmitVertex();
      gl_Position  =  mvpMatrix  *  vec4(x2*cos(angle),  y2,  -
x2*sin(angle), 1);
    EmitVertex();
  }
  EndPrimitive();
}
```

4.4 Billboards

A billboard is a screen aligned quad which is texture mapped with the image of a distant object such as a tree and placed in a three-dimensional scene to provide a visual representation of the object. The billboard is an example of a sampled representation of geometry where a three-dimensional model is replaced with its image mapped onto a quad [2, 3]. Objects such as sprites, billboards, and impostors are commonly used in image-based rendering methods, and they all share the property that they are view aligned texture mapped quads.

A geometry shader-based implementation of billboarding given below specifies only the positions of the billboards as inputs. The application contains only one vertex buffer object that stores the coordinates of the points. The geometry shader

(a)   (b)

Fig. 4.5 Construction of billboards using a geometry shader

receives the points and constructs a view-oriented quad at each point (Fig. 4.5a). It also specifies the texture coordinates at the vertices of the quads. A sample output is shown in (Fig. 4.5b).

The code for the geometry shader for a basic implementation of the billboarding algorithm is given in Listing 4.3.

Listing 4.3 Implementation of billboarding using a geometry shader

```
layout (points) in;
layout (triangle_strip, max_vertices = 4) out;
uniform mat4 mvpMatrix;
out vec2 texcoord;
void main()
{
  vec4 pos;
  vec4 p = gl_in[0].gl_Position;

  pos = vec4(p.x-0.5, p.y, p.z, 1);
  gl_Position = mvpMatrix * pos;
  texcoord = vec2(0, 0);
  EmitVertex();

  pos = vec4(p.x+0.5, p.y, p.z, 1);
  gl_Position = mvpMatrix * pos;
  texcoord = vec2(1, 0);
  EmitVertex();

  pos = vec4(p.x-0.5, p.y+1, p.z, 1);
  gl_Position = mvpMatrix * pos;
  texcoord = vec2(0, 1);
  EmitVertex();

  pos = vec4(p.x+0.5, p.y+1, p.z, 1);
  gl_Position = mvpMatrix * pos;
  texcoord = vec2(1, 1);
  EmitVertex();

  EndPrimitive();
}
```

Billboards can also be constructed using point sprites which are screen aligned square shaped regions. However, not all billboards are necessarily screen aligned.

View oriented billboards try to maintain an orientation that is perpendicular to the local view axis direction. Using a geometry shader we can easily implement more general methods for rendering various types of billboards and particles with only positions and orientations of such planar structures as inputs. The next section discusses one such application.

4.5 Modelling Trees

Three-dimensional models of trees are extensively used in the rendering of natural environments as parts of games or simulations [4]. The geometry shader provides the ability to design particles similar to billboards, with non-square shapes and arbitrary orientations. The method outlined above, with minor modifications, could be used to map textures of leaf images on a tree model consisting of the main trunk and the branches. Such models, where only the positions and orientations of leaves are specified as inputs, are particularly useful for real-time and photorealistic rendering of trees. The process of constructing a tree model using a geometry shader is discussed in the following sections.

4.5.1 Leaves

Assume that the position P and orientation n of each leaf is specified as three-dimensional vectors. In this model, we treat leaves as a stationary particle system, and the input consists of only the values of two parameters, position and orientation, each stored as a three-dimensional vector in vertex buffer objects. The vertex shader is a pass-thru shader that outputs these values to the geometry shader. The orientation of the leaf particle is defined based on a right-handed orthogonal triad of unit vectors u, v, n given in Eq. (4.1). The vectors satisfy the property

$$n = u \times v \tag{4.1}$$

The computation of these vectors using the vertices of a model of the stem is discussed in the next section. Similar to the implementation in Listing 4.3, the geometry shader constructs and emits a square-shaped quad (triangle strip) of size $2d$ units as shown in Fig. 4.6a. The vertices of the quad and the texture coordinates are computed as given in Eq. (4.2). The rendered leaf is shown in Fig. 4.6b.

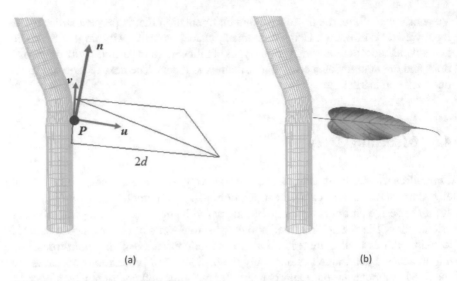

Fig. 4.6 Construction of a leaf particle using a geometry shader

$$
\begin{array}{ll}
\text{Vertex position} & \text{Texture coordinates} \\
\boldsymbol{p}_1 = \boldsymbol{P} - d\boldsymbol{v} & (1, 0) \\
\boldsymbol{p}_2 = \boldsymbol{P} + d\boldsymbol{v} & (0, 0) \\
\boldsymbol{p}_3 = \boldsymbol{P} - d\boldsymbol{v} + 2d\boldsymbol{u} & (1, 1) \\
\boldsymbol{p}_4 = \boldsymbol{P} + d\,\boldsymbol{v} + 2d\boldsymbol{u} & (0, 1)
\end{array}
\tag{4.2}
$$

Figure 4.7a shows the wireframe model of a tree, with several positions of leaves indicated by quads. A rendering of the tree with each quad texture mapped using a leaf image is given in Fig. 4.7b. The next section outlines a method to design the

Fig. 4.7 A model of a tree with a leaf texture mapped to quad regions

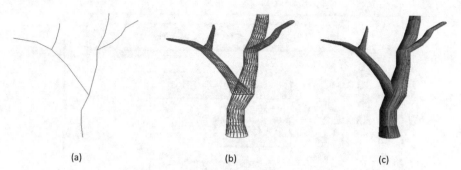

(a) (b) (c)

Fig. 4.8 Construction of a 3D model of a tree stem using a geometry shader: **a** skeleton, **b** wireframe, and **c** textured solid model

trunk and the branches. The positions and orientations of the leaves are defined based on the points on the mesh surface constructed using a geometry shader.

4.5.2 Stem

A fairly general structure of the trunk and branches of a tree with variations in size and orientation can be designed using minimal inputs with the help of a geometry shader. As in the case of a surface of revolution (Listing 4.2), the main input to the geometry shader is a set of line segments specifying the medial axis (skeleton) of the stem (Fig. 4.8a). The points along this polygonal line (the input vertices of the line segments) are used as centres of circular cross sections of the tree mesh. The radius of each circular section at an input vertex is also specified along with the vertex coordinates in the data file (Fig. 4.9). Variations in the shape of the stem can be easily created by modifying the values of the radius and vertex coordinates.

For each input line segment received, the geometry shader constructs a triangle strip between two circular sections, one at each end of the line segment (Fig. 4.8b). This method allows branching structures to be easily specified (see Fig. 4.9) and constructed. The endpoints of the branches are defined with a small value for the radius. A rendering of the model including lighting calculations and texture mapping is shown in Fig. 4.8c.

The model definition has a simple structure containing a vertex list which includes the coordinates and the radius at each vertex, and the vertex indices of the line segments. A sample model definition is given in Fig. 4.9. The skeleton model in this example contains eight nodes (vertices) and seven line segments connecting the vertices.

An implementation of the method described above in a geometry shader is given in Listing 4.4.

Listing 4.4 Modelling of a tree stem using a geometry shader

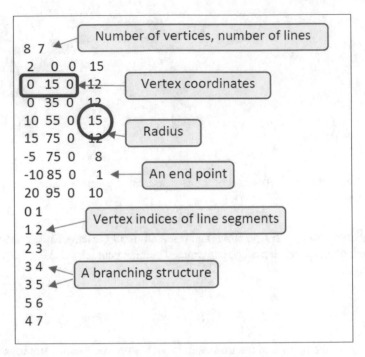

Fig. 4.9 Sample data specifying the skeleton of the tree model

```
layout (lines) in;
layout (triangle_strip, max_vertices = 144) out;
uniform mat4 mvpMatrix;  //The model-view-projection matrix
in float rad[];  //radius
void main()
{
  float angle, ca, sa;
  vec4 pos;
  vec4 p0 = gl_in[0].gl_Position;
  vec4 p1 = gl_in[1].gl_Position;
  for (int i = 0; i < 20; i++)  //circular sections
  {
    angle = radians(i*18);
    ca = cos(angle);
    sa = sin(angle);

    pos = vec4(rad[0]*ca+p0.x, p0.y, rad[0]*sa+p0.z, 1);
    gl_Position = mvpMatrix * pos;
    EmitVertex();

    pos = vec4(rad[1]*ca+p1.x, p1.y, rad[1]*sa+p1.z, 1);
    gl_Position = mvpMatrix * pos;
    EmitVertex();
  }
  EndPrimitive();
}
```

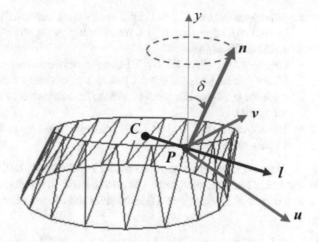

Fig. 4.10 Vectors defining the orientation of a leaf on a stem

Once a model of the trunk and the branches are constructed, the positions and orientations of leaves can be specified as previously shown in Fig. 4.6a, using a set of points on the mesh. Leaves are added to only thin branches where the radius is below a pre-specified threshold. For each of the circular sections, a few points on the circumference are randomly selected as the positions P of the leaves. The vector l from the centre of the circular section C towards the point P defines the approximate direction of the leaf. The orientation (or the normal vector) of the leaf n is computed as a random vector around the vertical direction $(0, 1, 0)$ using the declination angle δ (a random value between $0°$ and $30°$), and an azimuth angle α (a random value between $0°$ and $360°$). The computation of the vectors is given in Eq. (4.3). The u, v vectors specify the plane of the leaf, with normal vector n (Fig. 4.10).

$$n = (\sin\alpha \sin\delta, \cos\delta, \cos\alpha \sin\delta), 0 \leq \alpha \leq 360°, 0 \leq \delta \leq 30°$$
$$l = P - C$$
$$v = n \times l$$
$$u = v \times n \qquad\qquad (4.3)$$

4.6 Non-photorealistic Rendering

Non-photorealistic rendering (NPR) of three-dimensional mesh models tries to emulate artistic styles seen in cartoon drawings and paintings into the shading algorithm [2, 3, 5, 6]. An important characteristic of non-photorealistic rendering is the highlighting of predominant edges of the model to enhance the expressive styles used by the shading method. Three types of edges are usually considered in NPR algorithms:

- Silhouette edges (Fig. 4.11a): These edges separate the model from the background. An edge shared by a front-facing polygon and a back facing polygon is a silhouette edge.
- Crease edges (Fig. 4.11b): The angle between two adjacent planes is used to identify crease edges. The dot product of normal vectors of every pair of visible adjacent triangles in a model needs to be computed to identify all crease edges of the model.
- Border edges (Fig. 4.11c): These are boundary edges of a mesh model that belong to only one polygon.

Figure 4.12 shows a two-tone rendering of a wineglass model with its edges highlighted in black. Even though a two-tone shading method can be easily implemented in a fragment shader using a threshold for the diffuse reflection term (the dot product

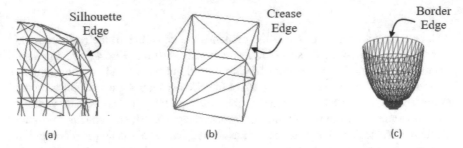

(a)   (b)   (c)

Fig. 4.11   Three types of edges on a mesh model

Fig. 4.12   Two-tone rendering of a wineglass model

of the normal vector and the light source vector), the detection and highlighting of edges will require a special primitive structure and a set of more complex processes as discussed below.

The detection of edges shown in Fig. 4.11 requires information on pairs of adjacent triangles on a mesh model. The geometry shader accepts a special type of primitive known as GL_TRIANGLES_ADJACENCY that contains six vertices representing a triangle and its three adjacent triangles (see Fig. 2.14). The triangle adjacency primitive is particularly useful for identifying edges in NPR applications. The properties of this primitive and the construction of the vertex buffer object containing six vertices per primitive were discussed in detail in Sect. 2.9. We now focus our attention on the geometry shader where the edges are detected and highlighted. We assume that the vertex shader is a pass-thru shader that outputs the vertex coordinates in the world coordinate space. In the geometry shader, the six input vertices are first converted to the eye coordinate space using the model-view matrix (mvMatrix). Listing 4.5 below gives the code for the detection of silhouette and crease edges. In this code, normMain denotes the face normal of the main triangle, and normAdj the face normal of an adjacent triangle. Please refer to Fig. 2.14 for the ordering of vertices used in the computation of face normal vectors. The functions drawSilhouetteEdge() and drawCreaseEdge() create a thin strip along the detected edge, as described below. The code for the function drawSilhouetteEdge() is given later in Listing 4.7.

Listing 4.5 Silhouette and crease edge detection in the geometry shader

```
layout (triangles_adjacency) in;
layout (triangle_strip, max_vertices = 27) out;
myPara

uniform mat4 mvMatrix;

void main()
{
    vec4 posn[6], posnAvg;
    vec3 normMain, normAdj;
    float angle[3];
    int k;

    posnAvg = vec4(0,0,0,1);
    for(int i = 0; i < 6; i++)
    {
        posn[i] = mvMatrix * gl_in[i].gl_Position;
        if(mod(i, 2) == 0) posnAvg = posnAvg + posn[i];
    }
    posnAvg = posnAvg/3.0;  //centroid in eye coords
    viewVec = - normalize(posnAvg.xyz);

    normMain = normalize(cross(posn[2].xyz-posn[0].xyz,
                    posn[4].xyz-posn[0].xyz));
    ndotV = dot(normMain, viewVec);
    for(int i = 0; i < 3; i++)
    {
```

```
      k = 2 * mod(i+1, 3);
      normAdj = normalize(cross(posn[k].xyz-posn[2*i+1].xyz,
                      posn[2*i].xyz-posn[2*i+1].xyz));
      angle = dot(normMain, normAdj);  //Dihedral angle

      //Silhouette edge detection
      if(dot(normAdj, viewVec) * ndotV < 0)
            drawSilhouetteEdge(posn[2*i], posn[k]);

      //Crease edge detection
      if(angle < 0.86) drawCreaseEdge(posn[2*i], posn[k]);
   }
}
```

Border edges are identified by the presence of repeated indices in the triangle adjacency primitive (see Listing 2.9). The code for detecting border edges in the geometry shader is given in Listing 4.6. Here, $vid[i], i = 0..5$ denotes the indices of the six input vertices of a triangle adjacency primitive.

Listing 4.6 Border edge detection in the geometry shader

```
if((vid[1] == vid[0]) || (vid[1] == vid[2]))
    drawBorderEdge(posn[0], posn[2]);
if((vid[3] == vid[2]) || (vid[3] == vid[4]))
    drawBorderEdge(posn[2], posn[4]);
if((vid[5] == vid[4]) || (vid[5] == vid[0]))
    drawBorderEdge(posn[4], posn[0]);
```

Once the important edges of the current primitive are detected, they are high-lighted by drawing a thin quad (a triangle strip) with a dark colour along the detected edge. This process uses the ability of a geometry shader to generate and emit additional primitives required in a rendering application. The orientation of a new quad constructed along an edge of the main triangle of a triangle adjacency primitive will vary depending on the type of the edge. The process of constructing this thin triangle strips for silhouette and crease edges is illustrated in Fig. 4.13. In both cases, the edge normal vector *u* is computed as the average of the normal vectors of the main triangle and the adjacent triangle, and four points near the edge are output as vertices of a triangle strip. In the case of a silhouette edge, the plane of the triangle strip contains the vector *u*. For a crease edge, the vector *u* is orthogonal to the plane of the strip. These specific orientations are chosen to give maximum visibility of the highlighted edge to the viewer.

Listing 4.7 provides a code example for generating a thin strip along a silhouette edge. The inputs to the function are the vertex coordinates of an edge that was identified as a silhouette edge. In this example, the vector *u* is chosen as the cross-product of the view vector and the edge vector in order to orient the strip perpendicular to the view direction.

Listing 4.7 Drawing a silhouette edge using a geometry shader

```
void drawSilhouetteEdge(vec4 posnA, vec4 posnB)
```

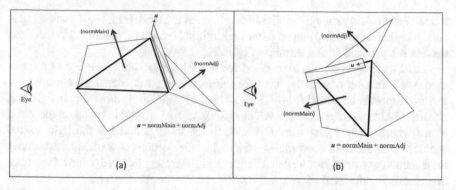

Fig. 4.13 Process of highlighting edges using a thin triangle strip. **a** Silhouette edge and **b** crease edge

```
{
  float epsd = 0.0005; //displacement
  vec3 p;
  vec3 edgeVec = normalize(posnB.xyz - posnA.xyz);
  vec3 perp = normalize(cross(edgeVec, viewVec));

  p = posnA.xyz - 0.001 * edgeVec;
      gl_Position = projMatrix * vec4(p, 1);
      EmitVertex();
  p = p + 0.01 * edgeNorm;
      gl_Position = projMatrix * vec4(p, 1);
      EmitVertex();
  p = posnB.xyz + 0.001 * edgeVec;
      gl_Position = projMatrix * vec4(p, 1);
      EmitVertex();
  p = p + 0.01 * edgeNorm;
      gl_Position = projMatrix * vec4(p, 1);
      EmitVertex();
  EndPrimitive();
}
```

Figure 4.14 shows the outputs of the application of the above discussed methods on a mesh model. Figure 4.14a shows the conventional Gouraud shading of the

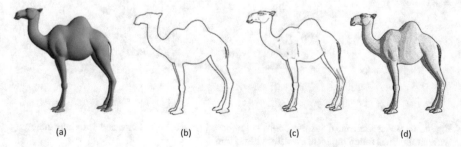

Fig. 4.14 Camel model rendered with **a** Gouraud shading and **d** pencil shading

model. Figure 4.14b shows the silhouette edges of the model. Figure 4.14c includes both silhouette and crease edges. After highlighting the edges, the model is rendered using a set of pencil stroke textures (Fig. 4.14d).

Pencil shading is a popular method for non-photorealistic rendering of a mesh model, where a set of mipmap textures with varying stroke densities are used for texture mapping the model (Fig. 4.15). The set of mipmap textures is called a tonal art map (TAM). A mipmap set is selected for texturing a triangle based on the value of $n.l$ where n is the face normal vector of the triangle and l is the light source vector [7]. The texture coordinates assigned to the vertices of a triangle determine the direction of stroke lines on that triangle. It is generally preferred to have the stroke lines following the local curvature directions on the model. A coarse estimate of the local curvature can be obtained using the dihedral angles between adjacent triangles in a triangle adjacency primitive.

An edge of the current triangle where the dihedral angle is maximum may be selected as the edge perpendicular to the stroke lines, and the texture coordinates for that triangle assigned as shown in Fig. 4.16a. The rendering of a model given in Fig. 4.16b clearly shows the stroke lines in the mapped textures following directions of curvature on the model.

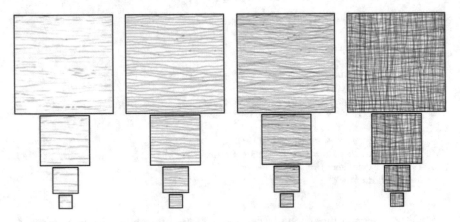

Fig. 4.15   A collection of mipmap sets (tonal art map) used for pencil shading

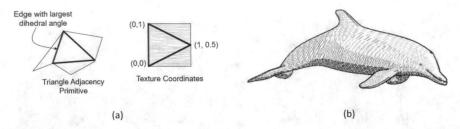

Fig. 4.16   a Assignment of texture coordinates based on local curvature and **b** texture mapping with stroke lines following local curvature directions

4.7 Chapter Resources

The folder "Chapter 4" on the companion website contains the following programs, associated shader files, and mesh data. The programs demonstrate the implementation and working of the algorithms presented in this chapter.

- BackfaceCulling.cpp: Implements the backface culling algorithm in a geometry shader (Listing 4.1).
- SurfaceRevln.cpp: Uses the geometry shader for creating a surface of revolution from a base polygonal line (Listing 4.2).
- Billboard.cpp: Generates texture mapped view-oriented billboards using a geometry shader that takes only the positional information of the billboards as inputs (Listing 4.3).
- TreeStem.cpp: Creates a three-dimensional model of a tree stem using a generic data structure specifying the positions and radii of axial sections (Listing 4.4).

References and Further Reading

1. D. Wolff, *OpenGL 4 Shading Language Cookbook*, 3rd ed. (Packt Publishing, 2018)
2. T. Akenine-Moller, E. Haines, *Real-Time Rendering*, 4th ed. (A K Peters/CRC Press, 2018)
3. A. Boreskov, E. Shikin, *Computer Graphics—From Pixels to Programmable Graphics Hardware.* (Chapman and Hall/CRC Press, 2013)
4. Q.L. Zhang, M.Y. Pang, A survey of modeling and rendering trees, in *Technologies for E-Learning and Digital Entertainment, Lecture Notes in Computer Science*, vol. 5093. (Springer, Berlin, Heidelberg, 2008), pp. 757–764. https://doi.org/10.1007/978-3-540-69736-7_80
5. T. Strohette, S. Schlechtweg, *Non-Photorealistic Computer Graphics: Modeling, Rendering, and Animation.* (Morgan Kaufmann, 2002)
6. B. Gooch, A. Gooch, *Non-Photorealistic Rendering.* (A K Peters/CRC Press, 2001)
7. R. Mukundan, Multi-level stroke textures for sketch based non-photorealistic rendering, in *2015 International Conference and Workshop on Computing and Communication (IEMCON)*, 15–17 October 2015 (2015), pp. 1–7. https://doi.org/10.1109/IEMCON.2015.7344505

Chapter 5
Mesh Tessellation

This chapter deals with methods for mesh surface modelling using the tessellation shader stage of the OpenGL-4 pipeline. This stage not only allows the construction of highly tessellated, complex, and smooth mesh surfaces from very basic, coarse geometrical structures (base or control polygons), but also provides the flexibility of rendering such surfaces with dynamic levels of detail. We consider two important applications of mesh tessellation and modelling in this chapter: (i) terrain rendering, and (ii) Bezier surface modelling. This chapter contains the following sections:

- **OpenGL-4 tessellation stages**: Gives an overview of the tessellation shader stage of the OpenGL-4 pipeline and discusses the computations performed in the shaders.
- **Terrain rendering**: Presents the complete algorithm for real-time rendering complex three-dimensional terrain models with dynamic levels of detail and surface texturing.
- **Procedural heightmap generation**: Presents algorithms for generating procedural heightmaps using organic noise models and random fractal generation methods.
- **Bezier surface patches**: Discusses methods for rendering popular Bezier surface models such as the teapot, using a tessellation evaluation shader.

5.1 OpenGL-4 Tessellation Stages

The tessellation stage is an optional shader stage in the OpenGL-4 pipeline—a user may write a program containing only the vertex and the fragment shader, bypassing the tessellation stage. This stage includes two programmable shaders: the tessellation control shader (TCS) and the tessellation evaluation shader (TES). Figure 5.1 shows the main components of the pipeline, with user defined shaders and structures highlighted in blue. Boxes with dotted lines indicate optional shader stages. Within the

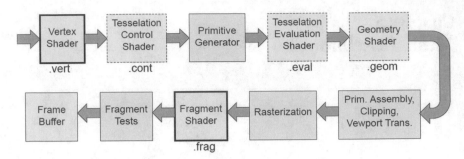

Fig. 5.1 Shader stages of the programmable pipeline

tessellation stage itself, the tessellation control shader is an optional stage, meaning that is possible to specify tessellation operations using only the evaluation shader.

If the tessellation shader stage is active (i.e. if the tessellation evaluation shader is present), then the type of the input primitive in the glDrawArrays() and glDrawElements() must be specified as GL_PATCHES. The next section outlines important properties of this primitive type.

5.1.1   Patches

GL_PATCHES is a special type of OpenGL-4 primitive that is valid only when the tessellation stage is active. This primitive defines the coarse structure of a base polygonal mesh used in the construction of the tessellated surface. Two important characteristics of a patch primitive are outlined below:

- A patch is not a renderable primitive. It is used only for controlling the shape of the tessellated surface. Its vertices are often used as inputs to polynomial blending functions to generate vertices of a triangle that forms part of a tessellated surface. Since patch vertices are never rendered, there is no need for converting them to the clip coordinate space. Therefore, in most applications where a tessellation shader is used, the vertex shader acts as just a pass-thru shader transferring the vertex coordinates directly to the next shader stage (Fig. 5.4).
- A patch is just an ordered list of vertices, where the ordering and the number of vertices are determined by the user. A patch does not have any mesh connectivity information. Depending on the application, control polygons may have varying number of vertices. A planar region may be tessellated using a patch containing only three or four vertices, while designing surfaces using higher order blending functions requires patches containing 9 or 16 vertices (Fig. 5.3). The number of vertices contained in the patch primitives must be specified using a separate OpenGL function, glPatchParameteri().

Some of the commonly used patch definitions are shown in Fig. 5.2.

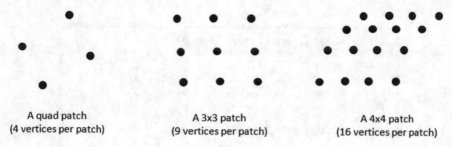

A quad patch | A 3x3 patch | A 4x4 patch
(4 vertices per patch) | (9 vertices per patch) | (16 vertices per patch)

Fig. 5.2 Few examples of patch definitions

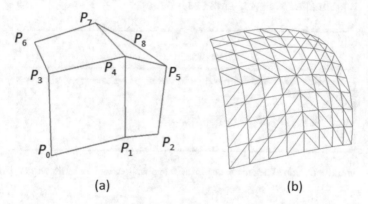

(a) (b)

Fig. 5.3 3×3 patch used as a control polygon for generating a smooth tessellated surface

A simple definition of a 3×3 patch in an OpenGL application is shown in Fig. 5.4. The vertex shader outputs the patch vertices in world coordinates without applying any transformation. These vertices are made available in a built-in array `gl_in[].gl_Position` of the control and evaluation shaders. Both these vertices therefore have access to all vertices of a current patch.

5.1.2 Tessellation Control Shader

The tessellation control shader is used for three purposes: to set the tessellation levels, to modify the positions of patch vertices, and to create new or remove existing patch vertices [1]. The tessellation control shader executes once for each output patch vertex. The output patch vertex currently processed by the shader is given by `gl_out[gl_InvocationID].gl_Position`. If the patch vertices are not modified, the coordinates of each patch vertex are directly copied over to the output vertex stream (`gl_out[gl_InvocationID].gl_Position = gl_in[gl_InvocationID].gl_Position`). If the tessellation levels are also not modified within the shader, they can be set by the application.

Application

```
float verts[] =        //Patch vertices
{
   -5, 0,  5,    0, 3,  5,      5, 0,  5,
   -5, 4,  0,    0, 6,  0,      5, 4,  0,
   -5, 0, -5,    0, 3, -5,      5, 0, -5
};


 . . . //VBO definition

// Draw commands
glPatchParameteri(GL_PATCH_VERTICES, 9);
glDrawArrays(GL_PATCHES, 0, 9);
```

Vertex Shader

```
layout (location = 0) in vec4 position;
void main()
{
     gl_Position = position;
}
```

Fig. 5.4 Simple definition of a patch in an OpenGL application, and its vertex shader

The inner and outer tessellation levels define the pattern of subdivision of a normalized two-dimensional parametric domain. OpenGL uses two types of parametric spaces: a quad domain and a triangle domain. A quad parametric domain is a square region of unit length with coordinate values (u, v) in the range [0, 1]. A triangle domain represents an equilateral triangle, where the coordinates (u, v, w) of a point are specified in barycentric coordinates (Fig. 5.5). The barycentric coordinates also have values in the range [0, 1] and satisfy the additional property that $u + v + w = 1$ (see Sect. 3.3.1). The coordinates of a vertex in these domains are called tessellation coordinates and used as parameters of blending functions that generate a linear

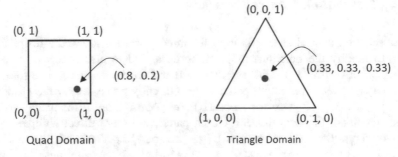

Fig. 5.5 Normalized parametric domains used for tessellation

combination of patch vertices to move that vertex from the two-dimensional space to the three-dimensional coordinate space of the input patch. This process is described in detail later in Sect. 5.1.5.

The way the above domains are tessellated depends on the outer and inner tessellation levels specified by the user. The outer tessellation levels define the number of subdivisions along the outer edges of the domain. A quad has 4 outer tessellation levels, while a triangle domain has 3. The fourth outer tessellation level for a triangle domain is always set to 0. The inner tessellation levels, on the other hand, are not so intuitively defined. For a quad domain, the inner tessellation level in the horizontal direction is the minimum number of subdivisions encountered as you move along an interior (non-boundary) polygonal line from the left edge to the right edge of the domain. The inner tessellation level in the vertical direction can also be similarly defined. Figure 5.6 tries to illustrate this interpretation of inner levels.

A few tessellated quad domains are shown in Fig. 5.7. It may be noted that all combinations of outer and inner levels may not yield the expected results. For example, specifying all outer tessellation levels as 2 and inner levels as 1 would still result in the rightmost output in Fig. 5.7, where both inner tessellation levels have a value 2.

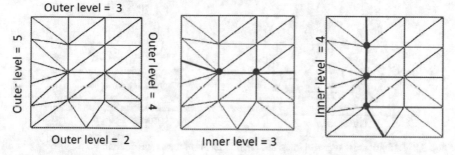

Fig. 5.6 Definition of outer and inner tessellation levels of a quad domain

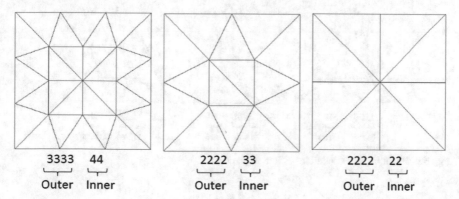

Fig. 5.7 Examples of tessellations of a quad domain

It may also be noted that both quad and triangle tessellations result in a triangle mesh. These triangles are generated by the primitive generator (see Fig. 5.1), and its vertices processed by the evaluation shader. The vertex coordinates will always have a value in the range [0, 1].

The inner tessellation levels of a triangle domain can also have an interpretation similar to that of the quad domain. It is important to note here that a triangle domain has only one inner tessellation level. The second inner tessellation level is always set to 0. The inner tessellation level is the minimum number of subdivisions encountered along an interior polygonal line path from any of the vertices of the triangle towards the opposite edge (Fig. 5.8).

Examples showing tessellations of a triangle domain with different outer and inner levels are given in Fig. 5.9.

As previously mentioned, the tessellation levels may be specified either in the OpenGL application itself (if they are constant and the control shader is not present), or within the tessellation control shader (if they vary with time—see next section) (Fig. 5.10).

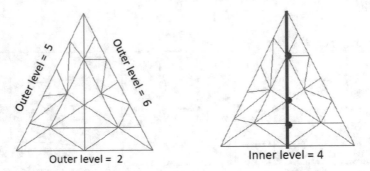

Fig. 5.8 Definition of outer and inner tessellation levels of a triangle domain

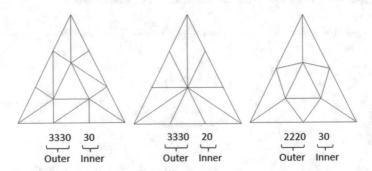

Fig. 5.9 Examples of tessellations of a triangle domain

```GLfloat outLvl[4]= {9, 2, 5, 0};``` ```GLfloat inLvl[2] = {4, 0};``` ```glPatchParameterfv``` ```(GL_PATCH_DEFAULT_OUTER_LEVEL, outLvl);``` ```glPatchParameterfv``` ```(GL_PATCH_DEFAULT_INNER_LEVEL, inLvl);```	```layout(vertices = 3) out;``` ```void main()``` ```{``` ``` gl_out[gl_InvocationID].gl_Position =``` ``` gl_in[gl_InvocationID].gl_Position;``` ``` gl_TessLevelOuter[0] = 9;``` ``` gl_TessLevelOuter[1] = 2;``` ``` gl_TessLevelOuter[2] = 5;``` ``` gl_TessLevelOuter[3] = 0;``` ``` gl_TessLevelInner[0] = 4;``` ``` gl_TessLevelInner[1] = 0;``` ```}```
(a)	(b)

Fig. 5.10 Definition of a set of tessellation levels for a triangle domain using **a** OpenGL application, and **b** control shader

5.1.3 Dynamic Level of Detail

One of the applications of the tessellation control shader in real-time rendering of large scene geometries such as terrains, is controlling the level of detail (LOD) based on the distance of a patch from the camera. Mesh objects that are modelled using control patches such as the teapot can also be rendered using a LOD-based tessellation method. Distant regions of the wireframe model of the terrain segment in Fig. 5.11a have lower levels of tessellation compared to regions located closer to the camera. The Bezier surface model of "Gumbo" shown in Fig. 5.11b has a LOD which dynamically varies based on the distance of the object from the camera.

If we assign a high level of tessellation L_{High} to regions that are at the closest distance d_{min} from the camera, and the lowest level of tessellation L_{low} to regions at the farthest distance d_{max}, a simple linear interpolation between the min–max values could be used to find the tessellation level L for a patch at a given distance d from the camera.

$$L = L_{\text{high}} - \frac{(d - d_{\min})(L_{\text{high}} - L_{\text{low}})}{(d_{\max} - d_{\min})} \tag{5.1}$$

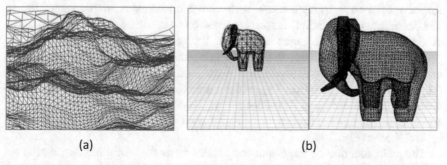

(a)   (b)

Fig. 5.11 Application of LOD in patch-based models of **a** a terrain, and **b** a Bezier surface

An implementation of the basic LOD algorithm as outlined above is given in Listing 5.1.

Listing 5.1: LOD implementation in a tessellation control shader

```
layout(vertices = 4) out;
uniform vec4 eyePos;                    //Camera position

void main()
{
    float l_low = 4, l_high = 50;  //Low, high tessellation levels
    float dmin = 5,  dmax = 200;   //min, max distance from camera
    float dist = 0, level = 0;
    vec4 centre;
    gl_out[gl_InvocationID].gl_Position
       = gl_in[gl_InvocationID].gl_Position;

    centre = (gl_in[0].gl_Position //Centroid of the current patch
            + gl_in[1].gl_Position
            + gl_in[2].gl_Position
            + gl_in[3].gl_Position)*0.25;

    dist = distance(eyePos, centre);

    level = l_high - (dist-dmin)*(l_high - l_low)/(dmax - dmin);
    gl_TessLevelOuter[0] = level;
    gl_TessLevelOuter[1] = level;
    gl_TessLevelOuter[2] = level;
    gl_TessLevelOuter[3] = level;
    gl_TessLevelInner[0] = level;
    gl_TessLevelInner[1] = level;
}
```

5.1.4 Tessellation Evaluation Shader

The tessellation of the parametric domain using the levels specified in the control shader results in a triangle mesh with vertex coordinates in the range [0, 1]. The tessellation evaluation shader receives one vertex of the tessellated mesh at a time—it acts as a vertex shader for the vertices emitted by the primitive generator. The coordinates of the tessellated mesh vertex in parametric space are called the tessellation coordinates. A quad domain generates two components (gl_TessCoord.u, gl_TessCoord.v), while a triangle domain generates three components (gl_TessCoord.u, gl_TessCoord.v, gl_TessCoord.w) which are barycentric coordinates. The evaluation shader also receives the patch vertices output by the control shader (Fig. 5.12).

The main function of the evaluation shader is, as the name implies, evaluate a blending function that combines the input patch vertices to map the tessellated mesh

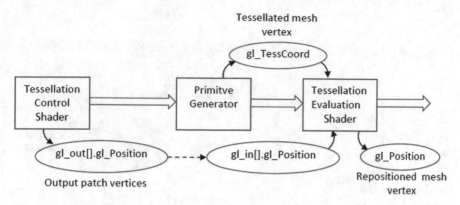

Fig. 5.12 Inputs to the tessellation evaluation shader

vertex to the world coordinate space of the patch vertices. This mapping process is also known as the repositioning of the mesh vertex from the parametric domain to the patch's coordinate space. The following section outlines this process using both quad and triangle domains. When every vertex of the tessellated mesh is mapped onto the patch's space, a triangle mesh surface in that three-dimensional space is formed. This surface may be transformed using the model-view-projection matrix inside the evaluation shader. Similar to a vertex shader, any vertex attribute output by the evaluation shader will be bi-linearly interpolated at the rasterization stage to get per-fragment values.

Like any vertex shader, the evaluation shader may also need to convert the repositioned mesh vertex to the clip coordinate space if it is the last shader stage before rasterization (i.e. the geometry shader is not present).

5.1.5 Blending Functions

Suppose a patch contains three vertices P_0, P_1, P_2, and that a triangle domain is tessellated at a certain level with the aim of subdividing the region between the patch vertices in exactly the same way, as shown in Fig. 5.13. Each tessellated mesh vertex with barycentric coordinates (u, v, w) can be mapped to a three-dimensional point P in the region of patch vertices using Eq. (5.2).

$$P = uP_0 + vP_1 + wP_2, \quad u, v, w \in [0, 1], \quad u + v + w = 1. \quad (5.2)$$

Listing 5.2 gives an implementation of the mapping using barycentric coordinates outlined above. Please note that the tessellation evaluation shader also transforms

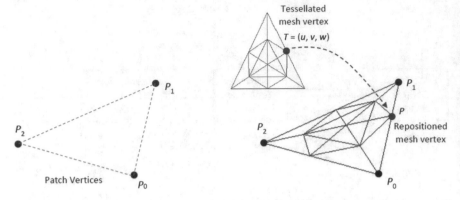

Fig. 5.13 Mapping of a tessellated vertex from a triangle domain to the world coordinate space

the repositioned mesh vertex to clip coordinates. This transformation is required if the geometry shader is not present.

Listing 5.2: Mapping of a tessellated vertex in a triangle domain

```
layout(triangles, equal_spacing, ccw) in;

uniform mat4 mvpMatrix;
vec4 posn;

void main()
{
    posn = gl_TessCoord.x * gl_in[0].gl_Position
         + gl_TessCoord.y * gl_in[1].gl_Position
         + gl_TessCoord.z * gl_in[2].gl_Position;
    gl_Position = mvpMatrix*posn;
}
```

The tessellation of a quad domain provides Cartesian coordinates (u, v) of the tessellated mesh vertex in the normalized parametric space. The repositioning of this vertex in the world coordinate space can be done using a variety of blending functions. In the following, we assume that the patch contains only four vertices P_0, P_1, P_2, P_3 as shown in Fig. 5.14. The tessellation coordinates (u, v) can be used as parameters of a bi-linear interpolation of the patch vertices to find the mapped position of the tessellated mesh vertex (Eq. 5.3).

$$P = (1 - u)(1 - v)P_0 + u(1 - v)P_1 + uvP_2 + (1 - u)vP_3 \quad u, v \in [0, 1]. \quad (5.3)$$

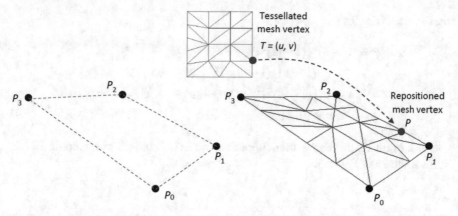

Fig. 5.14 Mapping of a tessellated vertex from a quad domain to the world coordinate space

Listing 5.3 gives an implementation of the above bi-linear mapping in a tessellation evaluation shader.

Listing 5.3: Bi-linear mapping of a tessellated vertex in a quad domain

```
layout(quads, equal_spacing, ccw) in;

uniform mat4 mvpMatrix;
vec4 posn;

void main()
{
    float u = gl_TessCoord.x;
    float v = gl_TessCoord.y;
    posn = (1-u)* (1-v) * gl_in[0].gl_Position
         + u * (1-v) *     gl_in[1].gl_Position
         + u * v *         gl_in[2].gl_Position
         + (1-u) * v *     gl_in[3].gl_Position;
    gl_Position = mvpMatrix * posn;
}
```

Please note that both the above mappings use only linear combinations of patch vertices to compute the interpolated position of the tessellated vertex. The triangle mesh thus formed will always lie on a planar surface whose position and orientation in the three-dimensional space are prespecified by the patch vertices. For generating curved surfaces whose shapes are given by control polygons defined using patch vertices, we require higher order blending functions and a larger number of patch vertices. Consider a patch formed by 9 vertices $P_0 \ldots P_8$, as shown in Fig. 5.3a. A bi-quadratic blending function in the tessellation coordinates u, v may be used to combine the patch vertices to generate the transformed position P of the tessellated mesh vertex (Eq. 5.4).

$$
\begin{aligned}
P =&(1-v)^2\{(1-u)^2 P_0 + 2u(1-u)P_1 + u^2 P_2\}\\
&+ 2v(1-v)\{(1-u)^2 P_3 + 2u(1-u)P_4 + u^2 P_5\}\\
&+ v^2\{(1-u)^2 P_6 + 2u(1-u)P_7 + u^2 P_8\}\\
&u, v \in [0, 1].
\end{aligned}
\tag{5.4}
$$

As a result of the above transformation, we get a smooth bi-quadratic Bezier surface shown in Fig. 5.3b.

5.1.6 Lighting Calculations

The tessellation evaluation shader receives only one vertex of the tessellated mesh at a time; information about the positions of neighbouring vertices is not available. To perform lighting calculations on the generated mesh, we require the surface normal vectors at the computed (repositioned) mesh vertices. Two ways to compute the normal vectors at a mesh vertex are given below:

- *Use a geometry shader*: A geometry shader, if added to the processing pipeline, will receive all three vertices of each triangle of the generated mesh surface. Geometry shaders are primarily designed for processing a primitive as a whole and to generate additional primitives if required. Using the vertices of a triangle, we can compute the components of the normal vector (face normal) using the cross product of two vectors on the plane of the triangle. Using face normal vectors in lighting calculations can result in a shading of the surface that has abrupt changes along the edges of the triangles (see Fig. 5.15c). Smooth shading of a polygonal surface requires a lighting calculation using per-vertex normals.

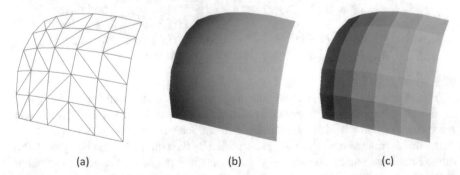

(a)   (b)   (c)

Fig. 5.15 **a** Wireframe of a tessellated mesh surface. **b** Lighting using evaluation shader. **c** Lighting using geometry shader

- *Use derivatives of blending functions*: As shown in Eq. (5.4), a second or higher order blending function uses continuous functions in the parameters u and v. The partial derivatives of the functions give the gradients along parametric directions. The gradient directions G_u, G_v at a point P in Eq. (5.4), are given in Eq. (5.5). The normalized cross-product of the two vectors gives the vertex normal vector at P.

$$
\begin{aligned}
G_u =&(1-v)^2\{(u-1)P_0 + (1-2u)P_1 + uP_2\} \\
&+ 2v(1-v)\{(u-1)P_3 + (1-2u)P_4 + uP_5\} \\
&+ v^2\{(u-1)P_6 + (1-2u)P_7 + uP_8\} \\
G_v =&(v-1)\{(1-u)^2 P_0 + 2u(1-u)P_1 + u^2 P_2\} \\
&+ 2(1-2v)\{(1-u)^2 P_3 + 2u(1-u)P_4 + u^2 P_5\} \\
&+ v\{(1-u)^2 P_6 + 2u(1-u)P_7 + u^2 P_8\}
\end{aligned}
\tag{5.5}
$$

Figure 5.15a shows a mesh surface generated using a bi-quadratic blending function in Eq. (5.4). A shaded rendering of the model with lighting calculations done using the derivatives of the blending functions (Eq. 5.5) is given in Fig. 5.15b. Figure 5.15c gives the output generated using lighting computations performed in a geometry shader

5.2 Terrain Rendering

Terrain rendering is a fascinating area of computer graphics that deals with the modelling and rendering of complex terrain geometries including several interesting surface features and rendering effects. In this section, we discuss important aspects of a terrain modelling and rendering algorithm that uses all shader stages given in Fig. 5.1.

5.2.1 A Patch-Based Terrain Model

Terrain modelling algorithms can leverage the power and versatility of the tessellation shader stage for generating a highly tessellated surface mesh with varying levels of detail. In the following, we shall consider the implementation aspects of such a method that uses the shader stages of the OpenGL-4 pipeline.

The base of our terrain model is a large horizontal planar region on the xz-plane consisting of a set of quadrilateral patches. Even though the entire base can be represented by a single patch and tessellated to the desired level, a subdivision of the base into a rectangular arrangement of small patches as shown in Fig. 5.16 allows each of those small segments of the terrain to have independent tessellation levels that can be adjusted based on the distance of the patch from the camera. Terrain

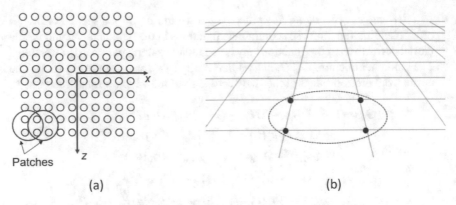

Fig. 5.16 **a** Patch-based modelling of terrain's base. **b** Each patch has 4 vertices

models must have dynamically changing levels of detail where regions farther away from the camera are rendered with very low levels of tessellation. The subdivision of the terrain base into an array of patches also helps in the computation of the texture coordinates for the vertices of the final terrain mesh. A patch provides a logical grouping of a bunch of triangles of the mesh. It can therefore represent a region of the terrain to which a set of textures must be mapped.

The vertex shader is a simple pass-thru shader (see Fig. 5.4) that outputs the patch vertices without any transformation. The tessellation control shader implements the level of detail (LOD) algorithm by computing the outer and inner tessellation levels for the patch based on its distance from the camera (Fig. 5.17). The formula given in Eq. (5.1) could be used to find the tessellation level of the current patch with parameters $(d_{min}: L_{high})$, $(d_{max}: L_{low})$ (Fig. 5.17a).

The tessellation evaluation shader uses a bi-linear mapping given in Eq. (5.3) to reposition a tessellated mesh vertex to a vertex P on the terrain base. The implementation of this mapping was given earlier in Listing 5.3. Figure 5.17b shows an example of a tessellated terrain base. The evaluation shader also accesses a height map texture similar to that given in Fig. 5.18a to modify the height values at each

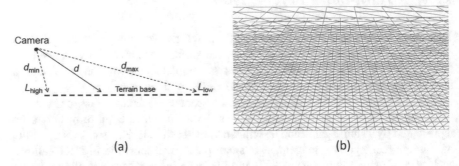

Fig. 5.17 **a** Terrain LOD parameters. **b** Tessellated terrain base

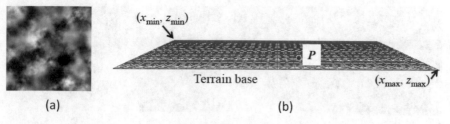

(a) (b)

Fig. 5.18 **a** Terrain height map. **b** Parameters used for texture mapping height map

vertex of the tessellated terrain base. Height maps are generally grey-level images with 8-bit intensity values in the range [0–255]. The height map is mapped to the whole terrain base. If the minimum and maximum extents of the terrain base are given by the coordinates (x_{min}, z_{min}), (x_{max}, z_{max}), respectively, and if the current vertex P on the terrain base has coordinates (x, z), its texture coordinates (s, t) for accessing the height map are computed as given in Eq. (5.6).

$$s = \frac{x - x_{min}}{x_{max} - x_{min}}$$
$$t = \frac{z - z_{min}}{z_{max} - z_{min}} \quad (5.6)$$

The terrain model is assigned a user specified maximum height value H. Intensity values sampled from the height map are scaled by the factor H, to convert them to the range [0-H]. This height value is then assigned as the y-coordinate value of the current point P. A height mapped terrain model with LOD is shown in Fig. 5.19. Note

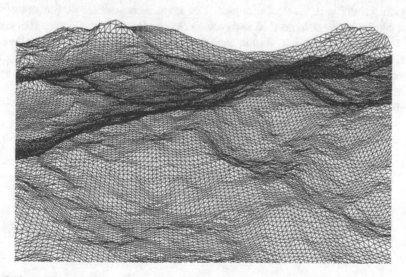

Fig. 5.19 Height mapped terrain model

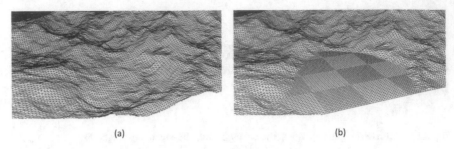

(a)   (b)

Fig. 5.20 Terrain mesh before and after adjusting vertex heights to form water regions

that a well-implemented terrain LOD algorithm will produce triangles with nearly equal projected area across the whole terrain.

Another height parameter used in terrain modelling is the height of the water level. Since water regions must have a flat surface, the coordinates of vertices that are below water level must be adjusted to form a planar surface. If the y-coordinate of the current vertex P is below a prespecified water level W, then the y-value is reset to W, moving the vertex P to the water surface (Fig. 5.20). Having a parameter for water level is very useful in a terrain model, to create different renderings of the terrain and simulate effects of flooding and water receding from parts of the terrain.

The tessellation evaluation shader may also be used to assign texture coordinates (for mapping surface textures) to each of the vertices of the tessellated mesh. If an image is individually mapped to each triangle of the mesh, the image features on surface textures such as grass, may not be clearly visible as the triangles generally have a very small projected area (see Fig. 5.19). A patch, on the other hand, has a much bigger size, and represents a region of the terrain, at the same time providing a logical grouping of a set of triangles. The texture coordinates at vertices of the mesh can be easily computed in such a way that an image is mapped to the whole area represented by a patch. Within each patch, the position of a vertex is given by two tessellation coordinates u and v. These values are normalized coordinates of the vertex on a patch and could be directly used as the texture coordinates of the vertex.

Listing 5.4 shows an implementation of the methods discussed above in a tessellation evaluation shader.

Listing 5.4: Tessellation evaluation shader for generating a terrain mesh

```
layout(quads, equal_spacing, ccw) in;

uniform sampler2D heightMap;
uniform float waterLevel;
uniform float maxHeight;
uniform float xmin, zmin;
uniform float base_len, base_wid;
out vec2 texCoord;

void main()
{
    vec4 posn, col;
    vec2 hmapCoord;

    float u = gl_TessCoord.x;
    float v = gl_TessCoord.y;

    posn = (1-u) * (1-v) * gl_in[0].gl_Position
         +    u  * (1-v) * gl_in[1].gl_Position
         +    u  *    v  * gl_in[2].gl_Position
         + (1-u) *    v  * gl_in[3].gl_Position;

    hmapCoord.s = (posn.x - xmin)/base_len;    //Eq.(5.6)
    hmapCoord.t = (posn.z - zmin)/base_wid;

    col = texture(heightMap, hmapCoord);
    posn.y - col.r * maxHeight;
    if(posn.y < waterLevel) posn.y = waterLevel;

    texCoord = gl_TessCoord.xy;   //for mapping surface textures
    gl_Position = posn;
}
```

A geometry shader is used to process the triangles of the terrain mesh. The main computation performed in the geometry shader is lighting. Face normal vectors of triangles of the tessellated mesh can be easily computed in the geometry shader. As previously described in Sect. 5.1.6, lighting computations using face normals in the geometry shader will not produce a smooth shading of the terrain. Discontinuities in shading along boundaries of triangles can be clearly seen in Fig. 5.22. Methods to estimate per-vertex normal vectors using the height map are discussed later in Sect. 5.2.3.

Surface texturing of a terrain model will require several textures corresponding to different height-based features of the terrain. Textures could contain images of snow, grass, rock and water. These textures are used in a multitexturing method in the fragment shader, where the textures selected for blending and the level of blending depend on the height of the current vertex. A sample set of textures, and the variations in their weights based on height values are shown in Fig. 5.21.

A terrain model rendered using lighting computations and texturing as discussed above is shown in Fig. 5.22.

Fig. 5.21 Computation of
texture weights for blending
surface textures

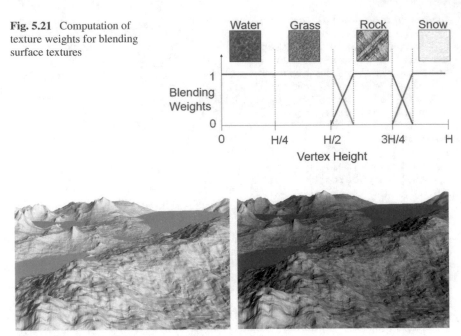

Fig. 5.22 Terrain model with **a** lighting, and **b** texturing

5.2.2 Micro-level Cracking

A common artefact seen in terrains modelled using patches that are tessellated with
varying levels of detail is micro-level cracking. When two adjacent patches have
unequal tessellation levels, triangles on either side of a common edge between the
patches may not have shared vertices along the edge. When the vertices are displaced
using height values from a terrain height map, cracks appear along the edge between
the patches (Fig. 5.23).

A terrain model with uneven tessellations and the presence of cracking can be
seen in Fig. 5.24.

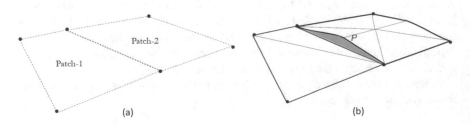

Fig. 5.23 a Two adjacent patches. **b** Uneven tessellation resulting in cracking

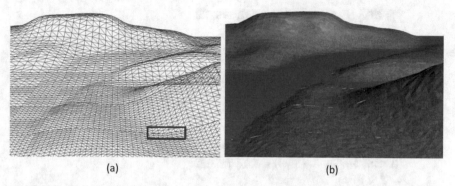

Fig. 5.24 **a** Wireframe model of a terrain showing unequal tessellation levels in patches. **b** Cracks apear along edges between patches

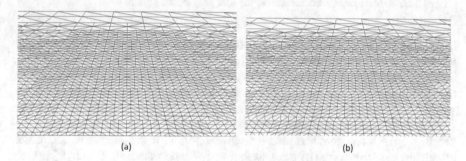

Fig. 5.25 Tessellations **a** without, and **b** with edge correction

Terrain level of detail will obviously generate uneven tessellations across a terrain model. The tessellation level for a region of the terrain was previously calculated using only the distance of the centre of the patch from the camera. We improve this method by using the distance of the centre of the patch from the camera to calculate only the inner tessellation levels. The outer tessellation levels are computed using the distance of the centre of the corresponding edge from the camera. Thus, along each common edge between patches, the same outer tessellation level is used on either side of the edge. This step is called edge correction in the process of tessellation. A wireframe model of a tessellated terrain base without and with edge correction are shown in Fig. 5.25.

5.2.3 Vertex Normal Computation

The terrain rendering algorithm discussed in Sect. 5.2.1 used the geometry shader for performing lighting calculations. The property that the geometry shader has access to all vertices of the triangles generated by the primitive generator was useful in

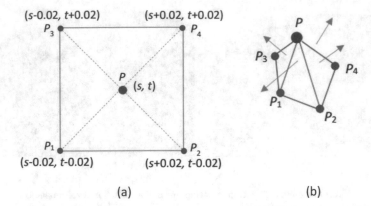

Fig. 5.26 **a** Four points around the current vertex P used for sampling the height map. **b** Vertex normal computation using the coordinates of the four neighbouring points

computing the face normal vectors of the triangles of the terrain mesh. In this section, we outline a method for improving the shading model using vertex normal vectors.

Computation of the surface normal vector at a vertex requires information about the triangles sharing that vertex. This information is not directly available until the whole terrain mesh is formed. However, we can obtain an approximation of the terrain mesh's geometry around a vertex by sampling the height values from the height map at a few points around the current vertex. If the current vertex of the tessellated mesh processed by the tessellation evaluation shader is P, and if (s, t) are its texture coordinates (see Eq. 5.6), then four fictitious points P_1, P_2, P_3, P_4 around P can be formed with texture coordinates $(s \pm 0.02, t \pm 0.02)$ as shown in Fig. 5.26a. The offset 0.02 in texture coordinates is computed based on the size of the height map. On a height map of size 256×256 pixels, an offset of 0.02 corresponds to approximately 5 pixels.

The coordinates of the four points surrounding P can be computed inside the tessellation evaluation shader as given in Eq. (5.7). The "heightmap()" function in the equation samples the height map and outputs a value in the range $[0, H]$, where H is the maximum height of the terrain.

$$P_1 = \begin{cases} x = x_{\min} + (s - 0.02)(x_{\max} - x_{\min}) \\ y = \text{heightmap}((s - 0.02, t - 0.02) \\ z = z_{\min} + (t - 0.02)(z_{\max} - z_{\min}) \end{cases}$$

$$P_2 = \begin{cases} x = x_{\min} + (s + 0.02)(x_{\max} - x_{\min}) \\ y = \text{heightmap}((s + 0.02, t - 0.02) \\ z = z_{\min} + (t - 0.02)(z_{\max} - z_{\min}) \end{cases}$$

$$P_3 = \begin{cases} x = x_{\min} + (s - 0.02)(x_{\max} - x_{\min}) \\ y = \text{heightmap}((s - 0.02, t + 0.02) \\ z = z_{\min} + (t + 0.02)(z_{\max} - z_{\min}) \end{cases}$$

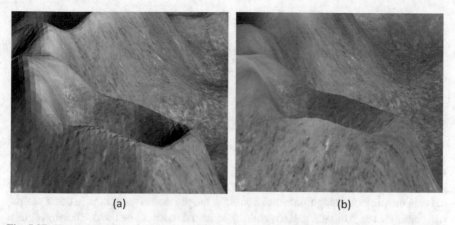

(a) (b)

Fig. 5.27 Terrain model rendered using. **a** Face normals computed in a geometry shader. **b** Vertex normals computed in a tessellation evaluation shader

$$P_4 = \begin{cases} x = x_{min} + (s + 0.02)(x_{max} - x_{min}) \\ y = \text{heightmap}((s + 0.02, t + 0.02) \\ z = z_{min} + (t + 0.02)(z_{max} - z_{min}) \end{cases} \quad (5.7)$$

The sum of the face normal vectors of the surrounding triangles computed using the vertex coordinates in Eq. (5.7) gives a fairly good approximation of the vertex normal vector at P. Figure 5.27 gives a comparison of outputs corresponding to lighting computation using face normal vectors and vertex normal vectors.

5.3 Procedural Heightmap Generation

In this section, we outline a few methods useful for generating procedural terrain heightmaps. We begin with a very coarse model of a terrain using sinusoidal functions and add randomness to this model using Perlin noise. We then explore a random fractal algorithm that is based on the same concept as Perlin noise.

5.3.1 Sum of Sinusoids

The undulations of a terrain have an intuitive and a highly coarse approximation in the form of a combination of sinusoidal functions. Consider a basic sine wave $g(t)$ as defined in Eq. (5.8).

$$g(t) = m \sin(2\pi ft), \quad t \in [0, 1]. \quad (5.8)$$

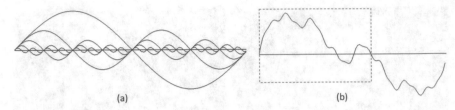

Fig. 5.28 a Sine wave and its higher harmonics, **b** the sum of the sinusoids

where m is the magnitude and f the frequency of the sine wave. We set the initial value of the frequency to 1. To this sine wave, we add more sinusoids, each time halving the previous magnitude and doubling the previous frequency. In other words, we combine the fundamental frequency sinusoid with its second, fourth, eighth, and sixteenth harmonics (Eq. 5.9). Note that higher frequency terms have lower magnitudes (weights).

$$g(t) = m \sin(2\pi t) + \left(\frac{m}{2}\right) \sin(4\pi t) + \left(\frac{m}{4}\right) \sin(8\pi t)$$
$$+ \left(\frac{m}{8}\right) \sin(16\pi t) + \left(\frac{m}{16}\right) \sin(32\pi t) \tag{5.9}$$

A plot of the individual sinusoids and the combined harmonics is given in Fig. 5.28. Since the frequency of each term in the above equation is double the frequency of the previous term, they are also referred to as octaves. We shall use the section of the graph within the dotted box in Fig. 5.28b, for generating a height map. This region is given by the t values in the range $0 \le t \le 0.6$.

The one-dimensional function in Eq. (5.9) may be extended in various ways to produce a two-dimensional image. As an example, consider Eq. (5.10).

$$I(x, y) = g\left(\sqrt{x^2 + y^2} \cos(2y)\right) \tag{5.10}$$

The above equation produces the image in Fig. 5.29a. The terrain model corresponding to this image is shown in Fig. 5.29b.

The images produced by the method described in this section always follow a sinusoidal pattern and lack the level of randomness required in terrain models. The following methods produce more realistic height maps.

5.3.2 Perlin Noise

The generation of Perlin noise uses a method similar to that outlined in the previous section, where signals at different octaves are combined in such a way that low frequency components have higher weights compared to high frequency components

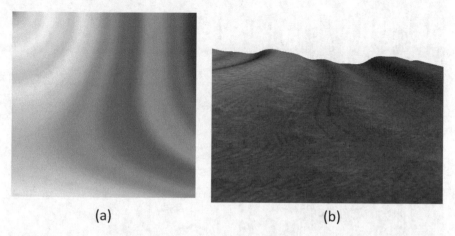

(a)   (b)

Fig. 5.29 a Height map generated using Eq. (5.10). **b** The corresponding terrain model

[2]. We replace the sine functions in Eq. (5.9) with functions that sample a random signal and produce another signal by interpolating between the sampled values. A one-dimensional example of this process is shown in Fig. 5.30. Let us assume that a uniformly distributed random value is generated at 256 points along the x-axis (Fig. 5.30a). This signal is sampled at 3 points (two end points and the middle point), at an interval of 128 points (first row of Fig. 5.30a), and the values at the intermediate points are computed by interpolating between the sampled values (first row of Fig. 5.30b). This polygonal line forms the signal $s_1(t)$ at the lowest frequency. We now sample the original random signal at an interval of 64 points, doubling the sampling frequency (second row of Fig. 5.30a), and generate another polygonal line $s_2(t)$ through the five sampled values. We continue this process of doubling the sampling frequency in each step and generating interpolated polygonal lines $s_3(t)$, $s_4(t)$, $s_5(t)$ etc., at higher octaves.

As in the case of the sum of sinusoids in Eq. (5.9), we combine the sampled and interpolated values at each octave using a set of weights that are halved as the frequency doubles (Eq. 5.11)

$$g(t) = s_1(t) + \left(\frac{1}{2}\right)s_2(t) + \left(\frac{1}{4}\right)s_3(t) + \left(\frac{1}{8}\right)s_4(t) + \left(\frac{1}{16}\right)s_5(t) \qquad (5.11)$$

The weighted sum $g(t)$ of the polygonal lines in Fig. 5.30b is shown in Fig. 5.31.

The extension of the 1D algorithm to 2D requires simple methods for (i) generating a single-valued two-dimensional random field, (ii) sampling values at different octaves in a two-dimensional image space, and (iii) bi-linear interpolation of the sampled values. Consider an image of size 257×257 pixels. At each pixel, we generate a random value in the range [0, 1], and scale it by 2π to convert it to an angle θ. A unit vector $(\cos\theta, \sin\theta)$ is formed at that pixel. Analogous to the 1D example, we first sample this vector field at the corner points and the midpoint with a

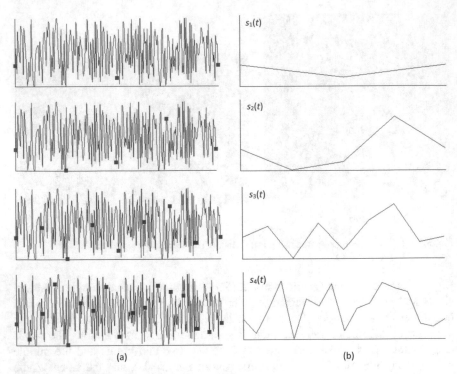

(a)   (b)

Fig. 5.30 **a** Random noise signal sampled with increasing frequency. **b** Polygonal line functions
obtained by interpolating between the sampled values

Fig. 5.31 Weighted sum of
signals sampled at different
octaves

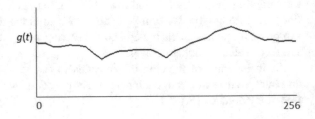

sampling interval of 128 pixels along both directions (Fig. 5.32a). At the next octave,
we have a set of samples with an interval of 64 points as shown in Fig. 5.32b. The
next octave with a sampling interval of 32 pixels is shown in Fig. 5.32c.

For each of the above sampling schemes, the value at any pixel $P(x, y)$ is computed
as follows: The four closest sampled pixels P_1, P_2, P_3, P_4, and the unit vectors u
$= (\cos\theta, \sin\theta)$ at those positions are first found. From each of these sampled pixels,
a vector v towards P is formed as shown in Fig. 5.33a. This vector v should not
be normalized, as we require the weightings of the distance of the pixel P from
the sampled pixels. The dot product of the two vectors $d = u.v$ is assigned to each
sampled pixel (Fig. 5.33b). A bi-linear interpolation between these four values d_1,

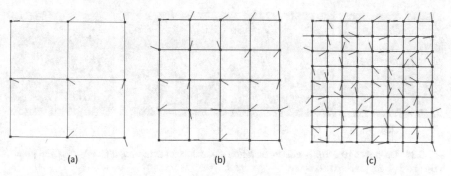

Fig. 5.32 Sampling of a 2D vector field on a 257×257 image using interval of **a** 128 pixels, **b** 64 pixels, **c** 32 pixels

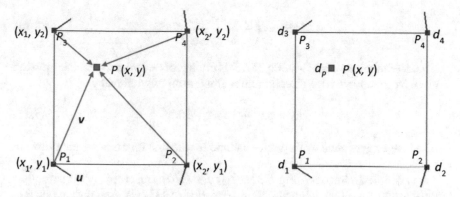

Fig. 5.33 Computation of a scalar value at a pixel P using vectors at four closest sampled pixels

d_2, d_3, d_4 (Fig. 5.33b) gives the scalar value d_P at the point P. This value is converted to the range $[0, 255]$ to get a grey-scale image. The computations performed are given in Eqs. (5.12)–(5.14).

Components of the unit vector $\boldsymbol{u}$ at a sampled pixel: (u_1, u_2)

$$\text{Vector } v = (v_1, v_2) = (x - x_1, y - y_1)$$
$$\text{Dot product } d = u_1 v_1 + u_2 v_2 \tag{5.12}$$

Bi-linear interpolation between d_1, d_2, d_3, d_4 with weight w:

$$d_{x12} = w(d_2 - d_1) + d_1, \quad w = \frac{x - x_1}{x_2 - x_1}$$
$$d_{x34} = w(d_4 - d_3) + d_3, \quad w = \frac{x - x_1}{x_2 - x_1}$$
$$d_P = w(d_{x34} - d_{x12}) + d_{x12}, \quad w = \frac{y - y_1}{y_2 - y_1} \tag{5.13}$$

Fig. 5.34 Outputs of the Perlin noise generation algorithm for sampling intervals of **a** 128 pixels, **b** 64 pixels, **c** 32 pixels, **d** 16 pixels

Intensity value at P is computed using the min, max values of d_p:

$$I(P) = \left(\frac{d_p - d_{\min}}{d_{\max} - d_{\min}} \right) 255 \qquad (5.14)$$

The interpolation weight w in Eq. (5.13) is often replaced with a smoothed version $\tilde{w}$ given by to remove edge discontinuities along sampling intervals.

$$\tilde{w} = 6w^5 - 15w^4 + 10w^3 \qquad (5.15)$$

The images generated by the above method for the first four octaves are shown in Fig. 5.34.

Let us denote the images in Fig. 5.34 as $I_{128}, I_{64}, I_{32}, I_{16}$, respectively, the subscripts indicating the sampling intervals. Similar to Eq. (5.11), we assign these images weights 1, 0.5, 0.25, 0.125, respectively, and add them to get the final height map.

$$I_{\text{hmap}} = I_{128} + \left(\frac{1}{2} \right) I_{64} + \left(\frac{1}{4} \right) I_{32} + \left(\frac{1}{8} \right) I_{16} \qquad (5.16)$$

The height map obtained using (5.16) and the corresponding terrain model are shown in Fig. 5.35.

5.3.3 Diamond-Square Algorithm

The diamond-square algorithm is the 2D version of the one-dimensional "midpoint displacement method" used for generating random fractals known as fractal Brownian motion [3, 4] . The methods discussed in the previous sections sampled a random signal at different frequencies, interpolated between the sampled values, and combined the resulting signals using weights that are scaled by powers of 2. The random fractal method iteratively displaces midpoints of sections of a base line or polygon using Gaussian random numbers, and the standard deviations of the random

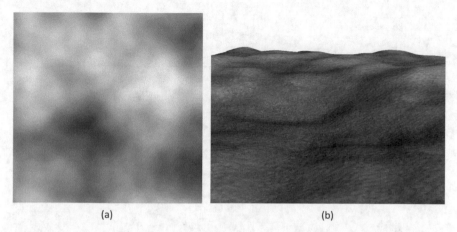

    (a)   (b)

Fig. 5.35 a Terrain height map generated using Perlin's algorithm. **b** The corresponding terrain model

numbers are scaled by powers of 2 in each iteration. Thus, with increasing subdivisions, we get progressively reducing range of displacements, providing fine grained variations on the final surface.

Figure 5.36 shows a few iterations of the midpoint displacement method. The method starts by displacing the midpoint P_1 of a line segment AB along the y-direction (Fig. 5.36i) by a Gaussian random number with a user specified standard deviation σ. The displacement splits the original segment into two, and the values at the points along each of these segments are obtained by a linear interpolation between the values at the end points. In the next iteration (Fig. 5.36ii), each of these segments AP_1 and BP_1 is further split into two by displacing their midpoints P_2 and P_3 by Gaussian random numbers with standard deviation $\sigma/2$. In the third iteration (Fig. 5.36iii), the midpoints of the current line segments are displaced using Gaussian numbers of standard deviation $\sigma/4$. Continuing this process of iterative subdivision a few more iterations result in a random fractal terrain shown in Fig. 5.36iv.

The diamond-square algorithm is an extension of the process described above to a two-dimensional planar section of the xz-plane. The first iteration of the algorithm displaces the midpoint P_1 of a square region given by vertices A, B, C, D (Fig. 5.37a). For convenience of iterative subdivision, the size s of this region is chosen as 2^n for some positive value of n. As in the case of the midpoint displacement method, a Gaussian random number with a user specified standard deviation σ is added to the average height of the vertices A, B, C, D to get the height at P_1. In the diamond step, a Gaussian random number with the same standard deviation σ is added to the average height of vertices A, B, P_1 to find the height at P_2. Similarly, the height values at the points P_3, P_4, P_5 are computed (Fig. 5.37b). The completion of the square and the diamond steps results in a set of square regions of size $s/2$, as shown in Fig. 5.37c, where s is the size of the original square $ABCD$. The height values at the interior points in each of these smaller squares are found by bi-linear interpolation of the height values at their corner vertices. The second iteration of the algorithm

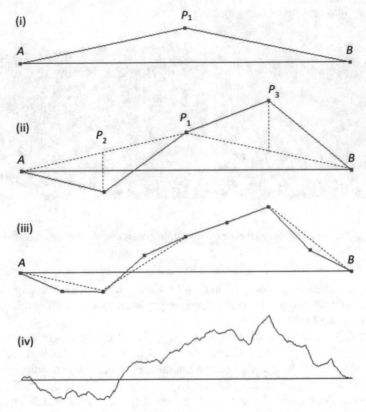

Fig. 5.36 Few iterations of the midpoint displacement algorithm in the constructions of a random fractal terrain

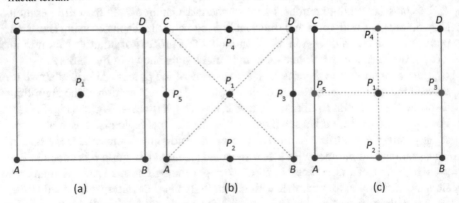

Fig. 5.37 First iteration of the diamond-square algorithm: **a** the square step, **b** the diamond step, **c** the interpolation step

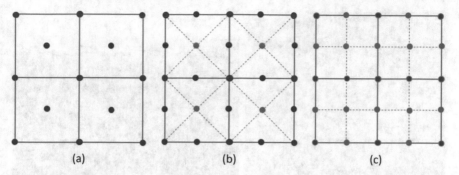

Fig. 5.38 Second iteration of the diamond-square algorithm: **a** the square step, **b** the diamond step, **c** the interpolation step

(see Fig. 5.38) proceeds with the subdivision of each of these smaller squares using a displacement of the midpoints of square and diamond regions with Gaussian random numbers of standard deviation $\sigma/2$. A pseudo-code of the diamond-square algorithm is given in Listing 5.5.

Listing 5.5: Pseudo-code of the iterative diamond-square algorithm

```
Listing 5-5: Pseudo-code of the iterative diamond-square algorithm
  for (int i = 0;  i < numIterations; i++)
  {
      Square(size);
      Diamond(size);
      size = size/2;
      Interpolate(size);
      σ = σ/2;
  }
```

A height map produced by the diamond-square algorithm and the corresponding terrain model are shown in Fig. 5.39.

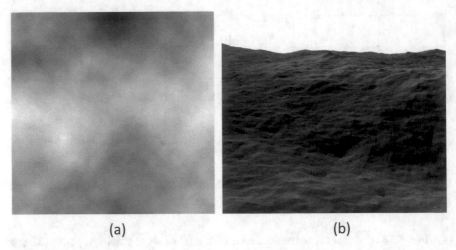

(a)   (b)

Fig. 5.39 Height map and the terrain model produced by the diamond-square algorithm

5.4 Bezier Surface Patches

Bezier surface patches [5] are extensively used in the modelling of three-dimensional objects, the most well-known example being the ubiquitous teapot. In this section, we explore the properties of Bezier surfaces and the ways of modelling surfaces using the tessellation shader stage of the OpenGL-4 pipeline.

An example of a 3×3 control patch containing 9 vertices and the corresponding tessellated mesh (Bezier surface patch) were shown earlier in Fig. 5.3. The bi-quadratic Bezier equations used for mapping vertices from the quad domain to the Bezier surface were given in Eq. (5.4). The bi-quadratic Bezier surface patches have parabolic shapes. A bicubic Bezier patch provides greater flexibility in a modelling application and requires a 4×4 control patch containing 16 vertices $P_0 \ldots P_{15}$ (Fig. 5.40a). Here, we use cubic Bernstein polynomials as blending functions in the tessellation coordinates (u, v) to form a combination of patch vertices that gives the map of the tessellated mesh vertex on the Bezier surface (Eq. 5.17).

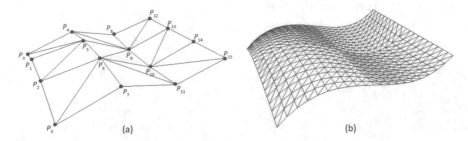

(a)   (b)

Fig. 5.40 **a** A 4×4 control patch. **b** Corresponding bi-cubic Bezier surface

$$P = (1-v)^3 \left\{ (1-u)^3 P_0 + 3u(1-u)^2 P_1 + 3u^2(1-u) P_2 + u^3 P_3 \right\}$$
$$+ 3v(1-v)^2 \left\{ (1-u)^3 P_4 + 3u(1-u)^2 P_5 + 3u^2(1-u) P_6 + u^3 P_7 \right\}$$
$$+ 3v^2(1-v) \left\{ (1-u)^3 P_8 + 3u(1-u)^2 P_9 + 3u^2(1-u) P_{10} + u^3 P_{11} \right\}$$
$$+ v^3 \left\{ (1-u)^3 P_{12} + 3u(1-u)^2 P_{13} + 3u^2(1-u) P_{14} + u^3 P_{15} \right\}$$
$$u, v \in [0, 1] \tag{5.17}$$

.

A 4×4 patch and its bi-cubic Bezier patch are shown in Fig. 5.40. Bezier surfaces (of all degrees) satisfy the following important properties:

- The Bezier surface passes through the corner points of the control patch. With reference to Eq. (5.17), a bi-cubic Bezier surface passes through the points P_0, P_3, P_{12}, and P_{15}.
- The edges at the corners of the control patch are tangential to the Bezier surface. With reference to Fig. 5.40a, the edges P_0P_1, P_0P_4, P_3P_7, P_3P_2, $P_{12}P_8$, $P_{12}P_{13}$, $P_{15}P_{11}$, and $P_{15}P_{14}$ are all tangential to the surface in Fig. 5.40b.
- The Bezier surface is fully contained within the convex hull of the vertices of the control patch.
- Any affine transformation of a Bezier surface can be obtained by applying the same transformation to the control patch vertices and computing the Bezier surface of the transformed patch.

The surface normal vectors at any point with tessellation coordinates (u, v) are computed using the principal gradient directions at each point, given by the partial derivatives G_u, G_v of the expression in Eq. (5.17) with respect to the parameters u and v. The normalized cross product of the two vectors $(G_u \times G_v)$ gives the vertex normal vector at the mapped vertex P.

$$G_u = (1-v)^3 \left\{ -(1-u)^2 P_0 + \left(1 - 4u + 3u^2\right) P_1 + \left(2u - 3u^2\right) P_2 + u^2 P_3 \right\}$$
$$+ 3v(1-v)^2 \{ -(1-u)^2 P_4 + \left(1 - 4u + 3u^2\right) P_5 + \left(2u - 3u^2\right) P_6 + u^2 P_7 \}$$
$$+ 3v^2(1-v) \left\{ -(1-u)^2 P_8 + \left(1 - 4u + 3u^2\right) P_9 + \left(2u - 3u^2\right) P_{10} + u^2 P_{11} \right\}$$
$$+ v^3 \left\{ -(1-u)^2 P_{12} + \left(1 - 4u + 3u^2\right) P_{13} + \left(2u - 3u^2\right) P_{14} + u^2 P_{15} \right\} \tag{5.18}$$

$$G_v = -(1-v)^2 \left\{ (1-u)^3 P_0 + 3u(1-u)^2 P_1 + 3u^2(1-u) P_2 + u^3 P_3 \right\}$$
$$+ \left(1 - 4v + 3v^2\right) \left\{ (1-u)^3 P_4 + 3u(1-u)^2 P_5 + 3u^2(1-u) P_6 + u^3 P_7 \right\}$$
$$+ \left(2v - 3v^2\right) \left\{ (1-u)^3 P_8 + 3u(1-u)^2 P_9 + 3u^2(1-u) P_{10} + u^3 P_{11} \right\}$$
$$+ v^2 \left\{ (1-u)^3 P_{12} + 3u(1-u)^2 P_{13} + 3u^2(1-u) P_{14} + u^3 P_{15} \right\} \tag{5.19}$$

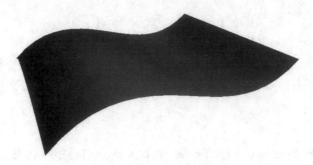

Fig. 5.41 Rendering of a bi-cubic Bezier surface patch using per-vertex normal vectors

The bi-cubic Bezier surface patch in Fig. 5.40b rendered with lighting calculations using per-vertex normal vectors computed as above, is shown in Fig. 5.41.

Listing 5.6 shows the implementation of Eqs. (5.17)–(5.19) in a tessellation evaluation shader.

Listing 5.6: Bi-cubic Bezier equations in a tessellation evaluation shader

```
//Cubic Bernstein polynomials
float Bez(int i, float u)
{
    float u1 = 1-u;
    switch (i) {
    case 0: return     u1 * u1 * u1;
    case 1: return 3 * u1 * u1 * u;
    case 2: return 3 * u1 * u  * u;
    case 3: return     u  * u  * u;
    default: return 0;
    }
}

//Derivatives of Bernstein polynomials
float dBez(int i, float u)
{
    float u1 = 1-u;
    switch (i) {
    case 0: return   - u1 * u1;
    case 1: return 1 - 4 * u + 3 * u * u;
    case 2: return     * u - 3 * u * u;
    case 3: return     u * u;
    default: return 0;
    }
}

void main()
{
    float u = gl_TessCoord.x;
    float v = gl_TessCoord.y;
    vec4 posn = vec4(0);
    vec4 gu = vec4(0);
    vec4 gv = vec4(0);
    vec3 vnorm;
    vec4 posnEye;

    for(int j = 0; j < 4; j++) {
        for(int i = 0; i < 4; i++) {
            posn += Bez(i, u) * Bez(j, v) * gl_in[4*j+i].gl_Position;
        }
    }

    for(int j = 0; j < 4; j++) {
        for(int i = 0; i < 4; i++)
        {
            gu += dBez(i, u) * Bez(j, v) * gl_in[4*j+i].gl_Position;
        }
    }

    for(int j = 0; j < 4; j++) {
        for(int i = 0; i < 4; i++) {
            gv += Bez(i, u) * dBez(j, v) * gl_in[4*j+i].gl_Position;
        }
    }
    posnEye = mvMatrix * posn;
    vnorm = normalize(cross(gu.xyz, gv.xyz));
}
```

5.4.1   The Teapot

The Utah Teapot is widely known as the computer graphics icon, as it is extensively used in computer graphics literature and courses as a demonstration piece to show the working of several fundamental methods such as transformations, modelling, illumination and texturing. This Bezier surface model is constructed using 32 control patches, each patch consisting of 16 vertices in a 4×4 grid format. The patch-based definition of the model therefore contains a total of 512 vertices. An exploded view of the teapot showing the control patches is given in Fig. 5.42a, and the locations of the patches on the model itself in Fig. 5.42b. The teapot model is constructed using bi-cubic Bezier equations (Eq. 5.17) to generate the vertices of the tessellated mesh surface. As in the case of a terrain model, a tessellation control shader could be used to adjust the level of detail of the model based on the distance of the model from the camera (Fig. 5.43a). All patches of the model are assigned the same tessellation level.

As discussed in Sect. 5.1.6, lighting calculations on a Bezier surface may be performed either in the geometry shader (using face normal vectors computed for each triangle primitive), or inside the tessellation evaluation shader (using vertex normal vectors computed using Eqs. (5.18), (5.19)).

Lighting calculations using vertex normal vectors provide a smoother shading of the surface as shown in Fig. 5.43b.

When a model like the teapot is constructed using a set of control patches, the control points (vertices of the control patch) are specified in such as way that they satisfy a set of boundary conditions required to ensure that the resulting Bezier surface does not have any discontinuities across common edges between the patches. A set of sufficient conditions for tangential continuity of a Bezier surface along boundaries between patches are given below:

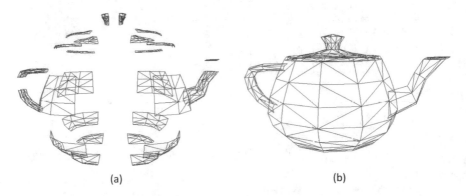

(a)   (b)

Fig. 5.42   Control patches of the teapot **a** exploded view, **b** model view

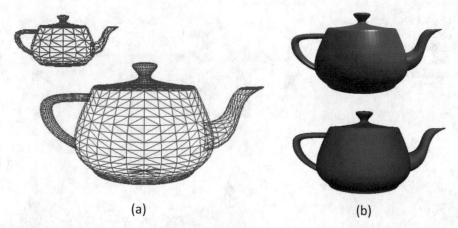

(a)   (b)

Fig. 5.43 **a** Changes in level of detail based on distance from camera. **b** Lighting using face normal and vertex normal vectors

- The vertices of two adjacent control patches must coincide along the common edge. This condition ensures that the resulting Bezier surface has C^0 continuity along the edge.
- The corresponding quadrilateral segments on either side of the common edge must be co-planar. This condition ensures that the resulting Bezier surface has tangential continuity across the edge.

Figure 5.44i shows two adjacent control patches on the surface of the teapot. The vertices of the patches satisfy the boundary conditions mentioned above. The tessellated Bezier surface mesh Fig. 5.44ii is both smooth and continuous across the edge. A shaded model of surface in Fig. 5.44iii show a seamless tiling of the two Bezier patches forming a smooth and continuous surface segment on the teapot model.

5.4.2 The Gumbo

After the teapot, the second most popular Bezier surface model in the field of computer graphics is the Gumbo [6] . It also is modelled using 4×4 control patches but contains 4 times the number of patches of the teapot (128 patches). The patch-based definition of the model contains 2048 vertices. A wireframe rendering of the model is shown in Fig. 5.45a. A shaded rendering of the model with lighting calculations performed in the geometry shader using face normal vectors is given in Fig. 5.45b. Figure 5.45c shows the output with lighting calculations using vertex normal vectors implemented in the tessellation evaluation shader.

Fig. 5.44 (i) Two adjacent control patches on the teapot model (ii) tessellated Bezier surfaces (iii) the shaded model of the Bezier surface

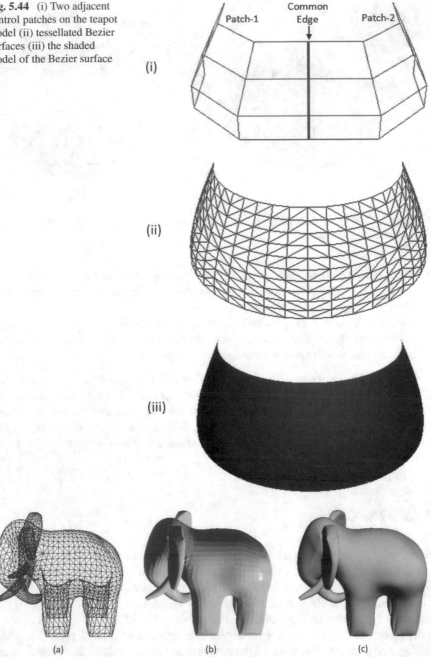

Fig. 5.45 **a** Wireframe model of Gumbo. **b** Lighting with face normal vectors. **c** Lighting with vertex normal vectors

Fig. 5.46 Parabolic
trajectories of control
patches

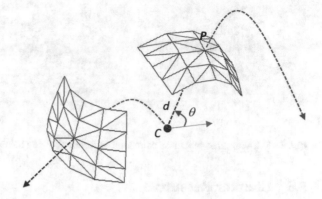

5.4.3 Mesh Explosion

A patch-based construction of a mesh model allows the movement of the Bezier patches away from the centre of the model providing an exploded view as previously shown in Fig. 5.42a. An animation of mesh explosion can be easily generated by continuously moving each 4×4 control patch away from the centre of the model along a parabolic path. The tessellation control shader allows the modification of the patch vertices—the shifting of a patch along its trajectory can be done by updating the vertex coordinates of the patch as below.

With reference to Fig. 5.46, if P denotes the centre vertex of a patch, and C the centre of the model, a unit vector d is defined in the direction from C to P. We assume that every patch is given an initial velocity of magnitude v along the unit vector d for that patch. If the vector d makes an angle θ with the local horizontal vector (the projection of d on the floor plane), the velocity vector may be resolved along the vertical and horizontal directions as given in Eq. (5.20).

$$v_y = v \sin(\theta), \ v_h = v \cos(\theta) \tag{5.20}$$

The update equations of the vertex P based on a simple model of a projectile's motion under gravity are given in Eq. (5.21).

$$P_y = P_y + v_y t - \frac{1}{2} g t^2$$
$$P_{xz} = P_{xz} + d_{xz} v_h t \tag{5.21}$$

where P_{xz} and d_{xz} denote the x, z components of the updated position P and the unit vector d, respectively. The movement of a control patch needs to be stopped when the patch hits the floor plane. A simple method for collision detection using the bounding volume of the patch and the floor plane's equation may be implemented for this purpose. Two frames of an animation sequence showing the explosion of the teapot's mesh are given in Fig. 5.47.

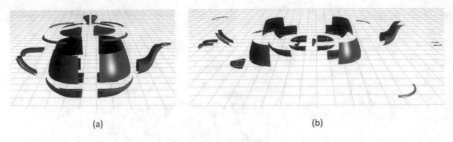

(a)   (b)

Fig. 5.47   Two frames of a mesh animation sequence showing the exploded views of the teapot

5.5   Chapter Resources

The folder "this Chapter" on the companion website contains the following programs, associated shader files, mesh and texture data. The programs demonstrate the implementation and working of the algorithms presented in this chapter.

- Terrain.cpp: Generates a terrain model from a height map using tessellation shaders, and renders the model using a set of surface textures (Listings 5.1, 5.3, 5.4). The model exhibits dynamic levels of detail corresponding to different positions of the camera.
- Perlin.cpp: Generates grey-level images corresponding to Perlin noise at different octaves (Fig. 5.34) and combines them to form a procedural height map (Fig. 5.35).
- Teapot.cpp: Displays the model of a Bezier teapot (Listing 5.6) constructed using 32 control patches. The wireframe mode of display shows varying levels of detail as the teapot is moved towards or away from the camera. The data file for the "Gumbo" model is also provided.

References and Further Reading

1. T. Akenine-Moller, E. Haines, *Real-Time Rendering* (4th ed. A K Peters/CRC Press, 2018)
2. A. Boreskov, E. Shikin, *Computer Graphics—From Pixels to Programmable Graphics Hardware* (Chapman and Hall/CRC Press, 2013)
3. K. Falconer, *Fractal Geometry—Mathematical Foundations and Applications* (2nd ed. Wiley, 2006)
4. M. Schroeder, *Fractals* (Dover Publications Inc., Chaos and Power Laws, 2009)
5. R. Mukundan, Chapter 7—curves and surfaces, in *Advanced Methods in Computer Graphics* (Springer, 2012)
6. Wikipedia. Bezier Surface. https://en.wikipedia.org/wiki/B%C3%A9zier_surface. Accessed 15 Feb 2020

Chapter 6
Quaternions

In computer graphics applications, general three-dimensional rotational transformations are often represented by quaternions. Quaternions provide some key advantages over the traditional ways of defining generic rotational transformations using Euler angles or angle-axis rotations. Quaternions are also extremely useful for interpolating between two orientations in three-dimensional space. Keyframe animations requiring orientation interpolation therefore find a very convenient mathematical tool in quaternions. This chapter gives an overview of the algebra of quaternions, the geometrical interpretation of quaternion transformations, and quaternion-based linear and spherical interpolation operations. A comparison of rotation interpolation methods using Euler angles, angle-axis representations, and quaternions is also given. This chapter has the following sections.

- **Generalized rotations**: Discusses important concepts behind the theory of three-dimensional rotational transformations.
- **Overview of quaternions**: Introduces quaternion algebra and outlines the applications of quaternions in specifying rotational transformations.
- **Rotation interpolation**: Discusses the usefulness of quaternions in rotation interpolations and provides the theory of quaternion linear and spherical linear interpolations.
- **Quaternion derivative**: Presents the mathematical equations for computing velocity vectors using quaternion components.
- **GLM quaternion class**: Provides a list of important functions in the GLM library [1] useful for quaternion computations.
- **Assimp quaternion class**: Provides a list of important functions in the Assimp library [2] useful for quaternion computations.

© The Author(s), under exclusive license to Springer Nature Switzerland AG 2022   129
R. Mukundan, *3D Mesh Processing and Character Animation*,
https://doi.org/10.1007/978-3-030-81354-3_6

6.1 Generalized Rotations

Any composite transformation that preserves length, angle and area is called a rigid-body transformation. If a rigid body transformation has also a fixed point (pivot), then it is a rotation. A rotation can be measured in terms of the angular deviation of an orthogonal right-handed system fixed on the rotating body relative to an inertial frame, with the origin of the system at the fixed point of rotation. In Fig. 6.1a, Ox, Oy, Oz are the axes of an orthogonal triad before rotation, and Ox_t, Oy_t, Oz_t denote the transformed axes directions after a rotation about O. The coordinate reference frame is inertially fixed and is represented by X, Y, Z axes.

A general rigid body transformation of an object without a fixed point can be treated as a rotation followed by a translation. Such a transformation can be considered as equivalent to a rotation that aligns the axes parallel to the final directions, followed by a translation that moves the fixed point O to its final position O_t (Fig. 6.1b). While any translation can be unambiguously represented by a three-component vector, a general rotation may be specified in several ways. In the following, we consider the Euler angle and angle-axis representations of three-dimensional rotations.

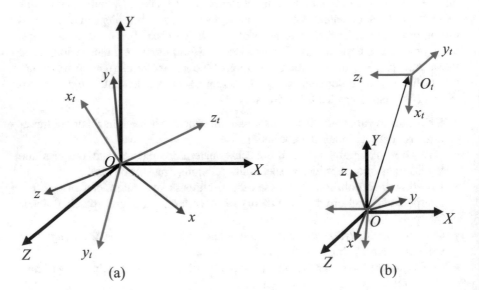

(a)   (b)

Fig. 6.1 Generalized rotational transform

6.1.1 Euler Angle Rotation

The Euler's theorem on rotations states that any general rotation can be performed using a sequence of elementary rotations about the coordinate axes passing through the fixed point. The theorem further states that if no two successive rotations are about the same axis, then the maximum number of rotations needed to achieve the transformation is three. Thus, any rotational transformation can be represented by a sequence of three rotations about mutually independent axes. These angles are called Euler angles. Before defining a Euler angle representation, we need to fix the sequence in which the rotations are performed. If we denote rotations about the X-axis by ψ, rotations about Y by ϕ, and rotations about Z by θ, a set of Euler angles can be defined using any of the following 12 sequences:

$\psi\,\phi\,\theta$	$\phi\,\theta\,\psi$	$\theta\,\psi\,\phi$
$\psi\,\theta\,\phi$	$\phi\,\psi\,\theta$	$\theta\,\phi\,\psi$
$\psi_1\,\phi\,\psi_2$	$\phi_1\,\theta\,\phi_2$	$\theta_1\,\psi\,\theta_2$
$\psi_1\,\theta\,\psi_2$	$\phi_1\,\psi\,\phi_2$	$\theta_1\,\phi\,\theta_2$

The Euler angle sequence $\{\psi\,\phi\,\theta\}$ represents a rotation about X followed by a second rotation about Y, followed by a third rotation about the Z-axis (Fig. 6.2). The sequence $\{\phi_1\,\psi\,\phi_2\}$ gives another Euler angle representation in terms of a rotation about the Y-axis, followed by a second rotation about the X-axis, and then a third rotation again about the Y-axis. The six sequences where each axis is used exactly once are called proper Euler angles.

The transformation matrix for the $\{\psi\,\phi\,\theta\}$ sequence is obtained by concatenating the transformation matrices corresponding to each principal axis rotation as shown below.

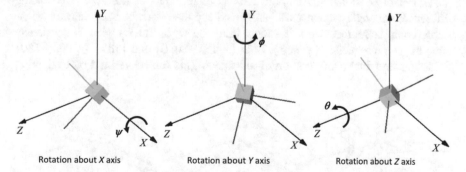

Rotation about X axis   Rotation about Y axis   Rotation about Z axis

Fig. 6.2 Euler angle sequence of rotations $\{\psi\,\phi\,\theta\}$ about X, Y, Z axes

$$
\begin{bmatrix} x' \\ y' \\ z' \\ 1 \end{bmatrix} = \begin{bmatrix} \cos\theta & -\sin\theta & 0 & 0 \\ \sin\theta & \cos\theta & 0 & 0 \\ 0 & 0 & 1 & 0 \\ 0 & 0 & 0 & 1 \end{bmatrix} \begin{bmatrix} \cos\phi & 0 & \sin\phi & 0 \\ 0 & 1 & 0 & 0 \\ -\sin\phi & 0 & \cos\phi & 0 \\ 0 & 0 & 0 & 1 \end{bmatrix} \begin{bmatrix} 1 & 0 & 0 & 0 \\ 0 & \cos\psi & -\sin\psi & 0 \\ 0 & \sin\psi & \cos\psi & 0 \\ 0 & 0 & 0 & 1 \end{bmatrix} \begin{bmatrix} x \\ y \\ z \\ 1 \end{bmatrix}
$$

$$(6.1)$$

The above equation can be interpreted as the transformation of any point (x, y, z) to (x', y', z') in a fixed coordinate frame. This interpretation does not use any information pertaining to body-fixed axes. The rotations are performed about inertially fixed principal axes directions X, Y, Z of the reference frame. Such a transformation is called an extrinsic composition of rotations. An intrinsic composition, on the other hand, uses rotations about body-fixed axes whose directions change in the reference frame after every rotation. For example, an aircraft's orientation in a three-dimensional space could be defined in this manner. In Fig. 6.3, the yaw rotation ψ is performed about the x-axis, the roll rotation ϕ about the transformed body y-axis, and the pitch rotation θ about the transformed body z-axis. For this sequence of intrinsic composition of rotations, the transformation from body frame to the coordinate reference frame is given by

$$
\begin{bmatrix} X \\ Y \\ Z \\ 1 \end{bmatrix} = \begin{bmatrix} 1 & 0 & 0 & 0 \\ 0 & \cos\psi & -\sin\psi & 0 \\ 0 & \sin\psi & \cos\psi & 0 \\ 0 & 0 & 0 & 1 \end{bmatrix} \begin{bmatrix} \cos\phi & 0 & \sin\phi & 0 \\ 0 & 1 & 0 & 0 \\ -\sin\phi & 0 & \cos\phi & 0 \\ 0 & 0 & 0 & 1 \end{bmatrix} \begin{bmatrix} \cos\theta & -\sin\theta & 0 & 0 \\ \sin\theta & \cos\theta & 0 & 0 \\ 0 & 0 & 1 & 0 \\ 0 & 0 & 0 & 1 \end{bmatrix} \begin{bmatrix} x \\ y \\ z \\ 1 \end{bmatrix}
$$

$$(6.2)$$

The above transformation equation for intrinsic rotations assumes that in the initial configuration, the body-fixed x, y, z axes coincide with the inertially fixed X, Y, Z axes directions.

A three-dimensional orientation can be represented in different ways using different Euler angle sequences. Even if we keep the sequence fixed, certain orientations could be represented using more than one set of Euler angles. For instance, using the same sequence $\{\psi\ \phi\ \theta\}$, both $\{-45, -80, 0\}$ and $\{135, -100, -180\}$ yield the same final configuration of an object. This can be verified by evaluating

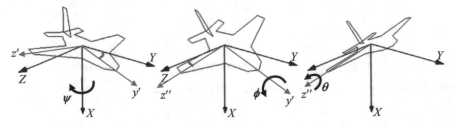

Fig. 6.3 Intrinsic composition of Euler angle rotations performed in the sequence $\{\psi\ \phi\ \theta\}$

Fig. 6.4 Two different Euler angle interpolation sequences generated for the same initial and target orientations

the product matrix in Eq. (6.1) for the two sets of angles. The non-uniqueness of the Euler angle representation also results in a non-unique interpolation path between two orientations in three-dimensional space (Fig. 6.4).

If we are given the transformation of a point (x, y, z) using a general 4×4 rotation matrix as below,

$$
\begin{bmatrix} x' \\ y' \\ z' \\ 1 \end{bmatrix} = \begin{bmatrix} m_{00} & m_{01} & m_{02} & 0 \\ m_{10} & m_{11} & m_{12} & 0 \\ m_{20} & m_{21} & m_{22} & 0 \\ 0 & 0 & 0 & 1 \end{bmatrix} \begin{bmatrix} x \\ y \\ z \\ 1 \end{bmatrix} \tag{6.3}
$$

we can extract the rotation angles of the Euler angle sequence $\{\psi \, \phi \, \theta\}$ by comparing the elements of the matrix with that of the product matrix in Eq. (6.1) as follows:

$$
\psi = \tan^{-1}\left(\frac{m_{21}}{m_{22}}\right)
$$

$$
\phi = \tan^{-1}\left(\frac{-m_{20}}{\sqrt{m_{00}^2 + m_{10}^2}}\right)
$$

$$
\theta = \tan^{-1}\left(\frac{m_{10}}{m_{00}}\right) \tag{6.4}
$$

When $\phi = 90°$, the terms m_{00}, m_{10}, m_{21}, and m_{22} become zero, leading to the singularity condition where the angles ψ and ϕ are indeterminate.

6.1.2 Angle-Axis Rotation

The Euler's theorem concerning three-dimensional rotations states that any number of rotational transformations with a single fixed point applied to an object can be replaced by a single rotation of the object about an axis passing through the fixed point. The axis is often called the equivalent axis of rotation. Any orientation of an object with the origin as a fixed point can therefore be specified using an angle

Fig. 6.5 General rotation about a vector $\boldsymbol{u}$ through the origin

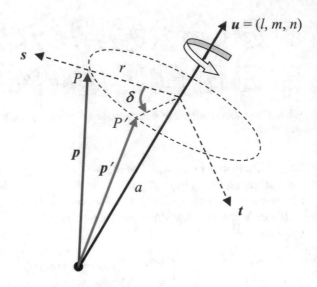

of rotation δ and an axis of rotation given by a unit vector $\boldsymbol{u} = (l, m, n)$. In the following discussion, we assume that the axis of rotation passes through the origin. Figure 6.5 depicts the rotational transformation applied to a vector $\boldsymbol{p}$ (or a point P). The transformed vector direction $\boldsymbol{p}'$ is given by the well-known Rodrigues' rotation formula [3] Given below.

$$\boldsymbol{p}' = \boldsymbol{p} \cos \delta + (1 - \cos \delta)(\boldsymbol{p} \cdot \boldsymbol{u})\boldsymbol{u} + (\boldsymbol{u} \times \boldsymbol{p}) \sin \delta \tag{6.5}$$

The terms in Eq. (6.5) can be rearranged to obtain t following matrix form for the angle-axis transformation of the point $P(x, y, z)$:

$$\begin{bmatrix} x' \\ y' \\ z' \\ 1 \end{bmatrix} =$$

$$\begin{bmatrix} l^2(1 - \cos \delta) + \cos \delta & lm(1 - \cos \delta) - n \sin \delta & ln(1 - \cos \delta) + m \sin \delta & 0 \\ lm(1 - \cos \delta) + n \sin \delta & m^2(1 - \cos \delta) + \cos \delta & mn(1 - \cos \delta) - l \sin \delta & 0 \\ ln(1 - \cos \delta) - m \sin \delta & mn(1 - \cos \delta) + l \sin \delta & n^2(1 - \cos \delta) + \cos \delta & 0 \\ 0 & 0 & 0 & 1 \end{bmatrix} \begin{bmatrix} x \\ y \\ z \\ 1 \end{bmatrix}.$$

$$\tag{6.6}$$

Given a general rotation matrix Eq. (6.3), we can derive expressions for the equivalent angle and axis of rotation by comparing the matrix with the rotation matrix in Eq. (6.6):

$$\delta = \tan^{-1}\left(\frac{\sqrt{(m_{21} - m_{12})^2 + (m_{02} - m_{20})^2 + (m_{10} - m_{01})^2}}{m_{00} + m_{11} + m_{22} - 1}\right)$$

$$l = \frac{m_{21} - m_{12}}{2 \sin \delta}$$

$$m = \frac{m_{02} - m_{20}}{2 \sin \delta}$$

$$n = \frac{m_{10} - m_{01}}{2 \sin \delta} \qquad (6.7)$$

6.2 Overview of Quaternions

This section provides an introduction to quaternion algebra and the applications of quaternions in transforming points and vectors in three-dimensional space.

6.2.1 Quaternion Algebra

The field of complex numbers has $1 = (1, 0)$, $i = (0, 1)$ as the two-dimensional orthogonal bases. Quaternions $Q = (q_0, q_1, q_2, q_3)$ are hyper-complex numbers of rank 4, defined using an extended orthogonal basis consisting of four elements $1 = (1, 0, 0, 0)$, $i = (0, 1, 0, 0)$, $j = (0, 0, 1, 0)$, $k = (0, 0, 0, 1)$. Thus, a quaternion $Q = (q_0, q_1, q_2, q_3)$ has an equivalent representation $q_0 + q_1 i + q_2 j + q_3 k$, where the quaternion components q_i are all real values. The term q_0 is called the scalar part of Q, and the 3-tuple (q_1, q_2, q_3) the vector part. The operations of addition, subtraction and scalar multiplication are defined as the usual element-wise operations as follows:

$$(p_0, p_1, p_2, p_3) \pm (q_0, q_1, q_2, q_3) = (p_0 \pm q_0, p_1 \pm q_1, p_2 \pm q_2, p_3 \pm q_3) \quad (6.8)$$

$$c(q_0, q_1, q_2, q_3) = (cq_0, cq_1, cq_2, cq_3) \qquad (6.9)$$

where c is any real number. The most important equation in the algebra of quaternions is the quaternion product PQ defined as follows:

$$\begin{aligned}(p_0, p_1, p_2, p_3)(q_0, q_1, q_2, q_3) = (&p_0 q_0 - p_1 q_1 - p_2 q_2 - p_3 q_3, \\ &p_0 q_1 + p_1 q_0 + p_2 q_3 - p_3 q_2, \\ &p_0 q_2 - p_1 q_3 + p_2 q_0 + p_3 q_1, \\ &p_0 q_3 + p_1 q_2 - p_2 q_1 + p_3 q_0) \qquad (6.10)\end{aligned}$$

From the above definition of a quaternion product, it is obvious that quaternion multiplication is not commutative. That is, for any two quaternions $P = (p_0, p_1, p_2, p_3)$, $Q = (q_0, q_1, q_2, q_3)$, the product PQ need not necessarily be the same as QP. If we denote the vector part of P by $v = (p_1, p_2, p_3)$ and the vector part of Q by $w = (q_1, q_2, q_3)$, then Eq. (6.10) becomes

$$(p_0, v)(q_0, w) = (p_0 q_0 - v \cdot w, \ldots p_0 w + q_0 v + v \times w) \tag{6.11}$$

where, $v \cdot w$ denotes the dot product and $v \times w$ the cross product of the two vectors. From Eq. (6.10), we can derive the following well-known properties satisfied by the quaternion bases:

$$
\begin{aligned}
i^2 &= j^2 = k^2 = ijk = -1 \\
ij &= - ji = k \\
jk &= - kj = i \\
ki &= - ik = j
\end{aligned}
\tag{6.12}
$$

The quaternion product formula in Eq. (6.10) can also be expressed in matrix form as

$$
PQ = \begin{bmatrix}
p_0 & -p_1 & -p_2 & -p_3 \\
p_1 & p_0 & -p_3 & p_2 \\
p_2 & p_3 & p_0 & -p_1 \\
p_3 & -p_2 & p_1 & p_0
\end{bmatrix}
\begin{bmatrix}
q_0 \\
q_1 \\
q_2 \\
q_3
\end{bmatrix}
\tag{6.13}
$$

We denote the quaternion dot product as $P \cdot Q$:

$$P \cdot Q = p_0 q_0 + p_1 q_1 + p_2 q_2 + p_3 q_3. \tag{6.14}$$

The conjugate $Q*$ of the quaternion $Q = (q_0, q_1, q_2, q_3)$ is defined as

$$Q* = (q_0, -q_1, -q_2, -q_3) \tag{6.15}$$

Thus, if $Q = (q_0, w)$, then $Q* = (q_0, - w)$. Also, $Q + Q* = 2q_0$. The magnitude (also called the length, or norm) of Q denoted by $|Q|$, is

$$|Q| = \sqrt{q_0^2 + q_1^2 + q_2^2 + q_3^2} \tag{6.16}$$

Quaternions of the type $(a, 0, 0, 0)$ with the vector component zero are called real quaternions and often denoted by a real number "a". For example, the product of a quaternion and its conjugate is a real quaternion:

$$QQ* = Q * Q = (|Q|^2, 0, 0, 0) = |Q|^2. \tag{6.17}$$

If Q is a unit quaternion ($|Q| = 1$), then the above equation implies that $Q^{-1} = Q*$. If the real part q_0 of a quaternion is zero, it represents a vector (q_1, q_2, q_3) in three-dimensional space. Such a quaternion that has the form $(0, q_1, q_2, q_3) = (0, \mathbf{q})$ is called a pure quaternion. Similarly, quaternions of the type $(a, b, 0, 0)$ behave exactly like complex numbers (a, b).

6.2.2 Quaternion Transformation

A special type of quaternion product in the form QPQ* plays an important role in three-dimensional transformations [3, 4] . We have just seen that a vector $\mathbf{p}$ in the three-dimensional space corresponds to a pure quaternion $P = (0, \mathbf{p})$. An interesting fact that leads to the notion of a quaternion transformation is that given any quaternion Q and a pure quaternion P, the product $P' = QPQ*$ is also a pure quaternion. Thus QPQ* can be viewed as the transformation of a pure quaternion $P = (0, p_1, p_2, p_3)$ using another quaternion Q. This transformation can be expressed in matrix form as follows:

$$\begin{bmatrix} 0 \\ p_1' \\ p_2' \\ p_3' \end{bmatrix} = \begin{bmatrix} 1 & 0 & 0 & 0 \\ 0 & q_0^2 + q_1^2 - q_2^2 - q_3^2 & 2(-q_0q_3 + q_1q_2) & 2(q_0q_2 + q_1q_3) \\ 0 & 2(q_0q_3 + q_1q_2) & q_0^2 - q_1^2 + q_2^2 - q_3^2 & 2(-q_0q_1 + q_2q_3) \\ 0 & 2(-q_0q_2 + q_1q_3) & 2(q_0q_1 + q_2q_3) & q_0^2 - q_1^2 - q_2^2 + q_3^2 \end{bmatrix} \begin{bmatrix} 0 \\ p_1 \\ p_2 \\ p_2 \end{bmatrix}$$

(6.18)

This equation defines the quaternion transformation of a three-dimensional point (or vector) $\mathbf{p} = (p_1, p_2, p_3)$ to another three-dimensional point (or vector) $\mathbf{p}' = (p_1', p_2', p_3')$. An alternative form of the equation can be derived as follows:

$$QPQ* = (q_0, \mathbf{w})(0, \mathbf{p})(-q_0, \mathbf{w}) \tag{6.19}$$

where, $\mathbf{w} = (q_1, q_2, q_3)$. Using Eq. (6.11) to expand the product term, we get

$$QPQ* = (0, \mathbf{p}') = (0, q_0^2\mathbf{p} + \mathbf{w}(\mathbf{p} \cdot \mathbf{w}) + 2q_0(\mathbf{w} \times \mathbf{p}) + \mathbf{w} \times (\mathbf{w} \times \mathbf{p})) \tag{6.20}$$

Further simplification of the right-hand side using vector algebra gives

$$\mathbf{p}' = (q_0^2 - \mathbf{w}^2)\mathbf{p} + 2\mathbf{w}(\mathbf{p} \cdot \mathbf{w}) + 2q_0(\mathbf{w} \times \mathbf{p}) \tag{6.21}$$

where $w^2 = |\mathbf{w}|^2 = q_1^2 + q_2^2 + q_3^2$. It should be noted that QPQ* generally is not a scale-preserving transformation because

$$|P'| = |Q|^2|P| \tag{6.22}$$

If we impose the constraint that Q is a unit quaternion (*i.e.* $|Q| = 1$), we get a scale-invariant (or length-preserving) transform. With this additional criterion, we can also write the inverse quaternion transform in a concise form as

$$P = Q * P'Q \tag{6.23}$$

We also note that when P is the zero-quaternion $(0, 0, 0, 0)$, so is P'. Therefore, the origin is a fixed point of the transformation. A length-preserving transformation with a fixed point is a rotation. In the following section, we will attempt to find a geometric interpretation of the quaternion transformation as a pure rotation in three-dimensional space and express the components of a unit quaternion in terms of the angle and the axis of rotation.

6.2.3   Quaternion Rotation

In the previous section, we saw that a quaternion transformation $P' = QPQ*$ transforms a point (or vector) $p = (p_1, p_2, p_3)$ to another three-dimensional point (or vector) $p' = (p_1', p_2', p_3')$ given by Eq. (6.21). Comparing this equation with the equation for the angle-axis transformation Eq. (6.5) we find that

$$\begin{aligned}
q_0^2 - w^2 &= \cos \delta \\
w &= k u, \text{ for some constant } k. \\
{}^0 - \cos \delta &= 2k^2 \\
2q_0 k &= \sin \delta
\end{aligned} \tag{6.24}$$

The above equations show that the vector component w of the quaternion $Q = (q_0, w)$, represents the axis of rotation. Let the unit vector u along the axis of rotation be given by $u = (l, m, n)$. We note from Eq. (6.24) that $k = \sin(\delta /2)$, and $q_0 = \cos(\delta /2)$. Therefore, the unit quaternion that represents a rotational transformation by an angle δ about the unit vector (l, m, n) through the origin is

$$Q = \left(\cos \frac{\delta}{2}, l \sin \frac{\delta}{2}, m \sin \frac{\delta}{2}, n \sin \frac{\delta}{2} \right) \tag{6.25}$$

This result is fundamental to the theory of generalized rotations, as it provides a direct mechanism for converting angle-axis representations of three-dimensional rotations into unit quaternions. Equation (6.25) also reveals a potential source of ambiguity or confusion in the mapping of a rotation to a quaternion. If we replace the rotation angle δ with $(2\pi) + \delta$, we get the same transformed configuration of the object in 3D space, but the sign of the quaternion Q in the above equation is reversed. Thus, both Q and $-Q$ represent the same rotational transformation.

From Eq. (6.25), we can also derive the relationship between the components of any unit quaternion $Q = (q_0, q_1, q_2, q_3)$ and the parameters of rotation it represents. The angle of rotation is given by

$$\delta = 2 \tan^{-1} \left(\frac{\sqrt{q_1^2 + q_2^2 + q_3^2}}{q_0} \right) \tag{6.26}$$

and the unit vector along the axis of rotation (l, m, n) can be obtained as

$$l = \frac{q_1}{\sqrt{q_1^2 + q_2^2 + q_3^2}}$$

$$m = \frac{q_2}{\sqrt{q_1^2 + q_2^2 + q_3^2}}$$

$$n = \frac{q_3}{\sqrt{q_1^2 + q_2^2 + q_3^2}} \tag{6.27}$$

In Eq. (6.18), we considered a 3D point as a pure quaternion of the type $(0, p_1, p_2, p_3)$, and gave the matrix form of the corresponding transformation. If we use the standard representation of a point in homogeneous coordinates as $P = (x, y, z, 1)$, the same transformation can be expressed as follows:

$$\begin{bmatrix} x' \\ y' \\ z' \\ 1 \end{bmatrix} = \begin{bmatrix} q_0^2 + q_1^2 - q_2^2 - q_3^2 & 2(-q_0q_3 + q_1q_2) & 2(q_0q_2 + q_1q_3) & 0 \\ 2(q_0q_3 + q_1q_2) & q_0^2 - q_1^2 + q_2^2 - q_3^2 & 2(-q_0q_1 + q_2q_3) & 0 \\ 2(-q_0q_2 + q_1q_3) & 2(q_0q_1 + q_2q_3) & q_0^2 - q_1^2 - q_2^2 + q_3^2 & 0 \\ 0 & 0 & 0 & 1 \end{bmatrix} \begin{bmatrix} x \\ y \\ z \\ 1 \end{bmatrix} \tag{6.28}$$

Using the additional requirement that Q is a unit vector, the diagonal elements of the above matrix can be further simplified as shown below:

$$\begin{bmatrix} x' \\ y' \\ z' \\ 1 \end{bmatrix} = \begin{bmatrix} 1 - 2q_2^2 - 2q_3^2 & 2(-q_0q_3 + q_1q_2) & 2(q_0q_2 + q_1q_3) & 0 \\ 2(q_0q_3 + q_1q_2) & 1 - 2q_1^2 - 2q_3^2 & 2(-q_0q_1 + q_2q_3) & 0 \\ 2(-q_0q_2 + q_1q_3) & 2(q_0q_1 + q_2q_3) & 1 - 2q_1^2 - 2q_2^2 & 0 \\ 0 & 0 & 0 & 1 \end{bmatrix} \begin{bmatrix} x \\ y \\ z \\ 1 \end{bmatrix} \tag{6.29}$$

If a general 4×4 rotation matrix is given as in Eq. (6.3), the following equivalence among the matrix elements can be easily established:

$$m_{00} + m_{11} + m_{22} + 1 = 4q_0^2$$

$$m_{21} - m_{12} = 4q_0q_1$$

$$m_{02} - m_{20} = 4q_0q_2$$
$$m_{10} - m_{01} = 4q_0q_3 \qquad (6.30)$$

The above equations are useful for extracting the quaternion elements from a given 4×4 rotational transformation matrix:

$$q_0 = \frac{\sqrt{1 + m_{00} + m_{11} + m_{22}}}{2}$$

$$q_1 = \frac{m_{21} - m_{12}}{4q_0}$$

$$q_2 = \frac{m_{02} - m_{20}}{4q_0}$$

$$q_3 = \frac{m_{10} - m_{01}}{4q_0} \qquad (6.31)$$

We will choose only the positive value of the square-root for computing q_0. A negative value for q_0 will change the sign of all remaining components and yield the quaternion $- Q$ in place of Q. Both Q and $- Q$ represent the same rotation, and therefore we can safely impose the constraint that the sign of q_0 is positive, and compute the remaining components from it. If a point (or a vector) P is first transformed by a quaternion Q_1 and then by a quaternion Q_2, the resulting point (or vector) P' is obtained by applying the transformation formula twice:

$$P' = Q_2(Q_1PQ_1*)Q_2* = (Q_2Q_1)P(Q_2Q_1)* \qquad (6.32)$$

The above equation shows that the composite rotation is given by the quaternion product Q_2Q_1. Generalizing this result, a series of rotational transformations performed using unit quaternions $Q_1, Q_2, \dots Q_k$ in that order, is equivalent to a single rotational transformation produced by the combined product quaternion $(Q_k \dots Q_2Q_1)$. We can use this result to find the quaternion equivalent of a Euler angle rotation sequence $\{\psi, \phi, \theta\}$, where the first rotation is performed about the x-axis by an angle ψ, the second about the y-axis by an angle ϕ, and finally about the z-axis by an angle θ. For each of the Euler angle rotations, we can write the corresponding quaternion (following Eq. 6.25) as below:

$$Q_\psi = \left(\cos\left(\frac{\psi}{2}\right), \sin\left(\frac{\psi}{2}\right), 0, 0\right)$$

$$Q_\phi = \left(\cos\left(\frac{\phi}{2}\right), 0, \sin\left(\frac{\phi}{2}\right), 0\right)$$

$$Q_\theta = \left(\cos\left(\frac{\theta}{2}\right), 0, 0, \sin\left(\frac{\theta}{2}\right)\right) \qquad (6.33)$$

The quaternion equivalent of the above Euler angle rotation sequence is given by the quaternion product $Q_\theta Q_\phi Q_\psi$.

6.3 Rotation Interpolatio

6.3.1 Linear Interpolation of Rotations

In the domain of computer animation, particularly in character animation, we commonly encounter the problem of interpolating between two orientations of an object. The orientations of an object or a part of a character model could be represented using Euler angles, angle-axis representations or quaternions. Given two sets of Euler angles $\{\psi_1, \phi_1, \theta_1\}$ and $\{\psi_2, \phi_2, \theta_2\}$, all intermediate sets can be obtained using a linear interpolation between the corresponding Euler angles:

$$\psi = (1 - t)\psi_1 + t\psi_2$$
$$\phi = (1 - t)\phi_1 + t\phi_2 \tag{6.34}$$
$$\theta = (1 - t)\theta_1 + t\theta_2, \quad 0 \le t \le 1.$$

As previously shown in Fig. 6.4, there may exist multiple Euler angle interpolation paths between two orientations. As an example, if the second orientation is given by $\{\psi_2 = 0, \phi_2 = 90, \theta_2 = 0\}$, the same orientation may be represented by an infinite number of Euler angles $\{\psi_2 = \lambda, \phi_2 = 90, \theta_2 = \lambda\}$, where λ is any value. Corresponding to each of these values representing the same target orientation, we get a different interpolation sequence. Even though the interpolated points $\{\psi, \phi, \theta\}$ lie along a straight line in the Euler angle space, the rotations produced by them may not yield a smooth and realistic motion between the two orientations.

Given two unit quaternions $Q_1 = \{q_0^{(1)}, q_1^{(1)}, q_2^{(1)}, q_3^{(1)}\}$ and $Q_2 = \{q_0^{(2)}, q_1^{(2)}, q_2^{(2)}, q_3^{(2)}\}$, a linear interpolation gives the quaternion

$$Q = (1 - t)Q_1 + t\, Q_2, \quad 0 \le t \le 1. \tag{6.35}$$

Since only unit quaternions represent rotational transformations, the quaternions resulting from the above equation must converted to unit quaternions before a transformation of the form QPQ* is applied to points P of an object. This quaternion linear interpolation scheme is often referred to as LERP.

The rotation interpolation sequence in Fig. 6.6a is generated using a linear interpolation between Euler angles $\{90, 40, 50\}$ and $\{-70, -130, -80\}$. The interpolation does not provide a realistic or desired motion between the initial and target orientations. A quaternion interpolation can give a proper transformation sequence as shown in Fig. 6.6b. In the previous section, we saw that quaternion representations exhibit a sign ambiguity, where both Q and $-Q$ represent the same rotational transformation in three-dimensional space. If this sign ambiguity is not taken care of, then even a

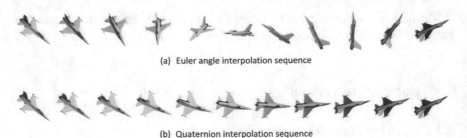

(a) Euler angle interpolation sequence

(b) Quaternion interpolation sequence

Fig. 6.6 Comparison of Euler angle and quaternion interpolation of rotations

quaternion linear interpolation can generate an improper transformation sequence as explained below.

Consider two quaternions Q_1 and Q_2 as shown in Fig. 6.7. The interpolated quaternions obtained from Eq. (6.35) lie on a straight line (shown in red) between the two points Q_1 and Q_2 in the four-dimensional space. We know that Q_2 and $-Q_2$ represent the same rotation. In our example, the angular separation between Q_1 and $-Q_2$ is smaller than the separation between Q_1 and Q_2. Therefore, we can get a shorter interpolation path (shown in blue) between Q_1 and $-Q_2$. In general, if the angle between Q_1 and Q_2 is greater than 90° (or equivalently, if the dot product $Q_1 \cdot Q_2$ is negative), we have to reverse the sign of one of the quaternions to get a proper linear interpolation path between the two orientations.

Figure 6.8a shows the sequence of orientations of an object generated by interpolating between two quaternions Q_1 and Q_2, and Fig. 6.8b the interpolation sequence between Q_1 and $-Q_2$. Note that the sign reversal does not change the target orientation, but causes an entirely new sequence to be generated.

Fig. 6.7 Selecton of a proper linear interpolation path between two quaternions

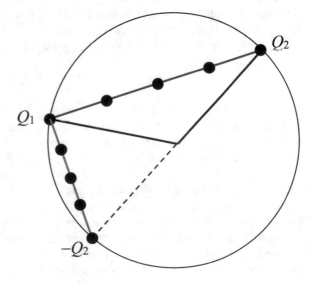

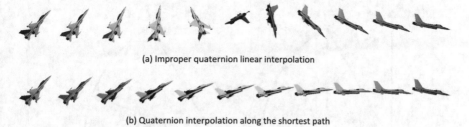

(a) Improper quaternion linear interpolation

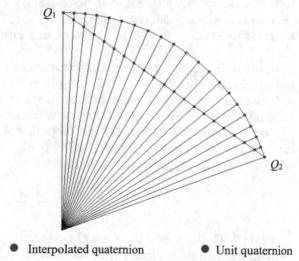

(b) Quaternion interpolation along the shortest path

Fig. 6.8 Two interpolation sequences generated by quaternion linear interpolation

An important drawback of the quaternion linear interpolation algorithm is the non-uniform distribution of rotations in quaternion space. When we convert the outputs of the linear interpolation formula (Eq. 6.35) to unit quaternions, the interpolated points move to the surface of a unit sphere in the four-dimensional space along a radial (Fig. 6.9). In other words, the interpolated quaternions after normalization lie on an arc of a great circle between Q_1 and Q_2. This transformation of quaternions resulting from normalization generates an uneven distribution of points and a corresponding non-uniformity in the angular velocity of the object. The speed in the middle of the interpolation path is generally much higher than the speed at the end points.

Fig. 6.9 Intermediate quaternions generated using linear interpolation

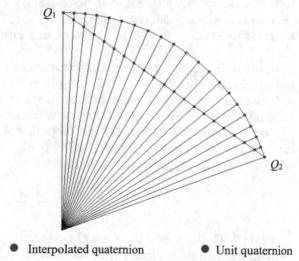

● Interpolated quaternion   ● Unit quaternion

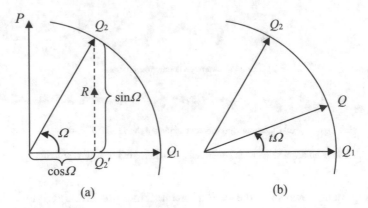

Fig. 6.10 Formulation of the SLERP interpolation scheme

6.3.2 Quaternion Spherical Linear Interpolation (SLERP)

In the previous section we saw that linear interpolation generates intermediate unit quaternions along an arc between Q_1 and Q_2 (Fig. 6.9) on the unit sphere in quaternion space, with unequal spacing between them. If we subdivide the angle between Q_1 and Q_2 uniformly, then we get an even distribution of points on the sphere. Such a distribution will also yield a smooth (torque-free) rotation of the object from one orientation to another with constant angular velocity. The spherical linear interpolation (SLERP) technique uses this approach to compute intermediate quaternions [3, 4].

Figure 6.10a shows the geometrical constructions needed to derive the SLERP formula. In the figure, $Q_1 = \{q_0^{(1)}, q_1^{(1)}, q_2^{(1)}, q_3^{(1)}\}$ and $Q_2 = \{q_0^{(2)}, q_1^{(2)}, q_2^{(2)}, q_3^{(2)}\}$ are any two unit quaternions and P another unit quaternion that is orthogonal to Q_1 (i.e. $P \cdot Q_{1} = 0$). Treating them as vectors in quaternion space, $Q_2 - Q_1 \cos\Omega$ is a vector (denoted by R) from Q_2' (the projection of Q_2 on Q_1) to Q_2, where Ω is the angle between Q_1 and Q_2. (i.e. $\cos\Omega = Q_1 \bullet Q_2$). Dividing R by its magnitude ($\sin\Omega$), we get the unit quaternion in the direction of R. Thus,

$$P = \frac{Q_2 - Q_1 \cos \Omega}{\sin \Omega} \tag{6.36}$$

Figure 6.10b shows how the angle Ω between Q_1 and Q_2 subdivided using an interpolation parameter t $(0 \le t \le 1)$, and the interpolated unit quaternion Q generated using this subdivision. Resolving Q along the orthogonal unit directions of Q_1 and P we get

$$Q = Q_1 \cos(t\Omega) + P \sin(t\Omega) \tag{6.37}$$

Substituting Eq. (6.36) and simplifying, we get the quaternion spherical linear interpolation formula [5].

$$Q = \frac{Q_1 \sin((1-t)\Omega) + Q_2 \sin(t\Omega)}{\sin \Omega} \tag{6.38}$$

The above equation has a singularity when $\Omega = 0$ or $\pm 180°$. When $\Omega = 0$, both the initial and final quaternions are the same, and therefore no interpolation is necessary. When $\Omega = \pm 180°$, $Q_2 = -Q_1$. In Sect. 6.2.3, we saw that this condition also corresponds to the situation where both orientations are the same.

As in the case of quaternion linear interpolation, we have to make sure that the spherical linear interpolation is also performed along the shorter arc on the great circle through the two points Q_1, Q_2 on the quaternion sphere. If the angle Ω between Q_1 and Q_2 is greater than $90°$ (i.e. $Q_1 . Q_2 = \cos\Omega < 0$), we reverse the sign of the target quaternion and interpolate between Q_1 and $-Q_2$.

6.4 Quaternion Derivative

A general three-dimensional motion of an object has an instantaneous linear velocity associated with positional changes and an angular velocity associated with rotational motion [6]. The computation of velocity components is required in application areas such as collision detection, character animation and kinematics. In this section, we derive the expression for angular velocity resulting from a rotational transformation expressed as a quaternion, and express the angular velocity in terms of the quaternion derivative.

Consider a rotation δ performed about the unit vector (l, m, n). The angular velocity vector ω for this rotation is given in terms of the derivative of the angle δ as

$$\omega = (l, m, n)\dot\delta \tag{6.39}$$

Let a unit quaternion Q represent the above rotation. We reproduce below the angle-axis representation of a quaternion given earlier in Eq. (6.25):

$$Q = \left(\cos \frac{\delta}{2}, l \sin \frac{\delta}{2}, m \sin \frac{\delta}{2}, n \sin \frac{\delta}{2} \right) \tag{6.40}$$

Differentiating the above equation, we get

$$\dot Q = \left(-\sin \frac{\delta}{2}, l \cos \frac{\delta}{2}, m \cos \frac{\delta}{2}, n \cos \frac{\delta}{2} \right) \frac{\dot\delta}{2} \tag{6.41}$$

Multiplying by the conjugate Q^*, and using Eq. (6.39), we get

$$\dot Q Q^* = \left(-\sin \frac{\delta}{2}, l \cos \frac{\delta}{2}, m \cos \frac{\delta}{2}, n \cos \frac{\delta}{2} \right) \left(\cos \frac{\delta}{2}, -l \sin \frac{\delta}{2}, -m \sin \frac{\delta}{2}, -n \sin \frac{\delta}{2} \right) \frac{\dot\delta}{2}$$

$$=(0, l, m, n)\frac{\dot{\delta}}{2} = \left(0, \frac{\omega}{2}\right) \tag{6.42}$$

In the above equation, we used the quaternion product formula given in Eq. (6.11). The above equation shows that the angular velocity corresponding to a quaternion rotation Q is given by

$$\omega = \text{The vector part of the quaternion} 2\dot{Q}Q^* \tag{6.43}$$

Post-multiplying both sides of Eq. (6.42) by Q, and noting that $Q^*Q = 1$, we get the following expression for the quaternion derivative in terms of the angular rate.

$$\dot{Q} = \left(0, \frac{\omega}{2}\right)Q \tag{6.44}$$

If an animation sequence generates quaternion values $Q(t)$ at small time intervals Δt, the instantaneous quaternion velocity at time t is given by the backward difference formula:

$$\dot{Q}(t) = \frac{Q(t) - Q(t - \Delta t)}{\Delta t} \tag{6.45}$$

6.5   GLM Quaternion Class

The OpenGL Mathematics Library (GLM) [1] contains the definitions of structures of quaternion types, and several functions providing the implementations of quaternion operations. Since GLM follows the naming conventions used in OpenGL shading language and supports interoperability features with OpenGL, graphics programmers and developers use GLM as a convenient library for performing vector and matrix operations. The following table (Table 6.1) provides a quick reference to the quaternion functions provided by the GLM library.

6.6   Assimp Quaternion Class

The Open Asset Import Library (Assimp) [2] is a popular library used for rendering and animation of character models. Algorithms for character animation using Assimp are discussed in detail in the next chapter. This section provides only a very brief overview of the quaternion functions used in applications based on Assimp library.

The animation of a character model involves a series of joint angle transformations applied on the mesh through a skeletal structure. An animation comprises of a set of keyframes, where each keyframe specifies the angles of rotations of every joint,

Table 6.1 GLM quaternion types and functions

#include < glm/glm.hpp > #include < glm/gtc/quaternion.hpp > #include < glm/gtc/matrix_transform.hpp > #include < glm/gtc/type_ptr.hpp >	These are the header files that should be included in the program

//Declaration of two quaternions
 glm::quat q1, q2;
 //Declaration and initialization
 glm::quat q(1, 0, 0, 0);
	The constructor takes arguments w, x, y, z. The first parameter is the scalar component of the quaternion. <u>Note:</u> The internal order is x, y, z, w. So, q[0] will return x, not w. Use component accessors q.w, q.x, q.y, q.z to retrieve component values from q

glm::quat prod = q1 * q2;	Quaternion product Eq. (6.10)– (6.13)
float dot = glm::dot(q1, q2);	Quaternion dot product Eq. (6.14)
glm::quat qc = glm::conjugate(q);	Quaternion conjugate Eq. (6.15)
float mag = glm::length(q);	Magnitude of a quaternion Eq. (6.16)
glm::quat q = glm::angleAxis(theta, x, y, z);	Formation of a quaternion using angle theta (in radians) and axis of rotation (x, y, z) Eq. (6.25)
glm::vec3 ax = glm::axis(q);	Function to obtain axis of rotation from a quaternion Eq. (6.27)
glm::mat4 qmat = glm::mat4_cast(q);	Function to obtain a quaternion transformation matrix Eq. (6.28)
float* mat = glm::value_ptr(qmat); glMultMatrixf(mat);	Conversion of the above quaternion matrix to a float array for use as an OpenGL transformation matrix
Glm::quat q = glm::toQuat(m);	Conversion of a rotational transformation matrix to a quaternion Eq. (6.31)
glm::quat q = glm::lerp(q1, q2, t);	Quaternion linear interpolation Eq. (6.35). *Note:* The output quaternion is not normalized
Glm::quat q = glm::slerp(q1, q2, t); OR glm::quat q = glm::mix(q1, q2, t);	Quaternion spherical linear interpolation Eq. (6.38)

and the global position of the model itself (root joint). Displaying an animation sequence will require an interpolation of joint angle rotations between consecutive keyframes. Since the quaternion spherical linear interpolation provides a smooth interpolation between two orientations, the joint angle rotations (which could be specified in terms of Euler angles) are first converted to quaternions, then interpolated and finally converted to transformation matrices. The Assimp library provides a set of convenient functions for these operations. Table 6.2 lists some of the functions defined in the Assimp library.

Table 6.2 Assimp quaternion functions

#include < assimp/types.h >	The main header file

//Declaration and initialization of
// identity quaternion
aiQuaternion q;
	Here "q" is initialized to the identity real quaternion given by (1, 0, 0, 0). The first element is the scalar component of the quaternion

//Declaration and initialization of
// a given quaternion
aiQuaternion q1(0.5, 0, 0.8666, 0);
	Declaration and initialization of a general quaternion. The first element is the scalar term. The quaternion components can be accessed as q1.w, q1.x, q1.y, q1.z

//Quaternion from Euler angles aiQuaternion q2(1.5707, 0, 0)	When initialized with three values, the parameters are interpreted as Euler angles roty, rotz, rotx in radians. In this example, roty $= \pi/2$, and the quaternion q2 is given by (0.707, 0, 0.707, 0)

//Quaternion from axis angle
aiVector3D axis(0.707, 0, 0.707);
aiQuaternion q3(axis, 0.7853);
	In this example, the axis of rotation is the unit vector (0.707, 0, 0.707), and the angle of rotation is $\pi/4$. The quaternion q3 is given by (0.9238, 0.2705, 0, 0.2705)

//Quaternion from a rotation matrix
aiMatrix3 $\times$ 3 mat
aiQuaternion q4(mat);
	The matrix must be an orthonormal matrix representing a rotational transformation

//Rotation matrix from a quaternion
aiMatrix3 $\times$ 3 mat
mat = q.GetMatrix();
	Given a quaternion q, this function returns the equivalent 3 $\times$ 3 rotation matrix

//Conversion to the conjugate
q.Congjugate();
	If q is a quaternion, q.Conjugate() converts q to q*

//Normalize a quaternion
q.Normalize();
	If q is any quaternion, q.Normalize() converts q to a unit quaternion

r = p * q;	Multiplies the quaternions p and q to yield the quaternion r. Note that quaternion multiplication is not commutative

//Transformation of a point or vector
aiVector3D p1(3, 5, -2);
aiVector3D p2;
aiQuaternion q(0.707, 0, 0, 0,707)
p2 = q.Rotate(p1)
	q.rotate(p1) performs the rotation of the point p1 using the quaternion q to yield the transformed point p2. This transformation is given by Eq. (6.18). In this example, the point p1 is rotated by 90 degs about the z-axis. The coordinates of p2 are (-5, 3, -2)

//Spherical linear interpolation
aiQuaternion qint;
aiQuaternion q1, q2;
float t;
qint.Interpolate(qint, q1, q2, t);
	The Interpolate() function performs a quaternion spherical linear interpolation Eq. (6.38) between two input quaternions q1, q2, using an interpolation parameter t $(0 \leq t \leq 1)$

//Rotation keys aiNodeAnim* ndAnim; aiQuaternion rotn; rotn = (ndAnim- > mRotationKeys[i]).mValue;	An animation node (aiNodeAnim) is a channel of an animation sequence. A channel consists of a set of keyframes containing position and rotation keys. Assimp represents rotation keys using quaternions

6.7 Chapter Resources

The folder "Chap. 6" on the companion website contains the following program and associated data files. The program demonstrates the usefulness of quaternions in rotation interpolation.

- Quat.cpp: Generates both Euler angle and quaternion rotation interpolation sequences similar to that shown in Fig. 6.6, between user-specified source and target orientations of an object model.

References and Further Reading

1. OpenGL Mathematics. https://glm.g-truc.net/0.9.9/index.html. Accessed 1 Mar 2020).
2. The Open Asset Importer Library. https://www.assimp.org/. Accessed 15 Nov 2021).
3. R. Mukundan, Chapter 5 – Quaternions, in *Advanced Methods in Computer Graphics* (Springer, 2012)
4. J.B. Kuipers, *Quaternions and Rotation Sequences* (Princeton University Press, New Jersey, 1998)
5. K. Shoemake, Animating rotation with quaternion curves. SIGGRAPH Comput. Graph. **19**(3), 245–254 (1985)
6. T. Haslwanter, *3D Kinematics* (Springer, 2018)

Chapter 7
Character Animation

Animations of three-dimensional character models are extensively used in computer generated feature films, games, simulations, and virtual environments. Depending on the application requirements, the character mesh and the animation sequence can have varying levels of complexity. While sophisticated virtual character agents incorporate several forms of articulation including facial expression animation, even the very basic character animation model requires fairly complex data structures and methods for implementing a proper transformation sequence.

In this chapter, we will look at the important parts of a character animation pipeline. Character animations involve joint angle transforms. Quaternions are therefore extensively used in both motion capture data and character animation (including inverse kinematics) algorithms. Scene graphs are data structures for storing hierarchical transformations applied to three-dimensional models along with material and scene properties. This chapter will study the main concepts and algorithms used for animating skeletal structures and character models.

This chapter has the following sections:

- **Scene graphs**: Explores the structure of a scene graph in general and the node hierarchy in particular, and discusses the representation of a joint chain and its transformations using a scene graph.
- **Assimp**: Introduces the main functions of the Assimp library that are useful for skeletal and character animations.
- **Motion capture data**: Gives an overview of motion capture data in BVH file format, and the mesh models generated by Assimp when motion capture data are loaded.
- **Skeletal animation**: Provides the details of methods used for animating a skeletal structure using motion capture data.
- **Bones**: Explains the components and properties of the bone data structure used in animations of rigged character models. Provides examples of character animations and discusses important aspects of keyframe interpolation.

© The Author(s), under exclusive license to Springer Nature Switzerland AG 2022
R. Mukundan, *3D Mesh Processing and Character Animation*,
https://doi.org/10.1007/978-3-030-81354-3_7

- **Vertex blending**: Outlines the need for associating multiple bones and weights to vertices near joints and gives examples of rendering artefacts introduced by joint angle transformations.
- **Animation retargeting**: Provides details of an algorithm for mapping an animation sequence from a source model (such as motion capture data) to a target character model.

7.1   Scene Graphs

A scene graph is a data structure commonly used to represent hierarchical relationships between transformations applied to a set of objects in a three-dimensional scene. It finds applications in a variety of acceleration and rendering algorithms. A scene graph could also be used to organize visual attributes, bounding volumes, and animations as a hierarchy in a collection of objects. In the most general form, any scene related information that can be organized in a hierarchical fashion can be stored in a scene graph. It also provides a convenient way of representing logical groups of objects formed using their spatial positions or attributes. In this chapter, we will outline the fundamental properties of scene graphs and look at some of the implementation aspects using the Open Asset Import (Assimp) [1] library.

7.1.1   Model Transformations

In this section, we analyse the hierarchical structure of series of transformations used for constructing (or representing) three-dimensional models. Transformations applied to different parts of a character model obviously have a hierarchical structure (e.g. the transformation applied to the shoulder joint affect not just the upper arm segment, but all its child segments such as the lower arm, hand, and fingers). Since character models generally have several joint chains forming a complex tree structure, we first consider a very simple model consisting of only very few levels in the hierarchy to explore the important parts of a scene graph.

The model in Fig. 7.1 consists of a dodecahedron, a torus, two cylindrical shapes, and a rectangular base. The following sequence of transformations may be used to specify the construction of the model, assuming that we are given the components in the required size and orientation. First, we create two copies of the cylindrical shape and transform each of them to their respective positions on the base. Then, we translate the torus and the dodecahedron together to their required position on the model. Finally, we rotate the whole model about the y-axis to get the desired orientation in the world coordinate space. A few transformation parameters are given in the figure for illustrative purposes.

The transformation associated with each node can be represented in a general form by a 4×4 matrix. In the above example, we also note that a node may contain

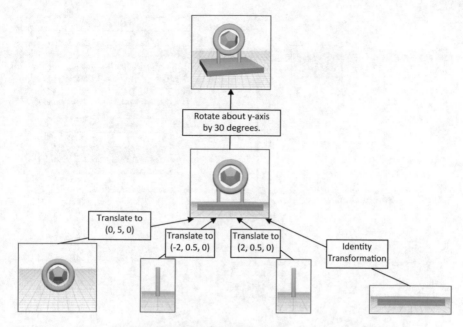

Fig. 7.1 A simple example of hierarchical transformations

multiple mesh objects, and multiple nodes may refer to the same mesh object. The mesh objects may be stored in a common array outside of the node hierarchy, and each node in the hierarchy may contain an array of mesh indices referring to one or more of the mesh objects in the common array. Each node matrix must be viewed as transforming the mesh objects belonging to that node from the node's reference frame to the parent node's reference frame. Each mesh object in the mesh array may also be associated with a "material" which is a collection of material properties such as ambient and diffuse colours. Since multiple mesh objects may share the same material property, the material data could also be stored in an array of structures, and a material index stored with each mesh object (we assume that a mesh is associated with only one material property; under this assumption, a mesh requiring more than one material will need to be split into a set of submeshes so that each submesh requires only one material). A scene graph can be viewed as a container that encapsulates the node hierarchy, the mesh array, and the material array. The node hierarchy in Fig. 7.1 augmented with the mesh and material arrays is shown in Fig. 7.2.

In the next section, we explore the properties of hierarchical transformations in a bit more detail using two-dimensional models of joint chains.

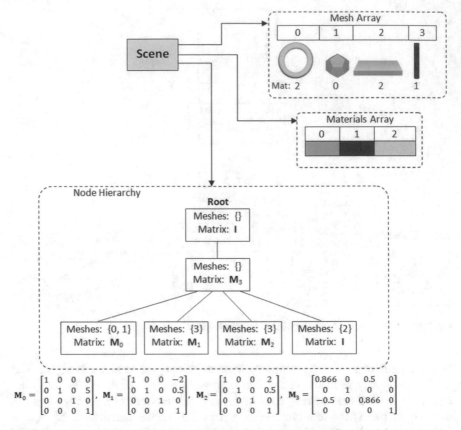

Fig. 7.2 A scene graph consisting of a node hierarchy, a mesh array, and a material array

7.1.2   A 2D Skeletal Structure

Two-dimensional skeletal structures are easier to understand, model, and visualize compared to their three-dimensional counterparts, and therefore used in the initial stages in the study of articulated character models. A simple joint chain representing an arm in two dimensions (on xy-plane) consists of three links, "upper arm", "lower arm", and "hand" as shown in Fig. 7.3. Each link is attached to its parent at a joint. The three joints of the model are named "shoulder", "elbow", and "wrist". The joints form the nodes of the transformation hierarchy which specifies how joint angle transformations must be applied to the model. As discussed in the previous section, each node contains the index of a mesh and a transformation matrix. For added convenience, we can also give a name to each node (e.g. "elbow") and to each mesh (e.g., "lower arm" or "L.arm"). We also create a special joint "end" at the end of the last link of the joint chain. This joint represents the end point of the chain and does not have any joint angle transformation associated with it. Figure 7.3 also shows the scene graph of the two-dimensional structure.

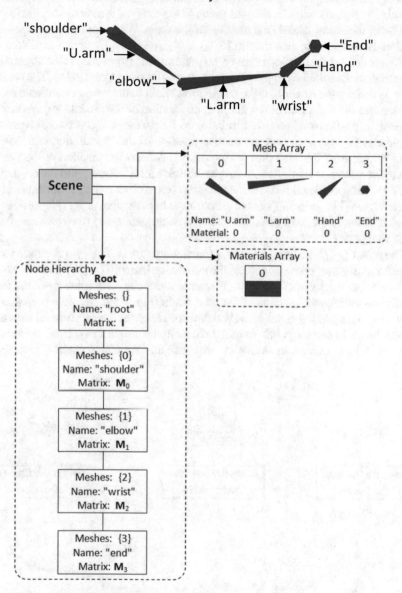

Fig. 7.3 A three-link joint chain and its scene graph

Being a 2D example, we assign only one rotational parameter to each joint and use the notation θ_0 to denote the rotation (about the z-axis) of the shoulder joint, θ_1 the rotation of the elbow, and θ_2 the rotation of the wrist. We denote the corresponding rotational transformation matrices as $\mathbf{R}(\theta_0)$, $\mathbf{R}(\theta_1)$, and $\mathbf{R}(\theta_2)$, respectively. Note that each angle defines the rotation of the corresponding link from its initial configuration. Therefore, in the initial configuration, all joint angles have a zero value. The rotation angle θ_0 defines the rotation of the whole joint chain in the world coordinate space. To complete the definition of the initial configuration of the model, we also require the relative positions of each link relative to its parent. We use two-dimensional coordinates (x_2, y_2) to denote the relative position of the "hand" link with respect to the "lower arm" link. In other words, (x_2, y_2) denotes the position of the "wrist" joint in the reference frame, where the parent link's joint "elbow" is at the origin (see Fig. 7.4). This positional offset means that the "hand" link must be translated to the position (x_2, y_2) in its parent's coordinate frame. In particular, (x_0, y_0) represents the global position of the joint chain in the world coordinate space (the reference frame of the root node).

The offset (x_2, y_2) corresponds to a translation matrix $\mathbf{T}(x_2, y_2)$ for the "wrist" node. Similarly, the "elbow" node has the translation matrix $\mathbf{T}(x_1, y_1)$, and the "shoulder" node has the matrix $\mathbf{T}(x_0, y_0)$. The node hierarchy with these matrices alone specify the initial configuration of the joint chain (Fig. 7.5a). We note here that the parameters $x_0, y_0, \ldots, x_3, y_3$ collectively define the shape (or the geometrical structure) of the joint chain and its global position in the initial configuration. These parameters remain fixed throughout an animation sequence and are called skeletal parameters

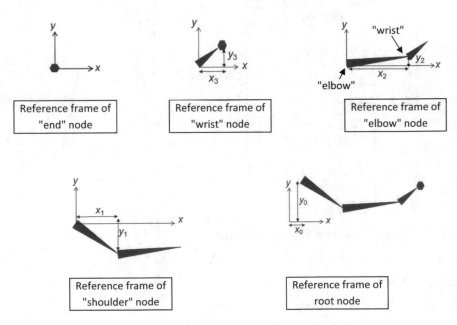

Fig. 7.4 Frames of reference of nodes and the corresponding transformations

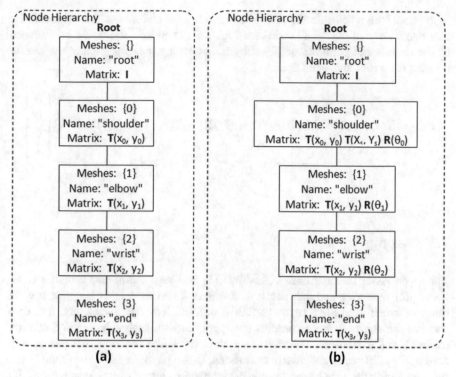

Fig. 7.5 Node hierarchy of the joint chain for its, **a** initial and **b** transformed configurations

of the joint chain. In contrast, the joint angles $\theta_0, \ldots, \theta_2$ may have a different set of values for each animation frame. These parameters are therefore referred to as the animation parameters. In addition to joint angle transformations, the chain may also undergo a global positional change (translational motion) in the world coordinate space. This motion is represented by a pair of translation parameters (X_s, Y_s) of the shoulder joint. Thus, the animation parameters of the chain shown in Fig. 7.3 are given by the set $\{X_s, Y_s, \theta_0, \theta_1, \theta_2\}$. For a given animation frame with a set of values for these parameters, the transformation matrices for each link are defined as shown in Fig. 7.5b.

A mesh belonging to a node is affected by transformations of not only that node, but also all its parent nodes. Therefore, in order to find the overall transformation to be applied to a mesh belonging to a node, we traverse the tree from the root node down to that node and concatenate all transformation matrices. From Fig. 7.5b, the transformation applied to vertices P of the mesh belonging to the "lower arm" is given by

$$P' = \mathbf{T}(x_0, y_0)\mathbf{T}(X_s, Y_s)\mathbf{R}(\theta_0)\mathbf{T}(x_1, y_1)\mathbf{R}(\theta_1)P \tag{7.1}$$

It should be noted that the end point of the joint chain is at the origin of the reference frame of the "end" node (see Fig. 7.5). Therefore, the world coordinates of the chain's end point are obtained by transforming the origin using the matrix product from root to the end node:

$$P_{\text{End}} = \mathbf{T}(x_0, y_0)\mathbf{T}(X_s, Y_s)\mathbf{R}(\theta_0)\mathbf{T}(x_1, y_1)\mathbf{R}(\theta_1)\mathbf{T}(x_2, y_2)\mathbf{R}(\theta_2)\mathbf{T}(x_3, y_3)\begin{bmatrix} 0 \\ 0 \\ 0 \\ 1 \end{bmatrix}$$

$$(7.2)$$

7.2 Assimp

The Open Asset Import Library (Assimp) [1] is a very useful and versatile C ++ library for rendering and animating three-dimensional models. It supports a wide range of model data file formats (e.g. 3ds, obj, off, bvh, dae, blend, ply, fbx, dxf) and has the ability to store complex mesh related data such as geometry, texture, material, and animations. It contains the data types and functions for performing commonly used vector and matrix operations. It also provides the scene graph structure containing the node hierarchy, mesh, and material arrays useful for rendering 3D models. These structures can be augmented with bone and animation data (discussed in the following sections of this chapter) for animating rigged character models. The library also supports several post-processing operations such as the construction of indexed meshes and the computation of normal and tangent vectors.

Table 7.1 provides a quick reference to the basic classes and functions in the Assimp library used for vector and matrix operations. Other important classes and functions used in both skeletal and character animation will be discussed in the sections that follow.

7.3 Motion Capture Data

Motion capture data (mocap, for short), as the name implies, provides a description of motion of objects and human actors within a three-dimensional space [2]. This motion is usually described using the changes in joint configurations (joint angles) within the body (or object), and the global position and orientation of the body (or object) itself. The recording of motion capture data involves the tracking of relative rotational motions of the joints and the changes in global positions and orientations using various markers and sensors placed on the body. In addition to animation data, a motion capture file also contains the definition of the skeletal structure in terms of a

Table 7.1 Assimp classes and functions

```#include <assimp/cimport.h>```
```#include <assimp/types.h>```
```#include <assimp/scene.h>```
```#include <assimp/postprocess.h>```
	These are the header files that should be included in the program

```//Declaration of a vector```
```aiVector3D vec;```
```//Declaration and initialization```
```aiVector3D v(1, 0, 2);```
```//Color```
```aiColor3D red(1, 0, 0);```
	These types are used to store three-dimensional vertex attributes such as position, colour, and normal components. Access elements using component accessors $v.x$, $v.y$, $v.z$ or indices $v[0]$, $v[1]$, $v[2]$

```//Vector dot product (scalar product)```
```float d = u * v;```
```//Vector cross product```
```aiVector3D w = u ^ v;```
	The dot and cross-products of vectors are not implemented as functions, but as operators as shown here

```v.Normalize();```	Converts the vector "v" to a unit vector
```float len = v.Length();```	Length of a vector

```//Declaration of a 4x4 matrix```
```aiMatrix4x4 mat;```
```//Declaration and initialization```
```aiMatrix4x4 m(11,12,13,14,```
```21,22,23,24,```
```31,32,33,34,```
```41,42,43,44);```
	Transformations may be represented by 3×3 or 4×4 matrices. Assimp stores matrices in **row-major order**. Use component accessors to retrieve matrix elements: $m.a1$, $m.a2$, $m.a3$, $m.a4$ for the first row $m.b1$, $m.b2$, $m.b3$, $m.b4$ for the second row, and so on

```//Identity matrix``` ```aiMatrix4x4 imat = aiMatrix4x4();```	Identity matrix

```//Conversion form 3x3 to 4x4 matrix```
```aiMatrix3x3 m3;```
```aiMatrix4x4 m4 = aiMatrix4x4(m3);```
	The vector $(0, 0, 0, 1)$ is added as the fourth row and fourth column to the 3×3 matrix

```//Transformation of a vector```
```aiVector3D v;```
```aiVector3D vt = m * v;```
	Here "m" is a 4×4 matrix. The 3D vector "v" is appended by the fourth element "1", prior to multiplication by the matrix. The first three elements of the output vector are returned in "vt"

```m.Transpose();```	Transposes the matrix "m"
```m.Inverse();```	Inverts the matrix "m"

```//Rotation matrix from angle and axis```
```aiMatrix3x3 rotn;```
```aiVector3D axis;```
```rotn.Rotation(angleRad, axis, rotn);```
	The "Rotation()" function returns a 3×3 rotation matrix given the axis and angle of rotation

```//Rotation of a vector to another```
```aiVector3D v1, v2;```
```aiMatrix3x3 rotn;```
```rotn =```
```rotn.FromToMatrix(v1,v2,rotn);```
	The "FromtoMatrix()" function returns a 3×3 rotation matrix that rotates a vector $v1$ to another vector $v2$

(continued)

Table 7.1 (continued)

``
//Assimp matrix to GLM matrix
#include <glm/gtc/type_ptr.hpp>
aiMatrix4x4 m;
glm::mat4   m_glm;
m_glm =
glm::transpose(glm::make_mat4(&m.a1))
``
	If the GLM library is used for mathematical functions, then it may be required to convert an Assimp matrix to a GLM matrix. Since GLM matrices are stored in column-major order, we also need to transpose the source matrix

joint hierarchy where the position of each joint is specified relative to its parent. This joint hierarchy can be directly mapped to the node hierarchy (Fig. 7.3) of the skeletal structure's scene graph. Once this mapping is established for a mesh structure of a skeleton model, the mesh can be animated by updating the transformation matrices of the node hierarchy. Highly realistic and complex animations of skeleton models can be easily generated in this manner. Skeletal animation using motion capture data is the first step towards understanding the concepts behind the algorithms used for animating rigged character models.

In this section, we will consider the structure of motion capture data in Biovision Hierarchy (BVH) [3] formats. Since BVH files are stored in ASCII format, they can be opened using any text editor. A BVH file organizes motion capture data in two sections: "Hierarchy" and "Motion". The Hierarchy section contains the definition of the skeletal structure. The Motion section contains animation data specified as keyframes. Each keyframe contains the rotation angles of joints and the global position and orientation of the root node. For small skeletal structures, the data contained in these two sections can be easily read, interpreted, and analysed. As an example, we consider below a BVH file for a simple test model of a skeleton containing only three joints (Fig. 7.6). As seen in the figure, the BVH format provides a straightforward definition of the hierarchical structure of the skeleton from which each joint's positional characteristics can be easily derived.

The skeletal model in the above file represents a human arm containing three joints, "Shoulder", "Elbow", and "Wrist" (Fig. 7.7). In addition to the three joints, the BVH file lists two special nodes: (i) the node with keyword "ROOT" denotes the root joint which does not have a parent. This joint has six degrees of freedom which gives the three-dimensional global position and orientation of the whole skeleton. The first six values in each keyframe give the three positional coordinates and three orientation angles of the skeleton. (ii) The node with keyword "End Site" denotes the end point of a joint chain. This node does not have any rotational transformation associated with it and therefore does not have any corresponding values in keyframes.

The position of each joint relative to its parent is specified using the "OFFSET" keyword. In the initial configuration of the skeleton, when all joint angles are zero, its geometrical shape is specified only by this positional information. In other words, the offset values uniquely specify the relative locations of the joints of the skeleton in the initial configuration, and they are often referred to as the skeleton parameters. The values of the skeleton parameters do not change during an animation sequence. Since each joint's offset is defined relative to its parent, we need to concatenate all

```
HIERARCHY
ROOT root
{
        OFFSET 0 0 0
        CHANNELS 6 Xposition Yposition Zposition Zrotation Yrotation Xrotation
        JOINT Shoulder
        {
                OFFSET 0.5  0.3  0
                CHANNELS 3 Zrotation Yrotation Xrotation
                JOINT Elbow
                {
                        OFFSET 1.0   -0.5 0
                        CHANNELS 3 Zrotation Yrotation Xrotation
                        JOINT Wrist
                        {
                                OFFSET 1.4  0.6 0
                                CHANNELS 3 Zrotation Yrotation Xrotation
                                End Site
                                {
                                        OFFSET 1.0 0.1 0
                                }
                        }
                }
        }
}
MOTION
Frames: 10
Frame Time: .1
0 0 0 0 0 0  3.0 0 0   8.0 0 0   -3.0 0 0
0 0 0 0 0 0  6.0 0 0  16.0 0 0   -6.0 0 0
0 0 0 0 0 0  9.0 0 0  24.0 0 0   -9.0 0 0
0 0 0 0 0 0 12.0 0 0  32.0 0 0  -12.0 0 0
0 0 0 0 0 0 15.0 0 0  40.0 0 0  -15.0 0 0
0 0 0 0 0 0 18.0 0 0  48.0 0 0  -18.0 0 0
0 0 0 0 0 0 21.0 0 0  56.0 0 0  -21.0 0 0
0 0 0 0 0 0 24.0 0 0  64.0 0 0  -24.0 0 0
0 0 0 0 0 0 27.0 0 0  72.0 0 0  -27.0 0 0
0 0 0 0 0 0 30.0 0 0  80.0 0 0  -30.0 0 0
```

Fig. 7.6 A sample BVH file for a three-link joint chain

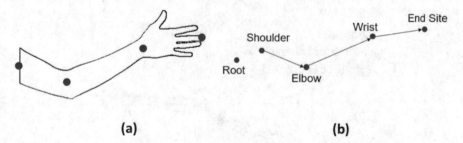

(a)   (b)

Fig. 7.7 A three-link joint chain representing a human arm and its skeletal structure

translational offsets from any given node to the root to find that joint's global position. In the example given in Fig. 7.6, the world coordinates of the elbow joint are (0.6, −0.2, 0).

The BVH format uses Euler angle sequences to represent rotations of joints. The initial configuration of the skeleton (Fig. 7.7b) where all joint angles are zero is known as the base pose or the zero pose. Each joint barring the end site has three values in each keyframe corresponding to the three Euler angles of rotation of that joint. The parameters used for specifying keyframes including rotation angles of all joints and the global position and orientation of the root node are collectively known as animatable parameters. Commonly used Euler angle sequences are Z, X, Y and Z, Y, X. The example in Fig. 7.6 uses a Z, Y, X sequence. The corresponding rotation matrix is given by

$$
\mathbf{R} = \begin{bmatrix} \cos\theta & -\sin\theta & 0 & 0 \\ \sin\theta & \cos\theta & 0 & 0 \\ 0 & 0 & 1 & 0 \\ 0 & 0 & 0 & 1 \end{bmatrix} \begin{bmatrix} \cos\phi & 0 & \sin\phi & 0 \\ 0 & 1 & 0 & 0 \\ -\sin\phi & 0 & \cos\phi & 0 \\ 0 & 0 & 0 & 1 \end{bmatrix} \begin{bmatrix} 1 & 0 & 0 & 0 \\ 0 & \cos\psi & -\sin\psi & 0 \\ 0 & \sin\psi & \cos\psi & 0 \\ 0 & 0 & 0 & 1 \end{bmatrix} \tag{7.3}
$$

where θ denotes the rotation about the Z-axis, ϕ the rotation about the Y-axis, and ψ the rotation about the X-axis. Note that the above sequence first performs a rotation about the X-axis, followed by a rotation about the Y-axis, followed by a rotation about the Z-axis.

Assimp generates a dummy mesh for the skeleton, with each link represented by a polyhedron (pyramid) with the centre of the base at the joint and the apex at the child node. The end site is represented by an octahedron (Fig. 7.8).

The base pose of skeletons of human characters has a few standard configurations defined by character modelling tools such as 3D Studio Max, DAZ Studio, and Motion Builder. The skeletal structure including the number of joints in the skeleton, and the Euler angle sequence used for representing joint angle rotations may differ between these applications. Figure 7.9 shows the base pose (zero pose) of skeletons used by three popular modelling tools. While 3DS-Max uses the Z, Y, X as the Euler angle sequence, both DAZ-Studio and Motion Builder use the Z, X, Y sequence.

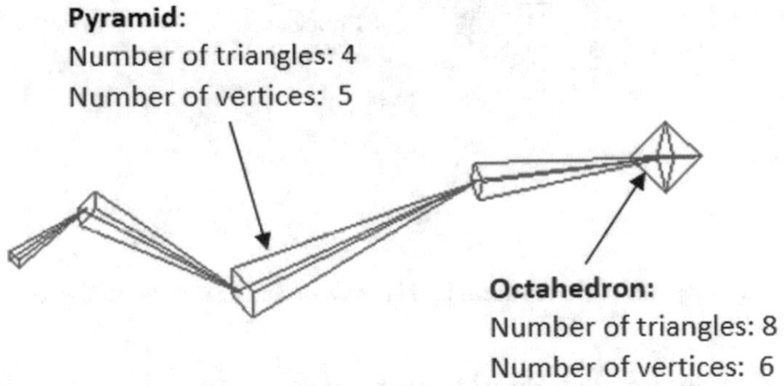

Pyramid:
Number of triangles: 4
Number of vertices: 5

Octahedron:
Number of triangles: 8
Number of vertices: 6

Fig. 7.8 A dummy mesh used by Assimp to represent the skeleton in Fig. 7.7b

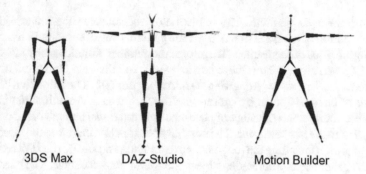

3DS Max   **DAZ-Studio**   **Motion Builder**

Fig. 7.9 Base pose of human skeletal structures used by modelling tools

7.4 Skeleton Animation

The important Assimp classes used for skeleton animation using the node hierarchy and motion data from a BVH file are shown in Fig. 7.10. A BVH file is loaded using the aiImportFile() function with the process preset aiProcess_Debone. This preset allows the mesh segment corresponding to each joint to be individually transformed using their joint angles and positional offsets. The scene object returned by this function contains references to the root (a Node object) of the node hierarchy and an Animation object. The data in the "Hierarchy" section of the BVH file are used

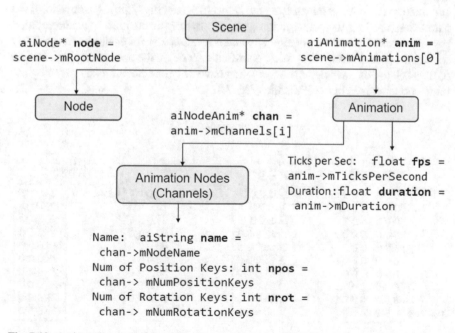

Fig. 7.10 Assimp classes used for skeleton animation using BVH files

to construct the node hierarchy. The animation object stores the data contained in the "Motion" section of the BVH file. A BVH file contains only one animation sequence consisting of a set of keyframes. Therefore, the number of animations always has a value 1 (scene->mNumAnimations = 1), and the only animation object is referenced using anim = scene->mAnimations[0]. The animation contains a number of channels given by anim->mNumChannels. An animation channel contains the complete set of values of positional and rotational parameters of one joint from the first to the last key frame. The number of channels is therefore the same as the number of joints (including the root joint, but excluding end sites). The BVH example in Fig. 7.6 generates one animation object containing four channels. The correspondence between a channel and a node in the hierarchy is established using the joint's name stored with each channel as anim->mChannels[i]->mNodeName. With reference to the example in Fig. 7.6, anim->mChannels[3]->mNodeName = "Wrist".

7.4.1   Updating Node Matrices

The offset positions of the joints (including both the root node and the end site) are directly represented by translation matrices and used in the node hierarchy (see Fig. 7.5a) to specify the initial configuration (base pose) of the skeleton. During an animation, these transformation matrices are replaced by the product of the translation and rotation matrices obtained from the keyframes (see Fig. 7.5b). Assimp stores the parameters used for the construction of these matrices as position keys and rotation keys. The root node has a position key and a rotation key for each key frame. They specify the global changes (in world coordinate space) in the position and orientation of the skeleton as a whole. All other joints have only one position key given by the joint's offset values in the BVH file (Fig. 7.11).

Channels

	[0] root		[1] Shoulder		[2] Elbow		[3] Wrist	
	T	R	T	R	T	R	T	R
Tick 0 ▶	0 0 0	0 0 0	0.5 0.3 0	3.0 0 0	1.0 -0.5 0	8.0 0 0	1.4 0.6 0	-3.0 0 0
	0 0 0	0 0 0		6.0 0 0		16.0 0 0		-6.0 0 0
	0 0 0	0 0 0		9.0 0 0		24.0 0 0		-9.0 0 0
	0 0 0	0 0 0		12.0 0 0		32.0 0 0		-12.0 0 0
	0 0 0	0 0 0		15.0 0 0		40.0 0 0		-15.0 0 0
	0 0 0	0 0 0		18.0 0 0		48.0 0 0		-18.0 0 0
	0 0 0	0 0 0		21.0 0 0		56.0 0 0		-21.0 0 0
	0 0 0	0 0 0		24.0 0 0		64.0 0 0		-24.0 0 0
	0 0 0	0 0 0		27.0 0 0		72.0 0 0		-27.0 0 0
Tick 9 ▶	0 0 0	0 0 0		30.0 0 0		80.0 0 0		-30.0 0 0

Fig. 7.11 Channels associated with joints defined in a sample BVH file given in Fig. 7.6

An animation sequence is given by a prespecified number of "ticks". Each frame of the animation increments the tick value. In other words, "tick" is an integer value that varies from 0 to n-1, where n is the total number of frames. For a BVH animation, we can use "tick" to index into the array of position keys and rotation keys of each channel to get the parameters for a particular keyframe.

Assimp uses quaternions to represent joint rotations (rotation keys). The quaternions are converted to rotational transformation matrices. The node hierarchy is updated using the product transformation matrix obtained from the position and rotation keys. Listing 7.1 gives a snippet of code that computes the transformation matrices for each channel for a keyframe given by the index "tick". After computing the product matrix, the node in the hierarchy with the same joint name is found and that node's transformation matrix replaced with the new product matrix.

Listing 7.1: Function for updating node matrices

```
void updateNodeMatrices(int tick)
{
  int index;
  aiAnimation* anim = scene->mAnimations[0];
  aiMatrix4x4 matPos, matRot, matProd;
  aiMatrix3x3 matRot3;
  aiNode* node;

  for (int i = 0; i < anim->mNumChannels; i++)
  {
      matPos = aiMatrix4x4();  //Identity
      matRot = aiMatrix4x4();
      aiNodeAnim* ndAnim = anim->mChannels[i]; //Channel

      if (ndAnim->mNumPositionKeys == 1) index = 0;
      else index = tick;
      aiVector3D posn = (ndAnim->mPositionKeys[index]).mValue;
      matPos.Translation(posn, matPos);

      if (ndAnim->mNumRotationKeys == 1) index = 0;
      else index = tick;
      aiQuaternion rotn = (ndAnim->mRotationKeys[index]).mValue;
      matRot3 = rotn.GetMatrix();
      matRot = aiMatrix4x4(matRot3);

      matProd = matPos * matRot;  //Product matrix
      node = scene->mRootNode->FindNode(ndAnim->mNodeName);
      node->mTransformation = matProd;
  }
}
```

The function in Listing 7.1 is called repeatedly for each key frame, typically inside a timer callback function. After updating the matrices of the node hierarchy, we need to update the display with the transformed configuration of the skeleton. The next section outlines this process.

7.4.2 *Updating the Display*

The postprocess preset aiProcess_Debone causes a dummy mesh (Fig. 7.8) to be generated for each joint of the node hierarchy. Each node will contain exactly one mesh index (nd->mMeshes[0]). This hierarchy can be recursively traversed from the root node, and the mesh stored in each node rendered to generate a display of the whole skeleton. The recursive function to render a skeleton mesh is given in Listing 7.2.

Listing 7.2: Recursive render function to draw a skeleton mesh

```
void render(const aiNode* nd)
{
  aiMatrix4x4 m;
  aiMesh* mesh;
  aiFace* face;
  int meshIndex;

  //----Section A: Transformation------
  m = nd->mTransformation;        //Get node's transformation
  m.Transpose();                  //Convert to column-major order
  glPushMatrix();
  glMultMatrixf((float*)&m);//Apply the transformation

  //----Section B: Draw the mesh---------
  if(nd->mNumMeshes > 0)
  {
    meshIndex = nd->mMeshes[0];
    mesh = scene->mMeshes[meshIndex];

    for (int k = 0; k < mesh->mNumFaces; k++)
    {
      face = &mesh->mFaces[k];
      glBegin(GL_TRIANGLES);
      for (int i = 0; i < face->mNumIndices; i++)
      {
        int vertexIndex = face->mIndices[i];
        if (mesh->HasNormals())
          glNormal3fv(&mesh->mNormals[vertexIndex].x);
        glVertex3fv(&mesh->mVertices[vertexIndex].x);
      }
      glEnd();
    }
  }

  //----Section C: Recursion------
  for (int i = 0; i < nd->mNumChildren; i++)
      render(nd->mChildren[i]);

  glPopMatrix();
}
```

The function in Listing 7.2 takes a reference to a node as input. This function is called inside the display callback of the application, with the root node as input. Starting from the root node, the program recursively visits all child nodes of the hierarchy, drawing the mesh stored in each node. The code given in the listing contains three sections: The first section specifies the transformation matrix of the node, and the second section renders the mesh stored in this node. It is assumed that each node contains exactly one index to a mesh. The third section recursively calls the function on each of the child nodes of the current node.

The development of a skeleton animation algorithm as outlined above is useful for.

- Visualizing an animation data stored in a motion capture file,
- Understanding the process of animating a segmented mesh object using only the node hierarchy, and
- Extending the skeleton animation algorithm to a more complex method for animating a rigged character model.

The initial and few transformed versions of the skeleton in Fig. 7.7b are shown below (Fig. 7.12).

The Carnegie Mellon University motion capture dataset available through cgspeed [4] provides an excellent repository of BVH files containing data for several realistic animation sequences performed by human actors. A few frames of a walk sequence are shown in Fig. 7.13.

The rendering quality of an animation of the dummy mesh structure generated by Assimp can be further enhanced by replacing the meshes with other shapes such as spheres, cylinders, and rectangular parallelopipeds, and by adding a few other mesh objects in the scene that are relevant to the animation. The built in objects in the OpenGL Utility Toolkit (glut, freeglut [5]) may be used for this purpose. As examples, two frames of animation sequence from the CMU dataset, and the corresponding enhanced versions of the skeleton model are shown in Fig. 7.14.

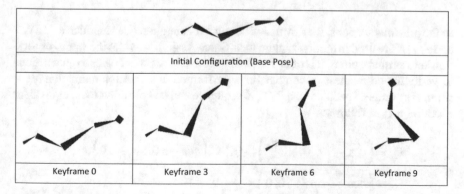

Fig. 7.12 Initial and transformed configurations of the skeleton in Fig. 7.7b

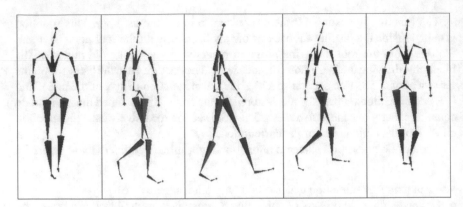

Fig. 7.13 A few frames of an animation sequence from the CMU dataset

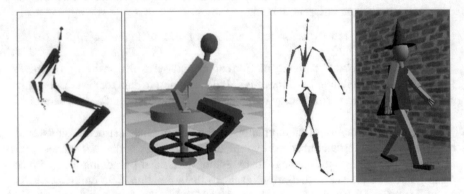

Fig. 7.14 Replacement of the mesh generated by Assimp with other geometrical shapes

7.4.3   Quaternion—Euler Angle Conversion

In the previous sections, we saw that different Euler angle sequences such as Z, X, Y and Z, Y, X are used in motion capture files. Since Assimp provides the values of rotation keys as quaternions, it is often required to convert the Euler angles to quaternions to verify the correctness of computations performed in a skeleton animation algorithm. The angles specified as a Z, Y, X sequence can be converted to an equivalent quaternion $\mathbf{Q}$ as follows:

$$\mathbf{Q_z} = \left(\cos \frac{\theta}{2},\ 0,\ 0,\ \sin \frac{\theta}{2} \right),\ \ \mathbf{Q_y} = \left(\cos \frac{\phi}{2},\ 0,\ \sin \frac{\phi}{2},\ 0 \right),$$
$$\mathbf{Q_x} = \left(\cos \frac{\psi}{2},\ \sin \frac{\psi}{2},\ 0, 0 \right) \tag{7.4}$$
$$\mathbf{Q} = \mathbf{Q_z} \mathbf{Q_y} \mathbf{Q_x}$$

Conversely, given a quaternion, we can use Assimp's `GetMatrix()` function to convert it to a rotation matrix. Assume that the elements of the matrix are given as in Eq. (6.3). The equations for the extraction of the Euler angle parameters $\{\psi \; \phi \; \theta\}$ from this matrix were given in Eq. (6.4). In a similar manner, we can find the rotation angles of a Z, Y, X sequence (3DS-Max) as follows:

$$Z \text{ rotation} = \tan^{-1}\left(\frac{m_{10}}{m_{00}}\right)$$
$$Y \text{ rotation} = \tan^{-1}\left(\frac{-m_{20}}{\sqrt{m_{00}^2 + m_{10}^2}}\right) \tag{7.5}$$
$$X \text{ rotation} = \tan^{-1}\left(\frac{m_{21}}{m_{22}}\right)$$

The rotation angles of a Z, X, Y sequence (DAZ-Studio and Motion Builder) can be obtained as follows:

$$Z \text{ rotation} = \tan^{-1}\left(\frac{-m_{01}}{m_{11}}\right)$$
$$X \text{ rotation} = \tan^{-1}\left(\frac{m_{21}}{\sqrt{m_{20}^2 + m_{22}^2}}\right) \tag{7.6}$$
$$Y \text{ rotation} = \tan^{-1}\left(\frac{-m_{20}}{m_{22}}\right)$$

7.5 Bones

The skeleton models shown in the previous section could be animated using motion capture data by applying each node's transformation directly on a segment of the mesh stored in that node (see Listing 7.2). This mode of animation is perhaps the simplest for articulated models. However, it requires a hierarchy of mesh structures closely following the node hierarchy, with each node storing its own part of the skeleton that could be transformed independently of other parts, as shown in Fig. 7.15a. A character model, on the other hand, may have only a single mesh containing all vertices of the model (Fig. 7.15b).

The node hierarchy in Fig. 7.15b could be further generalized with a set of nodes containing only joint transformations and a set of separate nodes storing only the character's mesh (Fig. 7.16). In this structure, the nodes containing joint transformations are called joint nodes, and the nodes storing the mesh structure are called mesh nodes. In order to animate the mesh using the transformations in the joint nodes, we need to segment the mesh into different parts that move with each joint. The joints themselves form a virtual skeleton that is attached to the mesh. As in the previous models, each joint's position is specified relative to its parent's position. A character model to which a skeleton is attached is called a rigged model. The pose of the character model to which the skeleton in its initial configuration (where all joint angles are zero) is attached is called the bind pose. Two examples are shown in Fig. 7.17.

Fig. 7.15 Comparison of
node hierarchies for a
skeleton and a character
mesh

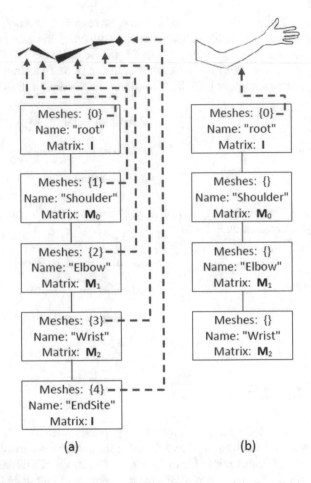

(a)   (b)

The "bones" of a mesh specify a partitioning of the mesh into groups of vertices that are associated with joints. A bone is a data structure that contains the following main components:

- An index: A rigged mesh, in general, contains an array of bones. Each bone is identified by an index from 0 to $n - 1$, where n is the number of bones of the mesh.
- A name: As mentioned above, each bone specifies a group of vertices that is associated with a joint (or moves with a joint). This association of a bone with a joint is established using a name. Each bone has a name of a joint which it represents.
- A vertex set: This is just an array of vertex indices. These vertex indices define a segment of the mesh that should move with the joint which the bone represents.
- An offset matrix: This matrix is used to transform the vertices belonging to the bone from the mesh space to the joint space (where the joint is at the origin). The offset matrix is discussed in detail in the next section.

Fig. 7.16 An alternative representation of node hierarchy using mesh nodes and joint nodes

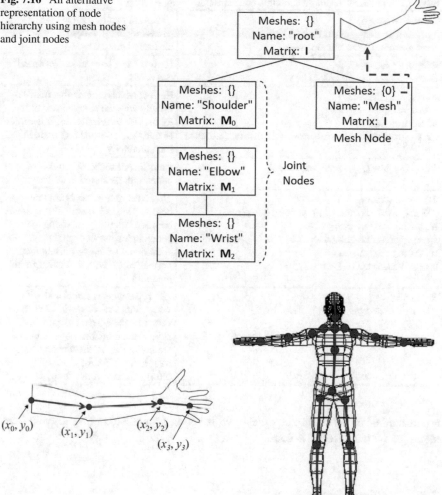

Fig. 7.17 Rigged mesh models with skeletons attached in bind pose

(a)   (b)

Table 7.2 provides a list of Assimp functions useful for retrieving the information stored in bones.

Bones are associated with mesh definitions, and they split the vertex set of the mesh into groups, so that each vertex group could be independently transformed using node matrices (Fig. 7.18).

The interpretation of bones as a partitioning of a character mesh is depicted in Fig. 7.19. A rigged character mesh is shown in Fig. 7.19a. Its wireframe display with the skeleton overlaid on the mesh is given in Fig. 7.19b. Figure 7.19c shows

Table 7.2 Functions for implementing a bone structure using Assimp

`aiMesh* mesh;`
`mesh = scene->mMeshes[i];`
`int n = mesh->mNumBones;`
	Bones are part of meshes. Here "i" is a mesh index. If a mesh does not have any bones, $n = 0$

`aiBone* bone;` `bone = mesh->mBones[k];`	Here "k" is a bone index between 0 and $n - 1$

`aiString name;`
`name = bone->mName;`
`aiNode* node;`
`node=scene->mRootNode->FindNode(name);`
	Each bone has a name that matches exactly with the name of one of the joints. Use the FindNode() function to find the corresponding node in the joint hierarchy

`int m = bone->mNumWeights;`	Here "m" denotes the number of vertex indices stored in a bone

`int vertId =`
`(bone->mWeights[j]).mVertexId;`
`aiVector3D vert =`
`mesh->mVertices[vertID];`
`aiVector3D norm =`
`mesh->mNormals[vertID];`
	The index of a vertex is obtained here as "vertId". Here, "j" is a value between 0 and $m - 1$. Using the vertex index, we can get the coordinates of the vertex and the normal vector with that index from the mesh

`float w =` `(bone->mWeights[j]).mWeight;`	"w" is the weight associated with the vertex with index "vertId". When the vertex is transformed using a bone's matrix, the transformed coordinates are multiplied by the weight. Please refer to Sect. 7.6 for more information on vertex weights

a partitioning of the character's mesh, with vertex groups belonging to each bone identified with a different colour.

7.5.1 Offset Matrix

As shown in the previous section, bones segment a mesh into different parts based on the configuration of joints in the skeleton. Each bone is also associated with a joint and contains that joint's name. In order to animate a mesh using node matrices (which are products of translation and rotation matrices), these mesh segments must be available at the nodes in their respective joint spaces (see Fig. 7.4). Since a rotation is always performed about a vector passing through the origin, a mesh segment can be rotated about a joint only if the joint is at the origin. In other words, the partitioned mesh segments must be translated to the joint space where the joint coincides with the origin. If a joint J has coordinates (x_J, y_J, z_J), then the offset matrix $\mathbf{F}$ of the corresponding bone may be given by a simple translation matrix in Eq. (7.7). In the most general case, an offset matrix may also involve a rotational transformation to

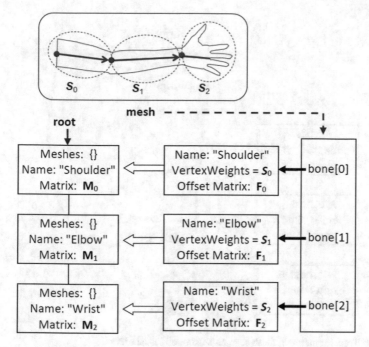

Fig. 7.18 Bones represent a partitioning of a mesh suitable for joint transformations

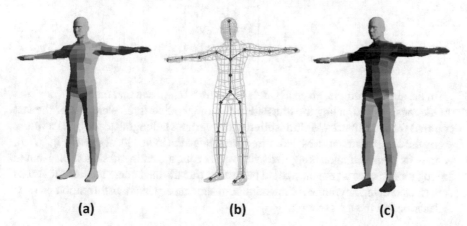

(a) (b) (c)

Fig. 7.19 **a** A character mesh, **b** the skeleton of the mesh, and **c** the vertex sets corresponding to the bones shown in different colours

align the axis of rotation with one of the principal axes.

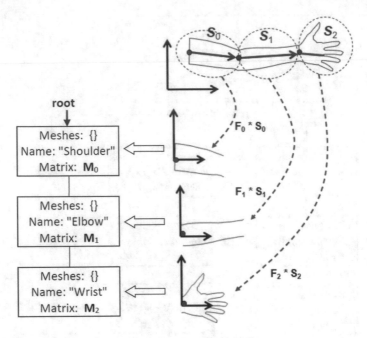

Fig. 7.20 Transformation of mesh segments using offset matrices

$$\mathbf{F} = \begin{bmatrix} 1 & 0 & 0 & -x_J \\ 0 & 1 & 0 & -y_J \\ 0 & 0 & 1 & -z_J \\ 0 & 0 & 0 & 1 \end{bmatrix} \tag{7.7}$$

In the above example, given a bone's offset matrix, we can find the joint's position on the mesh by extracting the translation vector (the first three elements of the last column) from the matrix. Multiplication of the vertices belonging to the bone's vertex set by the offset matrix moves the entire vertex set to the joint's local space (Fig. 7.20). When this transformation is applied to all vertex sets, the entire mesh gets distributed among joint spaces where they could be further transformed using the node matrices constructed using keyframes of an animation sequence. This transformation process is described in the next section.

7.5.2   *Vertex Transformation*

The processes described in the previous sections yield an "animatable" segmented mesh, where joint angle transformations defined by position and rotation keys of an animation sequence could be applied to the mesh segments to generate transformed configurations of a mesh. Using the example in Fig. 7.20, assume that each joint

Fig. 7.21 Transformation of mesh segments using position and rotation keys

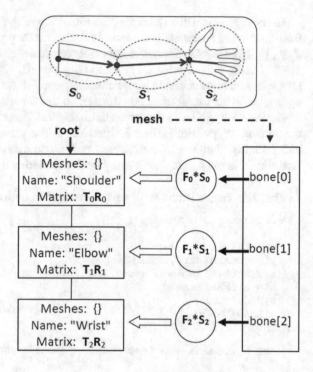

undergoes a transformation given by the product matrix **TR**, where **T** is a translation matrix obtained from the position key in the joint's channel, and **R** is a rotation matrix obtained from the rotation key of the channel for the current keyframe. The vertices of the mesh model can now be transformed using the node hierarchy as shown in Fig. 7.21.

The transformed configuration of the mesh in Fig. 7.21 is given by the following sets of vertices transformed using the offset matrices of bones and the **TR** matrices of the nodes for a given keyframe:

$$\text{Transformation of vertex set } \mathbf{S}_0 : \mathbf{S}_0' = \mathbf{T}_0\mathbf{R}_0\mathbf{F}_0\mathbf{S}_0$$
$$\text{Transformation of vertex set } \mathbf{S}_1 : \mathbf{S}_1' = \mathbf{T}_0\mathbf{R}_0\mathbf{T}_1\mathbf{R}_1\mathbf{F}_1\mathbf{S}_1$$
$$\text{Transformation of vertex set } \mathbf{S}_2 : \mathbf{S}_2' = \mathbf{T}_0\mathbf{R}_0\mathbf{T}_1\mathbf{R}_1\mathbf{T}_2\mathbf{R}_2\mathbf{F}_2\mathbf{S}_2 \qquad (7.8)$$

The repeated multiplications of **TR** matrices in Eq. (7.8) can be avoided by storing the product matrix used in the previous iteration as shown in Eq. (7.9):

$$\text{The } \mathbf{TR} \text{ matrix of the root node : } \quad \mathbf{L}_0 = \mathbf{T}_0\mathbf{R}_0$$
$$\text{The product of } \mathbf{TR} \text{ matrices : } \quad \mathbf{L}_k = \mathbf{L}_{k-1}\mathbf{T}_k\mathbf{R}_k, \quad k > 0$$
$$\text{Multiplication by the offset matrix : } \mathbf{J}_k = \mathbf{L}_k\mathbf{F}_k$$
$$\text{Transformation of vertex set } \mathbf{S}_k : \quad \mathbf{S}_k' = \mathbf{J}_k\mathbf{S}_k \qquad (7.9)$$

Every keyframe will require the transformation of the vertices given by Eq. (7.9) from their initial positions. The matrix $\mathbf{J}_k$ represents the product matrix $\mathbf{T}_0\mathbf{R}_0\,\mathbf{T}_1\mathbf{R}_1\ldots$ $\mathbf{T}_k\mathbf{R}_k\,\mathbf{F}_k$. Note that the normal vectors will require a transformation using the matrix $\mathbf{J}_k{}^{-T}$. If using a fixed-function pipeline (e.g. OpenGL-2), the initial vertex list for all meshes must be stored in a separate array and the Assimp's mesh data structure updated with the transformed coordinates, so that the mesh could be drawn using a render function similar to that given in Listing 7.2. A sample code for transforming the vertices as given in Listing 7.3 gets the initial vertex coordinates from a user defined array "initData". The updated vertex coordinates and normal vectors are stored back in the Assimp mesh array before rendering the mesh.

Listing 7.3: Transformation of vertices stored in bones

```
void transformVertices()
{
  aiMesh* mesh;
  aiVector3D vert, norm;
  aiMatrix4x4 offset, nodeTransf, matProd;
  aiMatrix3x3 norMat;
  aiNode* node;
  aiBone* bone;
  int vertId;

  for (int imesh = 0; imesh < scene->mNumMeshes; imesh++)
  {
        mesh = scene->mMeshes[imesh];

        for (int i = 0; i < mesh->mNumBones; i++)
        {
            bone = mesh->mBones[i];
            offset = bone->mOffsetMatrix;
            node = scene->mRootNode->FindNode(bone->mName);
            nodeTransf = node->mTransformation;

            while (node->mParent != NULL)
            {
                node = node->mParent;
                nodeTransf = (node->mTransformation) * nodeTransf;
            }

            matProd = nodeTransf * offset;

            norMat = aiMatrix3x3(matProd);
            norMat.Transpose();
            norMat.Inverse();

            for (int k = 0; k < bone->mNumWeights; k++)
            {
                vertId = (bone->mWeights[k]).mVertexId;
                vert = (initData + imesh)->mVertices[vertId];
                norm = (initData + imesh)->mNormals[vertId];
                mesh->mVertices[vertId] = matProd * vert ;
                mesh->mNormals[vertId] = norMat * norm;
```

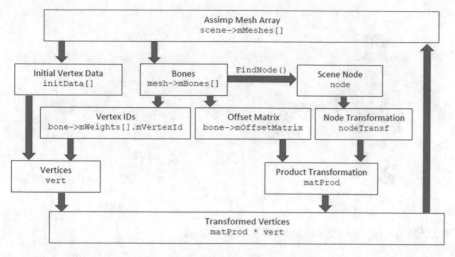

Fig. 7.22 Schematic of the computations needed for updating mesh vertices

```
        }
      }
    }

  }
```

A schematic of the process outlined above is given in Fig. 7.22.

An implementation using the programmable pipeline (e.g. OpenGL-4) could store the initial mesh vertices in a vertex buffer object and the coordinates transformed inside a shader [6, 7].

The Assimp library contains a rigged and animated character model "Dwarf" (Dwarf.x), which could be used to test the implementation of the character animation algorithm outlined above. Figure 7.23a shows a rendering of the mesh model, and Fig. 7.23b gives the skeletal structure of the model. A few animation frames of the model are shown in Fig. 7.24.

7.5.3 Keyframe Interpolation

The animation data contained in a BVH file has a uniform spacing of keyframes along the time axis given by "Frame Time" (see Fig. 7.6), where each tick corresponds to one keyframe (Fig. 7.11). Since the display of an animation sequence is updated for each tick, and a new keyframe is used for each display update, we do not require an interpolation between keyframes. The animation data embedded in a character model, however, may not have such a uniform distribution of keyframes. For example, the animation data of the "Dwarf" model in Fig. 7.24 has 56 frames ("ticks"), but the position key for Channel-1 has only 25 values unevenly distributed among the frames.

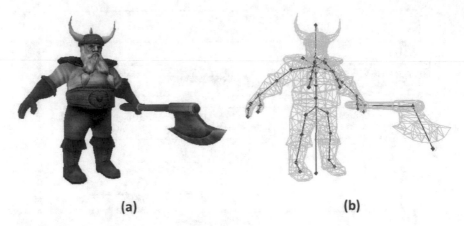

Fig. 7.23 **a** The "Dwarf" model and **b** its skeletal structure

Fig. 7.24 A few keyframes of the "Dwarf" model

The y-values of the position key are shown in Fig. 7.25. Similarly, the rotation key of Channel-2 has only 23 values. The distribution of values of the second quaternion component q_1 of the rotation key is shown in Fig. 7.26.

Both the above examples show the need for interpolating between successive position keys and successive rotation keys for each tick of an animation sequence. If a position key value is not be available for a given "tick", we use the previously found position key $P[k]$ and the next position key $P[k+1]$ and their corresponding times t_1, t_2 to find the interpolated value of the position key at the current time t:

$$P(t) = \left(\frac{t - t_1}{t_2 - t_1}\right)(P_2 - P_1) + P_1 \tag{7.10}$$

The implementation of the above method for position interpolation in Assimp is shown in Listing 7.4:

Listing 7.4: Interpolation of position keys

```
aiVector3D posn1 = (channel->mPositionKeys[k]).mValue;
```

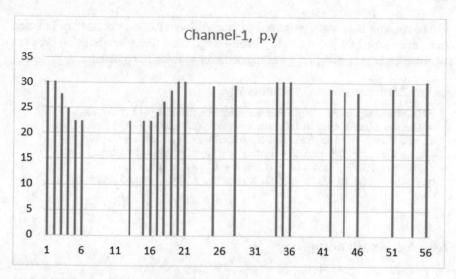

Fig. 7.25 Distribution of position keys for Channel-1 of the Dwarf model

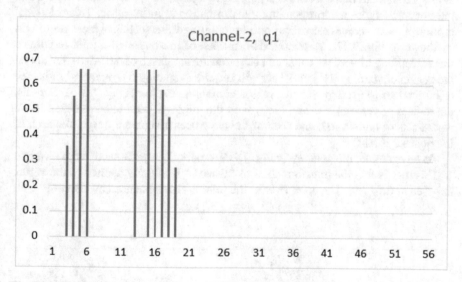

Fig. 7.26 Distribution of rotation keys for Channel-2 of the Dwarf model

```
aiVector3D posn2 = (channel->mPositionKeys[k+1]).mValue;
float time1 = (channel->mPositionKeys[k]).mTime;
float time2 = (channel->mPositionKeys[k+1]).mTime;
float factor = (tick - time1) / (time2 - time1);
aiVector3D posn = (1 - factor)*posn1 + factor * posn2;
```

The rotation keys are represented by quaternions. We use the Assimp function `Interpolate` (see Table 6.2) to perform a spherical linear interpolation between two rotation keys. Listing 7.5 gives the code for rotation interpolation:

Listing 7.5: Interpolation of rotation keys

```
aiQuaternion rotn1 = (channel->mRotationKeys[k]).mValue;
aiQuaternion rotn2 = (channel->mRotationKeys[k+1]).mValue;
float time1 = (channel->mRotationKeys[k]).mTime;
float time2 = (channel->mRotationKeys[k+1]).mTime;
factor = (tick - time1) / (time2 - time1);
aiQuaternion rotn.Interpolate(rotn, rotn1, rotn2, factor);
```

7.6   Vertex Blending

In Sect. 7.5.2, we discussed the process of transforming mesh vertices using bones. When a rotational transformation is applied to a joint, all mesh vertices attached to the bone undergoes a corresponding transformation in mesh space. This rotational motion of mesh vertices can cause both stretching and intersection of mesh primitives as shown in Fig. 7.27a. A smooth deformation of mesh around a joint requires a linear blending of vertices obtained using transformations by both bones that act on the region containing the joint. This will require extending the region of influence of both bones to overlap around a region containing the joint (Fig. 7.27b). For this, the indices of vertices in the region around the joint will need to be included in the vertex sets of both bones, and each of those vertices assigned a weight for each of the bones it is part of.

As an example, the point P_0 in Fig. 7.28a is part of only "Bone 0" with a weight 1. This means that the transformation of "Bone 0" is entirely applied to the vertex as given in Eq. (7.9). The point P_1 near the joint is also influenced by "Bone 1" with

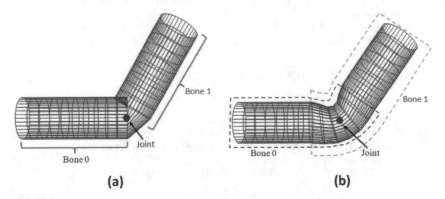

Fig. 7.27   Transformation of mesh vertices without **a** and with **b** vertex blending

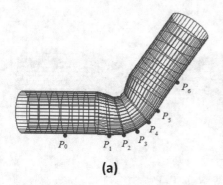

Vertex	Vertex Weights	
	Bone 0	Bone 1
P_0	1	-
P_1	0.9	0.1
P_2	0.7	0.3
P_3	0.5	0.5
P_4	0.3	0.7
P_5	0.1	0.9
P_6	-	1

(a)   **(b)**

Fig. 7.28 An example of a set of points around a joint with vertex weights assigned

a small weight 0.1. The transformation of "Bone 0" is applied to P_1 with a weight 0.9, and the transformation of "Bone 1" with a weight 0.1. The results of these two transformations are added together to get the final position of P_1. The addition of the two transformations is equivalent to blending the two vertices obtained using the transformations of each bone separately with the respective weights (0.9, 0.1 in this case). The weights of a vertex always have values in the range [0, 1], and the sum of weights is 1. Thus, the final vertex is always a convex combination of the vertices transformed individually by each bone. Note that the joint itself has an equal weight (0.5) for both bones.

Referring to Eq. (7.9), if a vertex v is transformed using bone-i with a matrix J_i and weight w_i, and bone k with a matrix J_k and weight w_k, then the final vertex position is given by Eq. (7.11).

$$v' = (w_i J_i + w_k J_k)v, \qquad w_i + w_k = 1. \tag{7.11}$$

Note that a linear combination of transformation matrices does not correspond to a linear combination of the respective normal matrices. The weighted sum of the matrices will need to be first computed and its inverse-transpose $(w_i J_i + w_k J_k)^{-1}$ must be used as the normal matrix.

As mentioned previously, a bone stores an array of vertex indices in the variable (bone->mWeights[i]).mVertexId. The corresponding weights are stored in the variable (bone->mWeights[i]).mWeights. Listing 7.6 gives an implementation of the vertex blending algorithm outlined above. It stores the weighted sum of the matrices in an array matArr, which is initialized with zero matrices. This array is used for computing the normal matrices as discussed in the previous paragraph.

Listing 7.6: Vertex Blending

```
for (int k = 0; k < bone->mNumWeights; k++)
{
    vid = (bone->mWeights[k]).mVertexId;   //Vertex index
    wt = (bone->mWeights[k]).mWeight;      //Vertex weight
    matArr[vid] += wt* matProd; //for matProd, see Listing 7.3.
```

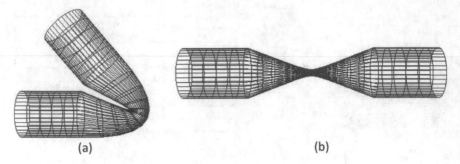

Fig. 7.29 **a** Collapsing elbow effect and **b** the candy wrapper effect

}

If a joint undergoes large angle rotations (typically beyond 90°), the region of overlap between bones must be considerably increased to prevent primitive intersections. Large overlap between bones results in an artefact known as the "collapsing elbow effect". Figure 7.29a shows this artefact using a cylindrical model, where the overlap between bones extends to almost half of the length of each cylindrical segment on either side of the joint. If an elbow or knee joint requires large angle rotations, the mesh structure on either side of the joint could be modelled in a way to minimize primitive intersections, and the overlap between bones could be kept at a minimum level.

Another artefact commonly found in character animations is the "candy wrapper effect" which occurs when a joint such as the elbow joint undergoes a rotation of 180° about its axis (Fig. 7.29b). Assuming that the joint has an equal weight of 0.5 for both bones, a 180° rotation of one of the bones results in a joint transformation given in Eq. (7.12). This transformation collapses all points on the yz-plane containing the joint to a single degenerate point.

$$v' = \left(0.5 \begin{bmatrix} 1 & 0 & 0 & 0 \\ 0 & 1 & 0 & 0 \\ 0 & 0 & 1 & 0 \\ 0 & 0 & 0 & 1 \end{bmatrix} + 0.5 \begin{bmatrix} 1 & 0 & 0 & 0 \\ 0 & -1 & 0 & 0 \\ 0 & 0 & -1 & 0 \\ 0 & 0 & 0 & 1 \end{bmatrix} \right) v$$

$$= \begin{bmatrix} 1 & 0 & 0 & 0 \\ 0 & 0 & 0 & 0 \\ 0 & 0 & 0 & 0 \\ 0 & 0 & 0 & 1 \end{bmatrix} v$$

(7.12)

The transformation resulting in the candy wrapper effect can be avoided by replacing the joint with several closely located joints and associated bones, thereby distributing the rotation among these multiple joints. Such joints used for distributing a large axial rotation of a link are called twist links.

7.7 Animation Retargeting

The process of remapping an animation specified for a skeleton or character model (source) to another skeleton or character model (target) is referred to as animation retargeting. In particular, using this method, we may be able to map motion capture data onto rigged character models that have the same bind pose as the skeleton in the BVH file. Animation retargeting thus greatly enhances the utility of motion capture data.

When we retarget an animation data from an external source to a character's skeletal structure, we keep the skeleton parameters of the target unchanged (i.e. we retain the offset values of each joint, maintaining relative positions of joints on the skeleton of the target model) and modify only the animation parameters (the rotation keys of the joints and the global positions of the root node). There are two key mapping functions involved in the process of animation retargeting:

1. Mapping of joint names (Map-JN): We require a one-to-one correspondence of joints in the source and target structures that take part in an animation sequence. This correspondence could be established using hash maps containing the joint names. Some of the joints that remain nearly stationary in an animation (e.g. spine joints, fingers) may not be used in the retargeting process. The absolute positions of the root joint may have to be scaled before mapping to the target skeleton to accommodate variations in height between the models.

2. Mapping of Euler angles (Map-EA): In addition to the mapping of joints using their names, we also require a mapping of joint angle rotations from the source to the target. A motion capture file may use the Z, X, Y rotation sequence for all joints. These Euler angle rotations may need to be applied along different axes in a different sequence for various joints on the target mesh. For example, a Z rotation of a joint on the source skeleton may have to be applied about the $-X$ axis at a joint on the target model to get the same motion (see Table 7.3). This Euler angle mapping will need to be generated using a careful observation and analysis of the target model's joint rotations. Since the bones' offset matrix and the node's transformation matrices may have a general structure (combinations of translations and rotations), it may be difficult to automatically extract this mapping from matrices. An easier method could be applying a 90° rotation about principal axes directions for each joint and observing how that joint responds to each rotation. If the skeleton in the bind pose of the target model does not match with the base pose of the source's skeleton, an additional rotational transformation will be required when transforming the corresponding bone of the target.

In the following, we use motion capture data from BVH files as the source. The corresponding skeleton in zero pose is shown in Fig. 7.30a. A character model "Mannequin" (Fig. 7.30c) is chosen as the target model. The configuration of the skeletal structure of the target (Fig. 7.30b) in the zero pose is very similar to that of the source. The source skeleton consists of 22 joints. On the other hand, the joint hierarchy of

Table 7.3 Joint mapping between source and target skeletons

| Map-JN | | Map-EA |
Source joint name	Target joint name	Input sequence: Z, X, Y *Mapped rotation axes*
0: Hips	hips	–
1: ToSpine	abdomen	Z, X, Y
2: Spine	abdomen2	Z, X, Y
3: Spine1	chest	Z, X, Y
4: Neck	neck	Z, X, Y
5: Head	head	Z, X, Y
6: LeftShoulder	Shoulder.L	X, Y, Z
7: LeftArm	upper_arm.L	$Z, Y, -X$
8: LeftForeArm	Forearm.L	$Z, Y, -X$
9: LeftHand	Hand.L	$-X, Y, -Z$
10: RightShoulder	Shoulder.R	$-X, -Y, Z$
11: RightArm	upper_arm.R	$Z, -Y, X$
12: RightForeArm	forearm.R	$Z, -Y, X$
13: RightHand	hand.R	$X, -Y, -Z$
14: LeftUpLeg	thigh.L	$-Z, X, -Y$
15: LeftLeg	shin.L	$-Z, X, -Y$
16: LeftFoot	foot.L	$Y, X, -Z$
17: LeftToeBase	toe.L	$Y, X, -Z$
18: RightUpLeg	thigh.R	$-Z, X, -Y$
19: RightLeg	shin.R	$-Z, X, -Y$
20: RightFoot	foot.R	$Y, X, -Z$
21: RightToeBase	toe.R	$Y, X, -Z$

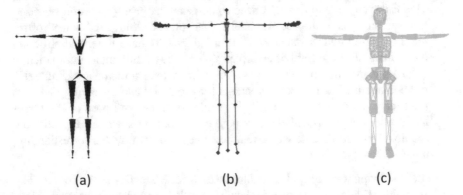

(a)   (b)   (c)

Fig. 7.30 **a** Source skeleton, **b** target skeleton, and **c** target mesh

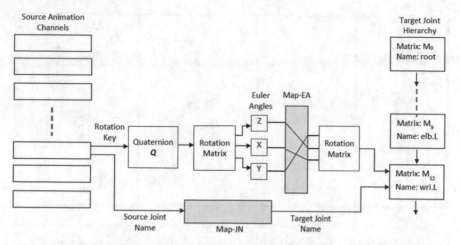

Fig. 7.31 Important steps and mapping in an animation retargeting algorithm

the target mesh consists of 54 joints. A mapping of the joints of the source skeleton to the target skeleton is shown in Table 7.3. A number of joints on the fingers of the target model have been left unmapped. The node transformation matrix of an unmapped joint will not be updated during a retargeted animation.

The requirement of mapping Euler angle rotation sequences between each pair of source and target joints leads to a few extra computations when updating node transformations. Since the rotation keys from the source channel are given as quaternions, we need to extract Euler angles from the corresponding rotation matrices. The computation of Euler angles from rotation matrices was discussed in Sect. 7.4.3 (Eqs. (7.5), (7.6)). The block schematic of the process of updating the transformation matrices in the target model's joint hierarchy using the joint angles of the source animation is given in Fig. 7.31.

Figure 7.32 gives a sample keyframe each from two BVH motion capture data files, the first corresponding to a walk sequence and the second corresponding to a boxing animation. The figure shows the skeletal model generated by Assimp for the BVH animations and the pose of the target character model after animation retargeting.

7.8 Chapter Resources

The folder "Chapter 7" on the companion website contains the following programs and data files. The programs demonstrate the working of some of the algorithms discussed in this chapter.

- Bvh.zip: A collection of motion capture data files in BVH format drawn from the cgspeed dataset [4].

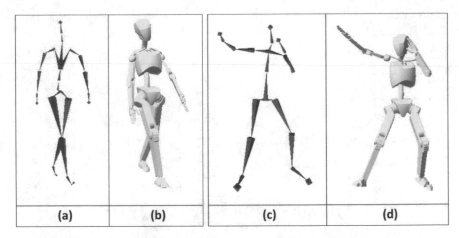

Fig. 7.32 Examples of keyframes from source and retargeted animations, using BVH files for **a**, **b** a walk animation and **c**, **d** a boxing animation

- Models.zip: Rigged and animated character models used as examples in this chapter.
- SkeletalAnimation.cpp: Loads a motion capture file in BVH format and displays the animation sequence using the skeleton model generated by Assimp.
- VertexBlending.cpp: Demonstrates joint transformations using vertex blending and the artefacts (collapsing elbow effect and candy wrapper effect) generated with large angle rotations.

References and Further Reading

1. The open asset importer library. https://www.assimp.org/. Accessed 15 Nov 2021
2. M. Kitagawa, in *MoCap for artists: workflow and techniques for motion capture* (Routledge, 2020)
3. Biovision BVH, https://research.cs.wisc.edu/graphics/Courses/cs-838-1999/Jeff/BVH.html. Accessed 20 Dec 2021
4. Motion capture, https://sites.google.com/a/cgspeed.com/cgspeed/motion-capture. Accessed 15 Nov 2021
5. Freeglut, http://freeglut.sourceforge.net/. Accessed 25 Sep 2021
6. A. Singh, Skeletal animation, https://learnopengl.com/Guest-Articles/2020/Skeletal-Animation. Accessed 15 Nov 2021
7. Skeletal animation, https://www.khronos.org/opengl/wiki/Skeletal_Animation. Accessed 1 Dec 2021

Chapter 8
Kinematics

The term "kinematics" refers to the study of the translational and rotational motion of objects without reference to mass, force, or torque. Kinematics equations are used to describe three-dimensional motion of a multibody system in terms of translational and rotational motions, and optionally, linear and angular velocities [1]. Kinematics analysis is extensively used in the animation of articulated models and skeletal structures for tracking the motion of joints in three-dimensional space and for generating goal direction motion of characters. This chapter presents important concepts, equations, and algorithms related to inverse kinematics motion of skeletal structures and contains the following sections:

- **Forward kinematics**: Gives the equations for the position and velocity of the end point in a forward kinematics motion of a joint chain.
- **Inverse kinematics**: Presents the "Cyclic Coordinate Descent" (CCD) algorithm and discusses its applications to goal-directed animations of a skeleton. Also presents the "Forward and Backward Reaching Inverse Kinematics" (FABRIK) algorithm.

8.1 Forward Kinematics

The term forward kinematics refers to the movement of a joint chain, given all the information about the relative position and orientation of each link with respect to its parent, and the absolute position of the root joint. Specifically, forward kinematics deals with methods for computing the motion (position and velocity) of the end point of a joint chain, given the chain's animation keyframes comprising of the positions of the root joint and the angles of rotations of the joints. The method for computing the end point's position in the world coordinate space was outlined in the previous chapter (see Eq. (7.2)). Listing 8.1 gives the code for computing the position of any joint (including the end point) in world coordinates.

Listing 8.1: Computation of a joint's position in world coordinates

```
aiNode* node;      //Input
aiMatrix4x4 nodeTransf;
aiVector3D joint(0);
nodeTransf = node->mTransformation;
while (node->mParent != NULL)
{
    node = node->mParent;
    nodeTransf = (node->mTransformation) * nodeTransf;
}
joint = nodeTransf * joint;
return joint;
```

Consider a chain consisting of a set of joints $J_0..J_3$ and the end point E as shown in Fig. 8.1. Given two consecutive positions of the end point E, its instantaneous velocity v_E is computed using the backward difference formula, using the current and the previous positions separated by a small time interval Δt:

$$v_E = \frac{E(t) - E(t - \Delta t)}{\Delta t} \tag{8.1}$$

Let the rotation of each joint J_i be denoted by a quaternion Q_i. Let u_i denote the offset of the joint J_i relative to J_{i-1}. The angular velocity of the joint J_i is given by (see Eq. (6.43))

$$\omega_i = \text{The vector part of the quaternion } 2\dot{Q_i}Q_i^* \tag{8.2}$$

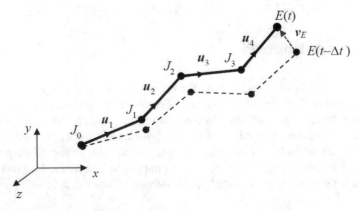

Fig. 8.1 Motion of end point of a joint chain

The linear velocity of joint J_i relative to J_{i-1} is then given by

$$v_i = u_i \times \omega_i \tag{8.3}$$

The linear velocity of the end point E with respect to the joint J_2 is the sum of the linear velocity (v_4) of E with respect to J_3 and the relative velocity (v_3) of J_3 with respect to J_2. Continuing in this manner, we find that

$$v_E = \sum_{i=0}^{4} v_i \tag{8.4}$$

8.2 Inverse Kinematics

Inverse kinematics (IK) deals with the process of computing the joint angles, given the world coordinates of the end point of a joint chain. Inverse kinematics solutions are needed for animating an articulated figure using only the desired world position of an end point as input [2]. For example, a user may interactively move the cursor or an object on the screen and may want a character to catch that object. Such goal-directed animations are commonly found in computer games.

For a general joint chain containing n joints, estimating all joint angles given only the end point's coordinates (xe, ye, ze) clearly leads to an under-determined system of equations when the number of joint angles is greater than 3. Such a system is called a redundant manipulator, implying that more than one set of joint angles could possibly lead to the same end effector position. A non-redundant manipulator in a two-dimensional space contains only two joints.

In the following sections, we discuss iterative algorithms for finding inverse kinematics solutions for a general n-link joint chain. The methods are particularly suitable for IK animations of skeletal structures and character models. In general, the number of joints on a character model could vary between 5 and 20 depending on the complexity of the skeleton. The spine segment may have 2–6 joints, and the hand segment may either have just one joint or up to 5 joints if fingers are included. The Cyclic Coordinate Descent algorithm discussed in the next section is a highly robust algorithm that can be easily implemented for skeletal models containing joint chains having a large number of joints.

8.2.1 Cyclic Coordinate Descent

The Cyclic Coordinate Descent (CCD) algorithm is a well-known method used for inverse kinematics solutions in computer graphics applications involving joint chains and moving targets [3, 4]. The CCD algorithm performs a series of rotations on the links of a joint chain, starting with the last joint (end point) towards the root, each time trying to move the end effector closer to the target.

A sequence of rotations performed by the CCD algorithm for a three-link chain on a two-dimensional plane is shown in Fig. 8.2. The joints of the links are denoted by J_0, J_1 ... etc., the target by T, and the end point by E. The last joint J_3 is rotated first by an angle θ_3, where θ_3 is the angle between the end point vector $\mathbf{u}_3 = E - J_3$ and the target vector $\mathbf{v}_3 = T - J_3$ (Fig. 8.2a). This rotation brings the end point E to a point on the target vector. The second rotation is performed about the next joint J_2, by an angle θ_2 between the two vectors towards the end point and target from that joint (Fig. 8.2b). This process of rotating joints is continued till the root joint J_0 is reached (Fig. 8.2d), and then repeated over, starting again from the last joint

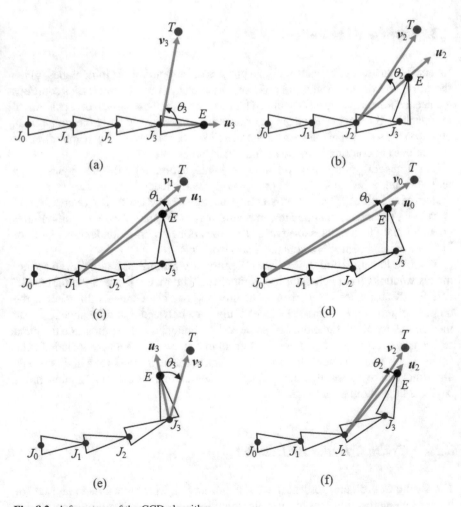

Fig. 8.2 A few steps of the CCD algorithm

J_3 (Fig. 8.2e). In a three-dimensional space, the axis of rotation for the ith joint at position J_i is calculated as the cross-product of the end point vector and the target vector at the joint. The angle of rotation θ_i at this joint is computed using the dot product of the two vectors (Listing 8.2).

Listing 8.2: Pseudo-code for the CCD algorithm

```
Inputs: Joint positions (J₀, J₁,…), Target position T
Input:  ε                //Error threshold
Input:  kmax             //Maximum number of iterations
i = n                    //Joint index.  Start from last link
iter = 0                 //Iteration count
Compute uᵢ,  ᵢ           //Unit vectors E-Jᵢ, T-Jᵢ
θᵢ = cos⁻¹(uᵢ•vᵢ)        //Angle of rotation
ωᵢ = uᵢ × vᵢ            //Axis of rotation
Perform angle-axis rotation (θᵢ, ωᵢ) of joint Jᵢ
Compute the new position of E
if (|T-E| < ε) STOP  //Reached target
i--                  //Next link
if (i < 0)
{
  i = n
  iter++;
}
if (iter > iterMax) STOP //Maximum iterations exceeded
else  repeat (GOTO step "Compute uᵢ, vᵢ")
```

Listing 8.2 gives an overview of the CCD algorithm. The terminating condition for the iterative algorithm can be defined based on the distance TE between the end point E and the target T, and also the number of iterations performed. The CCD algorithm can generate large angle rotations that may result in an unrealistic motion of the chain. In some cases, particularly when the target is located close to the root, the CCD algorithm causes the chain to form a loop, intersecting itself (Fig. 8.3a). Similarly, for certain target positions, the algorithm can take a large number of iterations resulting in a slow zigzag motion of the end point (Fig. 8.3b).

8.2.2 Skeleton IK

A skeleton structure or a rigged character model may be animated using the CCD algorithm to generate a goal-directed motion of the model, where the target position is interactively specified by the user [5]. There are a few important implementation aspects to be considered here:

- The end point used for the IK motion must be prespecified. Only the joint chain from this end point to the root joint will be processed by the algorithm.

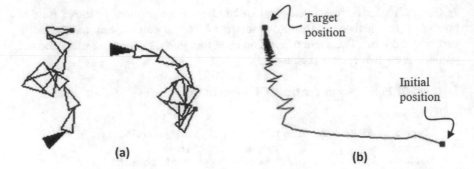

Fig. 8.3 Common problems associated with the CCD algorithm

- The computation of the end point vector u and the target vector v given in Fig. 8.2 requires the positions of the end point and the current joint in world coordinate space. We can use the Assimp function `FromToMatrix()` (see Table 7.1) to compute the transformation matrix that rotates the vector u to the vector v.
- The joint angle rotations of a skeleton are always defined with respect to the zero pose of the skeleton. They perform a transformation of the skeleton from the initial configuration. For a CCD algorithm, however, the rotation angles are defined with respect to the current (previously transformed) configuration of the skeleton. The rotation angles of each joint must be stored, and the current rotation of a joint added to its existing (accumulated) rotation. Alternatively, the rotation matrices of each joint may be stored in an array, and the existing rotation matrix updated in each iteration by premultiplying it by the current rotation matrix.
- When a character or skeleton model is animated using a set of keyframes, we can always assume that the animation data satisfies joint angle constraints. A CCD algorithm might generate an arbitrarily large rotation angle that falls outside the implicit min–max bounds of a joint's rotation angles. Therefore, while implementing an IK animation, the min–max values of each Euler rotation of each joint must be prespecified and used to limit the movement of a joint to ensure that the resulting animation looks realistic. This additional constraint at each joint will help avoid large angle rotations and the associated problems of self-intersections of the joint chain.
- Since Euler angles provide a decomposition of a rotation in terms of angles along principal directions, joint angle constraints are usually defined as min–max values of the Euler angles. After concatenating the current rotation matrix with the existing rotation matrix at each joint, the Euler angles are extracted and checked against their valid ranges, and converted back and stored as rotation matrices.
- The initial configuration (zero pose) of the skeleton or character may not be an appropriate start pose for the IK algorithm. In some cases, an intermediate transformation may be required to move the skeleton/character to the start pose.

A transformation from the initial configuration (zero pose) of a skeleton to the start pose of a CCD algorithm is shown in Figure 8.4. In this example, the shoulder

Fig. 8.4 a Zero pose and **b** the start pose of an IK animation

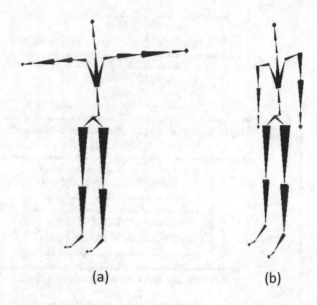

(a)   (b)

joints are rotated by 90 degrees and the corresponding rotation matrices stored in the array of initial matrices for the joints.

The node transformation matrices are updated in each iteration, and the method given in Listing 8.1 is used to obtain the updated positions of the current joint and the end point in world coordinates. A flow chart of one iteration of the CCD algorithm for animating a skeletal structure is given in Figure 8.5.

Figure 8.6 shows the names and locations of the joints on the skeletal model used for the implementation of the CCD algorithm. Table 8.1 gives a sample set of joint angle constraints for a human character model. In our example, the constraints are specified as the min–max values of the Euler angle rotations at each joint. These values, albeit approximations, have been found to be adequate for generating realistic looking goal-directed motion of the skeleton model.

The CCD algorithm in action can be seen in Fig. 8.7. The joint chain used for the animation consists of eight joints from the right hand to the root joint. The target position is indicated by a blue dot. The skeleton is first transformed into start pose as given in Fig. 8.4b, and then the joint angles updated in each step of the CCD algorithm.

8.2.3 FABRIK Algorithm

The "Forward and Backward Reaching Inverse Kinematics" (FABRIK) algorithm [6] is designed to circumvent some of the limitations of the CCD algorithm and to reduce computational cost. While the CCD algorithm performs a series of joint angle rotations to move the end point of a joint chain towards a target, the FABRIK

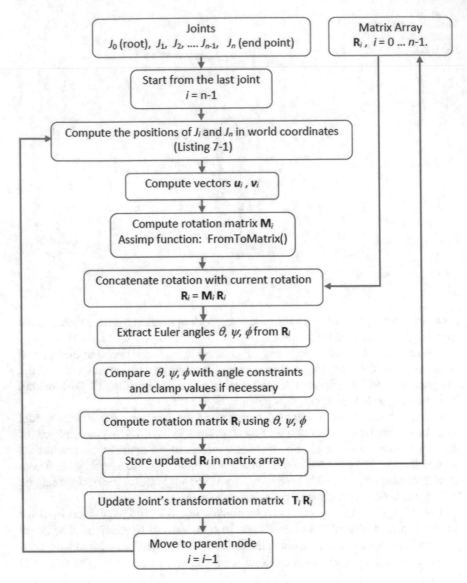

Fig. 8.5 One iteration of the CCD algorithm over a joint chain of a skeleton

algorithm computes only the updated positions of the joints to find a valid solution. The algorithm uses two passes in each iteration:

- Forward pass: The end point is moved to the target, and the remaining joint positions from end to the root are adjusted using a sequential update algorithm.
- Backward pass: The root joint position is moved back to its initial position, and the remaining joint positions from root to the end point are sequentially updated.

Fig. 8.6 Names and
locations of joints of the
skeleton model used for IK
animation

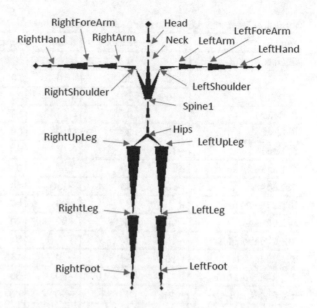

Figure 8.8a shows an example of a three-link joint chain in zero pose with root
joint R, end point E, and the intermediate joints denoted by A and B. The target
position is denoted by T. For simplicity, we assume that all links of the chain have
the same length d units. The forward pass of the FABRIK algorithm consists of the
following steps. The dotted red line TB in Fig. 8.8a shows the direction in which
the first two points of the joint chain are moved—the point E is moved to T and the
point B is repositioned at a distance d units from E along the line TB (Fig. 8.8b). The
dotted line BA in Fig. 8.8c shows the direction in which the point A is moved—the
point is repositioned at a distance d units from B along this line Fig. 8.8d. In a similar
fashion, the point R is moved along the dotted line AR in Fig. 8.8e and placed at a
distance d from A (Fig. 8.8f).

The backward pass of the FABRIK algorithm begins by moving the root R of the
joint chain to its initial position, and A to a point along the vector RA at a distance d
from R (Fig. 8.9a). The point B is then moved along AB such that B is positioned at a
distance d from A (Fig. 8.9b). Finally, the end point E is moved along the vector BE,
such that the distance BE is d (Fig. 8.9c). The updated positions of the joints define
the configuration of the joint chain after one iteration of the FABRIK algorithm
(Fig. 8.9d).

Compared to the CCD algorithm, the FABRIK method generally gives a faster
convergence and avoids the problems associated with large angle rotations.

The application of the FABRIK algorithm in animating character models is
discussed in [7].

Table 8.1 Joint angle constraints for a sample skeleton model

Joint	Zmin	Zmax	Xmin	Xmax	Ymin	Ymax
0: Hips	0	0	0	0	−20	20
1: ToSpine	−30	30	−10	50	−20	20
2: Spine	−10	10	0	30	−10	10
3: Spine1	0	0	0	50	−10	10
4: Neck	−20	20	−10	50	−30	30
5: Head	−10	10	−10	40	−20	20
6: LeftShoulder	0	10	0	0	−10	10
7: LeftArm	−90	80	−150	50	−120	20
8: LeftForeArm	0	0	−90	90	−140	0
9: LeftHand	−90	40	−90	90	−20	20
10: RightShoulder	−10	0	0	0	−10	10
11: RightArm	−80	90	−50	150	−20	120
12: RightForeArm	0	0	−90	90	0	140
13: RightHand	−40	90	−90	90	−20	20
14: LeftUpLeg	−10	40	−80	40	0	0
15: LeftLeg	0	0	0	130	−20	20
16: LeftFoot	0	0	−30	50	−20	20
17: LeftToeBase	0	0	0	0	0	0
18: RightUpLeg	−40	10	40	−80	0	0
19: RightLeg	0	0	0	130	−20	20
20: RightFoot	0	0	−30	50	−20	20
21: RightToeBase	0	0	0	0	0	0

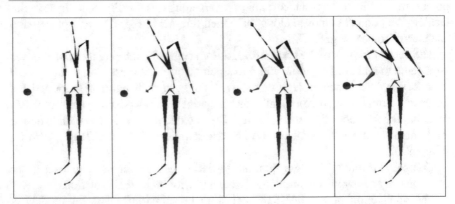

Fig. 8.7 A few frames of an IK animation sequence where the CCD algorithm is used to generate joint angle transformations

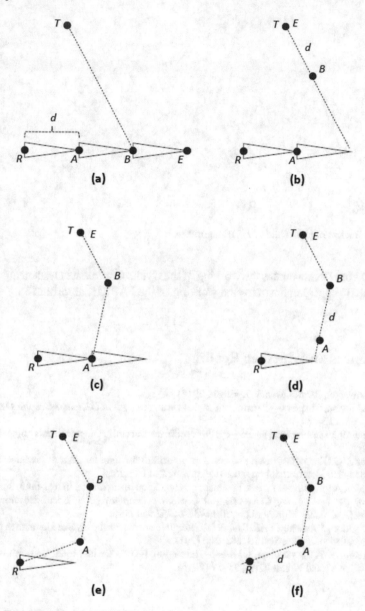

Fig. 8.8 Forward pass of the FABRIK algorithm

8.3 Chapter Resources

The folder "Chapter 8" on the companion website contains the following programs.
The programs demonstrate the working of inverse kinematics algorithms discussed
in this chapter.

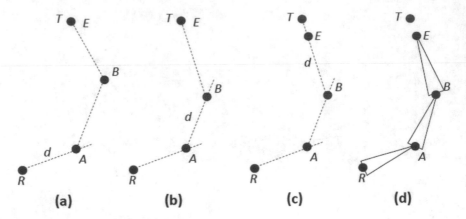

Fig. 8.9 Backward pass of the FABRIK algorithm

- CCD.cpp: Demonstrates the working of the Cyclic Coordinate Descent algorithm.
- FABRIK.cpp: Demonstrates the working of the FABRIK algorithm.

References and Further Reading

1. T. Haslwanter, *3D Kinematics* (Springer, 2018)
2. R. Mukundan, Chapter 6—Kinematics, in *Advanced Methods in Computer Graphics* (Springer, 2012), pp. 113–137
3. B. Kenwright, Inverse kinematics—cyclic coordinate descent. J. Graphics Tools **16**(4), 177–217 (2012)
4. W. Song, G. Hu, A fast inverse kinematics algorithm for joint animation. Procedia Eng. **24**, 350–354 (2011). https://doi.org/10.1016/j.proeng.2011.11.2655
5. M. Fêdor, Application of inverse kinematics for skeleton manipulation in real-time, in *Proceedings of the 19th Spring Conference on Computer Graphics* (Budmerice, Slovakia, 2003). [Online]. Available: https://doi.org/10.1145/984952.984986
6. A. Aristidou, J. Lasenby, FABRIK: A fast, iterative solver for the inverse kinematics problem. Graphical Models (Elsevier) **73**, 243–260 (2011)
7. A. Aristidou, Y. Chrysanthou, J. Lasenby, Extending FABRIK with Model Constraints. Comp. Animation Virtual Worlds **27**(1), 35–57 (2016)

Index

Printed in the United States
by Baker & Taylor Publisher Services